FREDDY

FREDDY

Brad Fittler & Richard Sleeman

THE
BRAD
FITTLER
STORY

Harper*Sports*
An imprint of HarperCollins*Publishers*

Harper*Sports*

An imprint of HarperCollins*Publishers*, Australia

First published in Australia in 2005
by HarperCollins*Publishers* Pty Limited
ABN 36 009 913 517
A member of the HarperCollins*Publishers* (Australia) Pty Limited Group
www.harpercollins.com.au

HarperCollins*Publishers*

25 Ryde Road, Pymble, Sydney NSW 2073, Australia
31 View Road, Glenfield, Auckland 10, New Zealand
77–85 Fulham Palace Road, London W6 8JB, United Kingdom
2 Bloor Street East, 20th floor, Toronto, Ontario M4W 1A8, Canada
10 East 53rd Street, New York, NY 10022, USA

National Library of Australia Cataloguing-in-publication data:

Fittler, Brad.
  Freddy: the Brad Fittler story.
  Includes index.
  ISBN 0 7322 8151 2.
  1. Fittler, Brad. 2. Rugby league football players –
  New South Wales – Biography. 3. Rugby League football –
  New South Wales – History. I. Sleeman, Richard. II. Title.

796.3338092

Cover design by Nada Backovic
Internal design by Christabella Designs
Cover image © Getty Images
Typeset in 11/15pt Sabon by Kirby Jones
Printed and bound in Australia by Griffin Press on 79gsm Bulky Paperback

5 4 3   05 06 07 08

To Marie and Demi,
for giving my life stability,
fulfilment and great happiness

There are things I've done that I'm not proud of and things I've done that I *am* proud of, but basically I'd like to thank everyone for allowing me to live a very fortunate life.

'No Regrets'

Brad

CONTENTS

starting out

I am standing at the front entrance of an old brown-brick block of public housing flats, probably built in the 1930s, in a suburb called Ashcroft in Sydney's southwest, near Liverpool. It's on the *other* side of Liverpool, really: the wrong side. Neighbouring suburbs have names that would be unfamiliar to the vast majority of Sydney residents — Busby, Cartwright, Sadleir, Green Valley and Miller. Little known yet notorious. I knew these places like the back of my hand when I was young.

When I lived in Ashcroft between the ages of two and twelve this block was full of Housing Commission flats, and nothing's changed here on the corner of Byrne Street and Strickland Crescent. There are six of these three-storey blocks scattered around a small area, each as unappealing as the next. If there were a high fence and razor wire around them, they'd fit in very comfortably as cell blocks at Long Bay. Each one is separated by Hills hoists and garbage bins. It hardly looks different to the way I remember it. The windows either have holes in them, shattered glass covered by masonite, or ripped curtains and blinds. Graffiti stains the walls. There are broken fences.

Ashcroft was not a rich man's world then, and it isn't now, all these years later. But as I search my memory for instances of childhood hardship, I can find none. As kids, we accepted what we had and made the most of it, and we didn't know any better

1

anyway. In my recollection, it was one giant playground. My thirty best friends lived within 100 metres of home — what else did an active young boy need? Now many of the former Housing Commission houses within a kilometre or two have been sold off and are being renovated by their new owners, but such modernisation hasn't come to the flats where I spent most of my childhood. I've come to Ashcroft for a bit of soul-searching as I prepare to write the story of my life.

I thought about starting off this book with the words 'Once upon a time', because my whole life's been a fairytale. I've heard that over and over recently, and it was true for my State of Origin comeback, but not so for my retirement Grand Final. So the 'Fittler fairytale' has been everywhere. Well, this is where the fairytale begins. And where my earliest memories start.

There is one difference I notice right away: it's deserted. Where there were once kids everywhere, now there are scarcely any on the street — I guess parents don't want to let their kids out unsupervised any more. They seem to think it's not safe. I often wonder whether that's paranoia; certainly it's a sign of the times. But was it ever any less safe then than now? We used to play all around the area until it got dark, and then we came home. Surely there were bad people at that time too. Maybe it was safety in numbers — there were never less than a dozen of us running and screaming and shouting. Not a young person in sight now. Are they inside playing with computers? Or just being kept close by nervous parents who are wary of the gangs that roam the streets at night?

So here I am, at the front entrance of my old block, pressing the button for ground floor flat 17, 34 Byrne Street. How about that — a security entrance! There was none of that in my day. It takes ten minutes to convince a very sweet-sounding young woman to open the door for me so I can take a nostalgic look inside.

'Can I come in, please, and have a look?' I ask first over the intercom. 'I used to live here.' A sign of the uncertain times we live in, I guess, but she tells me flat out 'No'. I try a more intelligent approach, which isn't all that easy for me: 'I'm writing a book about my life and want to have a little look at the place ... see if it's how I remember it as a child.' That doesn't work either. So I play my trump card.

'Do you follow the rugby league? My name's Brad Fittler. I play for the Roosters.'

'Who?' she says. 'What roosters? Sorry, never heard of you. Go away.'

I keep pleading, and eventually this faceless voice at the other end of the intercom agrees to let me in. The woman turns out be a charming and caring young mother — a single mother, as it turns out, like my mum was then — named Kristie. She has a beautiful, well-cared-for daughter, Madison, who has a ponytail and is wearing the uniform of my old school, Ashcroft Public. The three of us practically fill the lounge room, just as the three members of my family — my mum, Christine, my older brother by two years, Nathan, and I — did all those years earlier. At a later time there were four us in that tiny flat when my half-sister, Kate, came along.

The hallway is dark, just as I remember it. God it was dark, even in the middle of the day. Pitch black. Couldn't see a thing. And the lights hardly ever worked — we could never get anyone to fix them. I'd always stub my toe bringing in the pushbike, and once I ran in after school and smashed my head on the corner of a wall because I couldn't see where I was going. I had five stitches, and still have the scar to prove it.

It's been twenty years since I was last here, and the only two big changes are the security entrance and the lack of the sights and sounds of children playing. No kids on the lawn, as there used to be by the dozens. But the front lawn is still there, about 15 metres square. To us kids it was the Sydney Cricket Ground in the summer and a footy stadium in the winter. That's where I kicked a football for the first time — a little plastic one Mum bought from the neighbourhood service station. They say you don't remember much before the age of five, but I remember some futile efforts at kicking and passing that plastic ball. And wrestling the local mutt to get to it first. It had no bladder or laces, but plenty of fang marks from the dog. Still, I must have kicked it pretty well, because one of the blokes in an upstairs flat, Phillip Arrandale, convinced Mum that, at all of four years of age, I should go and play with a club called the Sadleir Bulldogs.

I caught up with Phillip while preparing this book; I hadn't seen him in twenty-two years. He's still fit and rakish, an amiable, caring man now in his sixties and living the comfortable life at Currumbin on Queensland's Gold Coast. Back then he was a hard-working storeman and packer, doing it tough like everyone in those Ashcroft Housing Commission flats. Phillip tells me:

I could see you were a bit of a goer, just by the way you ran around and kicked at the ball in the front yard. You were at least as good as my son, Jason, and a lot bigger, even though he was a year older. So I went downstairs and knocked on your mum's door. I said: 'How about you let him play football with Jason at Sadleir in the under-sixes team I manage?' Your mum wouldn't have a bar of it. 'No way,' she told me. 'Brad's too young. He'll get hurt. He's just a baby.'

Well it took a few weeks, but I convinced her to let you have a try at it. And she insisted on coming along to see that her 'baby' was OK. We all piled into the Valiant station wagon and off we went to Wheat Park, Sadleir, about four or five blocks from home. I think Christine warned you about tackling anyone in case you injured yourself, and you just stood there for most of the first game, watching the boys in the other team rush past. I swear it just clicked in your head that it made no sense to stand there and let them run past. So you hit one, and hit him hard. Very hard. No one ran past you again as long as you played with Sadleir. Running with the ball was never a problem. I'll tell you something: that big, left-foot step ... you had it even then, at four years of age.

Don't tell anyone, but in that very first game I ran off crying because I needed to go to the toilet. I was running, bawling and holding my willy, all at the same time. What a sight that must've been — not that I remember it, but it doesn't surprise me.

I reckon Phil Arrandale only wanted me to go somewhere else to kick the ball because we were always breaking windows — his, and our own. Windows copped a hammering, winter and summer. We kids were always smashing them with a wayward kick or cricket shot. The truth is, though, that Phillip was typical of the warmth and plentiful care that existed among the struggling families in those flats then, and which, by the look of Kristie and young Madison, still does. Money was in short supply, but care and compassion were in abundance. If it wasn't football in winter, they'd take us off to Cronulla Beach for nippers on a summer Sunday. It was a couple of hours there and back, and no matter that the Valiant coughed and spluttered all the way in the scorching heat. Many were the times we'd be stuck on the side of the road with the radiator boiling over. Any spare time and spare cash for petrol money and playing or training fees was spent on us, and nothing ever asked for in return.

At those ages — four, five and six — you don't know the effort and cost others are putting into your development. You accept it, and relish it as terrific fun, and then, decades later, appreciate it. I found the same unflinching concern and desire to help in a number of adults who knew our situation. My first coach at the Sadleir Bullogs, Mick Steward, was one. I caught up with him again too — twenty-five years down the track — while gathering information for this story. To be able to thank people like Phillip Arrandale and Mick Steward personally, as an adult and family man myself, and again in these pages, is a rare treat.

The woman in flat 17, Kristie, tells me how 'bad young men' in the area now terrorise the elderly and other people in the blocks. There is serious gang-related crime; police are always coming around. 'The block's a mess,' she says, 'torn blinds, broken windows, fights and arguments all the time.' The official figures

5

back her up: the NSW Bureau of Crime Statistics says assaults in the Liverpool area are up 10 per cent in the past five years, and sexual assaults are up 17 per cent. The instances of robbery without a weapon are 50 per cent higher than the NSW average; break-and-enters are 16 per cent more prevalent than average.

Yet this tiny flat is clearly a refuge from all of that. I stay about ten minutes and enjoy the trip down memory lane. Kristie could not be more pleasant, and obviously adores Madison. The two of them are side by side while we talk. Mum rubs her fingers through her daughter's hair and tells me how well the girl's doing at school. It is a heartwarming few minutes. As I leave Kristie confides, 'I really do know who you are, Brad. My brother won't believe you were here today. I'm sorry I didn't let you in at first, but around here, and with a small daughter, and on your own, you can't take any chances.'

I suppose it was like that when I was a child, but I don't ever remember being scared. Not once. I never went short of a meal. I always had clothes on my back. There was always something in the fridge when I came home from school. There was lots of love, friends everywhere, and room to roam. It's only recently that I've come to understand how much Mum went without. And only in putting this book together that I learned the truth about the first two years of my life, before I made it to the relative luxury of Ashcroft.

My first home was the kitchen table of a tiny flat in Regents Park, where my grandparents lived. There were three adults and two kids, and only two bedrooms. So they put my bassinette on the kitchen table, and that's where I slept. At dinner time and breakfast time, they shifted me aside — young Brad had to go on the floor.

That arrangement was only temporary, though; next we moved to Mum's aunty and uncle's house in Greystanes for a while. Mum tells me now: 'Your dad left me when I was pregnant with you — we had nowhere to go and no money to live on. We stayed where we could. I survived — I had to. I had no choice.' At Greystanes Mum paid her way by looking after her four cousins as well as Nathan and me. And Mum worked when she could, off and on. She never had any help at all. Not many of Dad's family were ever sighted — only Dad's sister, Narelle. I never knew the rest of them. I never even knew what my father looked like — there were never any photos of him about. Mum never spoke about him either, at least, not that I remember.

It wasn't until I was almost nineteen that I finally met my father, Rob, and that encounter came out of the blue when I returned from the 1990 Kangaroo tour. I didn't know much about him, other than that he used to ride in the Hell's Angels; I never heard any more than that. I never saw a picture. I never wanted to find out. He was just a bloke my mum had met and had a couple of kids to. That was all. That's life. I was happy as a kid, and never cared to find out any other details. My father meant nothing to me all those years.

I guess Mum thought it would be a good thing if my brother and I met him after I came back from the Kangaroo tour. The meeting would be a bit more emotional for Nathan, because he'd known our father as a baby, although he also had fewer older male influences than I did.

While I was away in England, Mum tracked down our father somewhere in Queensland. I didn't know we were going to meet, but there he was waiting for me at the house in the cul-de-sac off Albert Street, Werrington, where I'd lived since I was twelve.

I got out of a cab loaded down with footy gear and presents for Mum and my family, looking more like a pack mule than a human. And there was this total stranger who happened to be my father standing on the front lawn. He stood out from everyone else because of his long beard and the tension around him — everyone and everything seemed to point in his direction. It's not that I never wanted to meet my father, more that the period when I needed a father the most had passed. So seeing him was a complete surprise to me.

After I handed Mum her present, she just said, 'This is your father, Robert.' I shook his hand and said, 'G'day.' Nothing more than that. No emotional attachment, certainly. I wasn't sure what was supposed to happen next. It's not the way you see it in the soapies. I'd imagined the meeting a couple of times in my head over the years, but I seemed an awful lot calmer in reality. He didn't apologise for leaving us or anything — I didn't want to hear any of that anyway. I appreciated his honesty, or at least his lack of an attempt to make excuses for leaving us.

He had the big beard, done up like the bikie club member he was, and still is. I was clean-shaven, and in my Australian Rugby League team uniform. The two of us were so different in appearance alone that it was difficult to believe he was my old man. I was tired and jet lagged, I guess, from a long flight, and it all seemed a little unreal, like it was happening in a fog. He stayed for a couple of hours, and we traded small talk over a few beers with friends. It didn't feel uncomfortable or anything. It just felt like ... well, a vacuum. He was just some man who was briefly a guest in my house; that was all. I figured it might be a momentous occasion when I finally met my father, but in fact my life wasn't changed one bit.

These days we do speak occasionally and catch up when we can, even more regularly since he and his partner, Jenny, moved closer to Sydney. To say everything is patched up between us would be wrong, because there was nothing to patch up. We have become mates, and I'm happy about that.

I don't say he's a bad person for running off when Mum was pregnant with me. I don't say he's a terrible letdown for having stayed away all those years. It's not my place to judge. He chose his path and, I guess, figured it was right for him at the time to clear out. As for Mum, she's not the first single mother in the world — and not the last. This is what I know and this is what really counts: I could not have had a better mum. Now I have a dad as a mate as well, and that's a good thing.

I asked my father, Rob Fittler, for his recollection of our first meeting, and to explain a little of his life during those 'lost years'. This is his response:

Running off like that was the stupidest thing I've ever done. I listened to some mates who weren't really mates at all about how we'd go to the Northern Territory, drive trucks around and get rich quick. It didn't work out. I paid the price.

I've cursed myself many times in my life for taking off and missing the childhood of you and your brother. And your grandfather Arthur missed out too, and he gave me a thick ear a few times over it, don't worry. He died just before you made it to first grade, and missed that as well. Old Dad worked in timber mills and the slaughterhouse and still played first grade league on the north coast, near Kempsey, when he was forty-two. I played a bit at high school and junior rep stuff at Parramatta, and then discovered motorbikes. I've had a few run-ins with the law, riding bikes, driving trucks, and had a few assault charges. But I've mellowed. A couple of heart attacks shortened me up.

A lot of times when you were a junior I went to watch you play, either on my own or with a couple of mates who knew I was your father. I never made myself known to you. Never dared. I wanted to. Lots of times, I got up to go and see you and just didn't do it. I was apprehensive when we eventually met. I guess I just looked different. I was in the bike club — still am — and, well, I'm not the handsomest bloke around. You made me feel comfortable. I remember that part the most. I didn't go to the Grand Finals or State of Origins. They were your days, not mine. But I'd watch on the TV wherever I was. I really am proud of you. As you say, we're mates now and that's good.

Anyway, back to that first place I remember living in, the flat at Ashcroft. I really did love that place.

I don't remember the absence of furniture and food in that little flat in the early days, so I'll let Mum tell the story:

I was so glad when the flat became available through the Housing Commission, but there was one big problem: I didn't own a stick of furniture. I went to the Smith Family to get a couch and a bunk bed for the boys, and we made do with milk crates for a dining table and chairs. I fed the boys off milk crates for more than a year. After that, on hire purchase, I bought a little laminated table and chairs and some bright yellow cushions, then a fridge, a twin tub washing machine, and eventually a Rank Arena television. Wow, that was a red-letter day when the colour TV arrived.

There was no money for toys, or Easter eggs. I'd buy them a pair of pyjamas or a tracksuit and put a small chocolate or tiny plastic toy inside them. Treats — and they were small — came only on birthdays or at Christmas. As for food, we'd eat well only every second night. That was all I could afford. There'd be meat and vegetables one night, baked beans on toast the next. Clothes were mostly hand-me-downs.

I'd put the boys to bed, then work from 9 p.m. till midnight packing shelves at Franklins, come home to check on the children, then work on a tucker truck making breakfast for factory workers from 4 a.m. until 8 a.m. Then back to wake the kids, give them some breakfast and care for them during the day. That's how we lived. It was day to day, and hand to mouth. But everyone in the flats was in the same boat. It seemed normal. You look back now and say, well, how did we get by? But it didn't seem so tough at the time, because everyone I knew lived that way.

My mum's father, Toby, would come around often. Pop worked in a smash repair place in Regents Park. I loved it when Mum took us there. I liked the fumes — they sent me off. I enjoyed the smell and the light-headed feeling that went with breathing in deeply — not unlike fumes at the petrol pump. Or maybe it

was the naked girls in the calendars on the walls. Whichever —
it looked like a pretty good place to work and spend some time.
The workshop had a distinctive smell and feel and sound that
engrossed me. Sometimes, even now, I can stop at a garage or
workshop of some kind, and when a similar smell wafts into my
nasal passages those images from long past flash through my
mind.

Pop loved a drink. Way too much. We'd go down to the
baseball to watch the Auburn Orioles play, right next to Auburn
RSL, and that's where Pop spent most of his time, at the bar.
Mum started seeing less and less of Pop because of his devotion
to drink. It killed him in the end. Sadly, my last memory of the
man is him sitting at our dining table accusing Dianne
Goodwin, a friend of Mum's, of being a Communist spy. Then
he ran outside in his pyjamas, pointing behind every bush and
calling for the spies to come out of hiding. Nathan and I found
this behaviour odd, of course, but hilarious. I had a good idea
that my pop had some serious problems and that what was
happening wasn't funny at all — but I was eight years old, and
there's my pop running around searching for Communist spies
in the bushes at Ashcroft. In his PJs. What was a young boy to
do but laugh?

Mum encouraged me to go to training and keep playing footy
at four and five as an outlet from our difficult life in Ashcroft. I
took to it straightaway, for some reason. There certainly aren't
any great football skills in the family tree. Well, except for Uncle
Ross. He'll kill me if I didn't mention that he played for
Telecom (as Telstra used to be called) in the business houses
competition. I used to love watching him play. But basically
there are no league or union heroes in the family. None at all.
Mum didn't follow it. Nathan, my brother, never cared for it.
Nor was there much on my father's side.

But for some reason no one could comprehend, I started to
dominate games. From four years of age it was like I was born
to do one thing, and that was play football. I'd run from one
end of the field to the other scoring tries at will. Phil Arrandale,

the neighbour who introduced me to the game, told Mum: 'Your boy's going to play for Australia one day.'

Not all the parents were as sweet and innocent as my mother. When I was six, I had my fingers taped for a game against Green Valley, after fracturing one of them. Mothers of the kids on the other team were screaming out, 'Kick the little bastard in the hand! Break his fingers! He's got a bad hand. Go on son, smash his fingers. Get him!' Six years old we were. But that's the area I lived in.

I wasn't too brave — not now, and certainly not then. In the under-nines, a boy much bigger than me kicked me in the face. We used to get a cup of cordial at half-time, and when it came my turn this same boy and a couple of his mates tipped theirs all over me. I burst out crying.

Violence was not restricted to the footy field. There were some bad people in the house opposite. I came out one night and there were sixty or seventy people in a wild brawl — guns, knives, the lot. Blood and police everywhere. But none of that mattered to me — it was just a bit of excitement. We had all we needed: Mum, Ashcroft Public School, the front yard-cum-footy field, a proper footy field (Stanwell Oval) just down the road, the creek at the back, and the pushbike track. I thought I was the luckiest kid in the world.

But it wasn't all fun and games. Cheap highs ruined a lot of young lives then. Glue sniffing was all the rage; now it's ecstasy and ice and uppers. A lot of the neighbourhood kids would put Tarzan's Grip into a plastic sandwich bag and sniff the fumes. You'd walk over to the creek and the park, and the ground would be covered in sandwich bags, and there were kids staggering about. For the first of a host of times throughout my life, it was sport that saved me. I couldn't sniff glue and play footy at the same time. My neighbours got out of it on the stuff sometimes, but not me. You wouldn't think you'd be forced to make choices like that at such a young age. But in that welfare wasteland where I lived I was forced to make life-changing decisions pretty much every day of my life as temptation loomed large. School was a welcome distraction. Most of the local kids hated it, and still do, I suppose. For me, it was a place to satisfy my natural curiosity and, more than anything else, to play football.

I was never unhappy at Ashcroft Public School, which was just two blocks away from home. And when I look at my old report cards, which Mum has lovingly kept, I can see I wasn't the sort of kid who disliked school or disrupted classes too much. Quite the opposite: I lapped it up. Here's one report card from Miss Roberts at Ashcroft Infants School — I was six years old: 'Bradley is inclined to be cheaky [sic]' — so the teachers couldn't spell either in those days, apparently — 'Bradley's tendency to dominate spoils group activity'. I like this half-yearly report from Miss Roberts that year: 'Bradley is always willing to help the slower children'. And this, in Year Three: 'Apart from showing leadership in class, Bradley's attitudes towards his school, learning, his teacher and other pupils are of a very good nature'. One more, if you'll excuse the indulgence, from Class 3C at Ashcroft Public School: 'Bradley's sporting achievements match his academic achievements and hopefully, if he can combine the two in the future, he will develop into a fine young man'. Very prophetic. I'm joking, of course, but I did like school. I enjoyed learning, and always found time for homework and study in between footy and playing up.

go west,
young man

When I was twelve we moved to a cul-de-sac — no more than a driveway, really — in Werrington. It's not Sydney's most sought-after suburb either, then or now. It's well west of centre, with Penrith on one boundary, St Marys on another, and the other side of places like Mt Druitt, Blackett, Bidwill, Whalan and Emerton. It's foreign soil to most Sydneysiders. And so it was for me, too, when I first arrived. The residence itself was not so much a house with no name as an entire street with no name. It was a laneway off Albert Street, number 117F. No one could ever find it. It was a free-standing house with three bedrooms.

We had to get out of Ashcroft because Mum was having huge problems with the father of my half-sister, Kate, who's ten years younger than me. Mum was on the verge of a nervous breakdown. We lived in fear for a while. But it took months and months of arguing with the NSW Department of Housing to get something suitable.

I want to make the point — and I guess this is as good a place as any since I'm talking about us all living together — that Kate and Nathan must have felt left out and ignored at times in our lives. As my footy career blossomed, all the attention was on me. It must have been hard for them, and I only realise now that there must have been occasions when they felt left in the shadows a bit. I'd like to say to them that if that has ever been the case, then as young kids, and now as adults, I'm sorry. I was good at football, and people liked me for it, and I can't help that. I've tried to make it up to you as adults. I hope I've been successful.

Moving to Werrington was traumatic for me; I was apprehensive. I'd had a lot of respect at Ashcroft — I was the football and swimming kingpin, won all the events at sports carnivals, was vice-captain at school, kissed any girl I wanted to — and when you're a kid it's important to have self-respect and be liked. I was considered the toughest kid in school, but I'd never had a fight. Kids in the playground are like pups in a litter: a pecking order is established, and you want to be top dog, not the runt. I was top dog at Ashcroft, and I felt like I was king.

Moving was going to be an exciting new chapter in our lives, but we couldn't help having nagging doubts about leaving that Ashcroft safety net behind. Mum took us to look at prospective new Housing Commission places. We knew the rules: you were allowed to turn down two, but you had to take the third. The first wasn't too bad — an old fibro house in St Marys, not far from the shops. It had a fireplace and a chimney, something I'd never seen before in my life. Mum sat us all down and asked the question: 'What do you think?' We agreed to take the risk and look at one more. They showed us Werrington. It was brand new, and a palace compared with Ashcroft, so we thought we'd struck gold. It had a back garden, for God's sake! Absolute luxury!

We were almost at the end of the cul-de-sac, and next door was an arm's length away on both sides. The Werrington surrounds used to flood like a busted sink, in the house and all around that area. It was just so dead flat and basic. The local park, Werrington Park, would often be under a metre of water. They were the best days. We'd climb up on the goalposts — we had to swim out to them. No football on flooded days like that, just water polo. By that age we were smoking like chimneys, all of us. The trick was to swim out on flooded days with your head held high so the cigarette you had in your mouth didn't get wet, and the rest in the packet would be delicately balanced on your head. The matches, too.

Recently I took a drive past the park, and the row of single-storey shops at the Werrington shopping centre looks no less depressing than I suppose it was then. To us kids, though, it was a great place to hang out. These days the only store that appears to be booming is the bottle-o. What do they say? The more things change, the more they stay the same.

It wasn't only cigarettes, I have to say. I was a curious kid with a very inquiring mind. Marijuana was readily available. And I wasn't about to miss out on the opportunity to try it. Often. I won't name him, but there was one mate of ours whose house we'd go to for a blast. His parents would let you have a choof in the back room. While they were there! I guess their theory was that it was better to do it while they were around than to be sneaking out and off your face in some strange place. Either that or they were just another rung in the ladder of the welfare society we lived in back then, put through the wringer by a life that can wear you down. There were lots of families like that in Werrington in the eighties, and there probably still are.

I smoked cigarettes from the time I was thirteen; marijuana came along soon as well. I was in Katoomba at a mate's house when I tried marijuana for the first time. I was nearly fourteen, maybe. There weren't many of us in that part of the west of Sydney who hadn't tried marijuana or worse by the time we reached our teens. You couldn't escape it if you wanted to. It didn't do a lot for me, actually, that first time. I pretended to fall back and giggle, because that's what I'd seen everyone else do. That's what happened in the Cheech and Chong movies, anyway. But to be honest, I got a bigger kick out of regular cigarettes (that didn't stop me sucking on a bong from time to time, though). Truthfully, I got bigger headspins from cigarettes. We smoked cigarettes when we could get away with it, from a very young age.

I watched guys inject heroin, and listened while they tried to convince me how good it was. But I also watched them fall down and throw up, so I figured it couldn't be *that* good. I never tried it, but I'll admit I came close on occasions. The opportunity certainly presented itself several times. Right next door there was a kid a few years younger than me. He was no different from me, experimenting with smokes and drugs. I came to meet up with him years later in circumstances that I'll never forget.

I was helping out the former great rugby league Test player Ron Coote in a charity role for the homeless and hopeless. The charity had a car that went around the streets of Sydney's inner east, offering kids an opportunity to get a lift home so they wouldn't be in danger as they slept in parks or on the streets. Not just kids, either, but the down and out of all ages, men and women. 'Cootey' and the car gave them a chance to go home to their families, or simply go off to a shelter for the night. This kid walked past me. I looked at him. He looked at me. He recognised me for sure. He was in a terrible state, a junkie probably. It was the boy who lived next door to me in that cul-de-sac in Werrington.

I have no idea how many of the kids I used to hang out with ended up the same way. I wanted to talk with him, but he kept on walking; maybe he was embarrassed. You know, it could've been me. I did feel at the time, though, that I was never out of control. But what do they say? There but for the grace of God go I. I know that bloke started off the same way, doing cigarettes, marijuana and beer.

I'll get to this mostly later, but the thought strikes me now, so please allow me to jump ahead briefly to State of Origin 2004. I said at the start that I should've kicked off this whole story with the words 'Once upon a time' because of all this talk about a Brad Fittler fairytale. Could I come back and go out on a winning note? And when I did so, scoring a try in the decider, the papers were full of it: 'Freddy's Fairytale', the headlines screamed.

17

Hey, the fairytale had come true a while ago. I was long gone from that flat in Ashcroft and the cul-de-sac in Werrington — while my former next-door neighbour was shooting up and living off the streets. I had been one step away from it. One step, that's all. I was good at footy, and someone noticed it and nurtured it. I kept control — barely. And after that, I found myself in the right place at the right time more often than not. I knew at that moment, when I saw that boy in the dead of night in inner Sydney, that I'd won the lottery. Fate? Luck? I don't know.

I returned to those depressing inner-city streets leading up to the Grand Final the Roosters won in 2002. It was for Father Chris Riley and his Youth Off The Streets program. At around 9 p.m. I'd go out with a few counsellors and talk to sad-faced, pale-skinned young people, some with eyes spinning in their heads like the reels of a poker machine. It was the blank, purposeless looks on their faces that I couldn't get out of my mind. Watching their eyes light up, however briefly, as we talked made it worthwhile. I befriended a guy called George who was about as good a fortune teller as any man I've ever met. Right through that finals series he'd tell me in advance what the score would be, and he was accurate to within a couple of points every time. I made a special trip to see him before we came up against the Auckland Warriors in the big one that year. He told me the Roosters would win, and he nominated the score, and the margin, getting it so close it didn't matter. You wonder what cruel hand fate had dealt people like him — people clearly with talent, and rotting away on the streets. But I'm getting maudlin. Let's go back to those wild days at Werrington.

My mates and I would go out and buy cheap grog — Passion Pop champagne at $1.99 was a favourite — and smokes, then head down to Werrington Creek, where they had a bike track and a Rambo-type course. I slept out there one night, too drunk to make it home. Mum thought I was at a mate's place. Her boyfriend, Kevin, caught me out when he cruised past the local shops, trying to track me down. But we never hurt anyone, or anyone's property. We kept to ourselves. I wouldn't say anyone in my group was a bad kid; we were just larrikins.

There was a stage there — I suppose I was fourteen — when Mum used to work in a nursing home on weekends. It was the greatest thing — sorry, Mum, but it was — when she walked out the door on a Friday arvo, and bad little Bradley knew she wouldn't be back until Sunday night. When the cat's away, the mice will play. And boy, did we play! Five of us — four mates and I — would stay in that house all weekend. Mum would be gone by the time I got home on Fridays. The five of us would stride down Albert Street, bags slung over our shoulders, like Mr Pink and his devious pals in the movie *Reservoir Dogs*, heading straight to my empty house. We'd get on the phone and track down some girls and necessities — it was party time for a bunch of teenage reprobates. My job, together with Nathan, who was also there, was supposed to be to look after baby Kate. Truth is, we terrorised the poor child.

There'd be this mad rush on a Sunday afternoon to clean up before Mum came home. It was always spotless when she walked in, so she thought we were angels. Little did she know! It wasn't until Kate was old enough to rat on us that Mum found out what we were getting up to while she was away. But I will say this in our favour: all of us — my mates and I — respected what Mum worked so hard for, and we'd never have damaged anything of hers, or hurt her feelings. In all that mayhem, there was a lot of love and respect for her. Mum says now that she'd come home from working at the nursing home praying we hadn't burned the house down, or killed poor Kate.

We might know a teenager who had a car. And if we did, we'd spin around the streets of Werrington. One time we were desperate to take a drive. Mum was gone, but she'd left behind her yellow Gemini station wagon, the one she'd saved up for years to buy. I was too young to have a driver's licence, but once I found where she'd hidden the keys, that was not about to stop me. With four mates in the car, I did burnouts and wheelies from one end of Werrington Park to the other until the whole bottom fell out of it. One of my mates had a brother who was a mechanic, so we got the car fixed before Mum got home, but it was a real patch-up job. When she drove over a pothole the next day, the rear axle dropped off again.

A couple of years later I made up for it. I borrowed Mum's car to drive to Penrith to sign my first contract. I came home in a different car — a brand new Corolla. Mum went off her head. 'Brad!' she yelled. 'Don't tell me you've wrecked another one of my cars! Where's my car? Have you had another bloody accident?' I said, 'This is it, Mum. I've just bought you a brand new one — Happy Mother's Day.' She fainted on the front lawn. I mean, literally — she fainted and hit the deck. She gets a bit emotional; that must be where I get it from. I had to carry her inside and revive her.

We'd do anything to take someone's car, whether they wanted us to or not. I'll never forget the night we got caught in the driveway of my mate Jason's house. His parents were asleep — supposedly — and we had their car in neutral, pushing it down the driveway and out into the street to take it for a drive. He'd lifted the keys from the mantelpiece. The plan was to push it to the end of the street, start it up and off we'd go. Only trouble was that his old man loomed up out of the darkness and took to us like a madman.

Sometimes, with a few mates, I'd jump on the train and go to Newtown or Penrith. We knew all the places where the train would stop, and we could jump off without having to go through the station and pay. For years we never paid a cent to travel on the train. It was considered a rite of passage, I guess, to avoid paying on a train. A sort of a dare every time you got on board. You just didn't pay. And the truth is, some of my mates couldn't afford to pay. I didn't have much money either. Anyway, we always figured there were better things to spend our money on than the trains. Occasionally we'd get caught, and then we'd give a false name. Anyway, they'd have been hard-pressed to track me down in that cul-de-sac without a name in Werrington.

For a year or more when I was young we'd often wag school and go to the city or Newtown and steal stuff from the stores. I'd wag for several days straight and never get caught — I can't believe they didn't miss me. I don't know why, but I got into stealing in a pretty big way around the time I turned fourteen. When I was quite young I'd religiously steal loose change from Mum's purse to get a vanilla Paddle Pop every day. I never took a note — she would've noticed that. Some of my mates, on the other hand, knew every technique of theft.

I was a good sneak-thief then, and a good sneak-thief in my early teens, too. I'd shoplift clothes mostly. I'd go out looking scruffy, and come home in the latest gear. I'd stick the clothes around my waist, or hide them up the sleeve, or inside the thigh of my jeans, or in the hood of my jacket. I don't know how Mum never twigged, but the fact is, I was a bloody good thief. No kidding. I got away with it all the time. It was almost like a compulsion to steal.

When I was on a school camp at Jindabyne in the NSW Snowy Mountains, I shoplifted these terrible sunglasses. Dirty brown ones. You wouldn't wear them in a pink fit. It was a damned stupid thing to do. It wasn't like I was so young that I didn't understand it was wrong to steal — I was in Year 11. I knew what I was doing. Anyway, they had an alarm, which went off when I walked out of the store. I hurled the sunnies away, but the teachers and the store owner demanded to know who the culprit was. The store wanted to press charges and everything. So I owned up. Mum had to go and see the principal and I was on detention for weeks. Not for the last time, I made a serious mistake in my life — but I learned from it. I never stole again, not once.

There was an earlier time when I almost got caught, at Walton's in Penrith. I used to love stealing penguin shirts. I was stuffing them down my pants when the security guard tapped me on the shoulder and said, 'Come with me', taking my arm. I figured he was old and out of condition, and I was young and fit and fast. So I backed myself to beat him — I broke away and took off, running for the lick of my life straight down Penrith Mall, weaving in and out of people. I think that's the fastest I've ever moved, and the best series of sidesteps I've ever put on. If you asked me when I perfected the big sidestep that would become the trademark of my career, I'd say it was right there on my zigzag escape route. If I'd crashed into a pedestrian, it would have been the end of my run. But I successfully sidestepped every one of them — man, woman, child, and the occasional dog on a lead. And strollers and pushbikes. I was so scared that I don't think I looked around until I was back at Werrington. The penguin shirts were lost, but I gained the sidestep from hell.

When I look back on it now, I can see I was probably stealing just because my mates were. I've never had a criminal mind as such. I'm not a sinister person; I don't have dark thoughts. Could I have become a famous crook, rather than a famous footballer? No. It's not in my make-up to be dishonest.

Football was my saviour from a life of crime, poverty, drunkenness, drugs and the dole queue, or all of the above. I'm sure of that. But even football wasn't always free of troubled times and anti-social behaviour. One memory sticks vividly in my mind. I was playing with the Mount Pritchard team, aged eight. At the end of the season awards were being handed out at the park where we used to play. Some parents objected to the choice of prizewinners — and suddenly there was this massive brawl. Every parent was into it. It was terrible. Horrible. And it's locked in my memory. Dozens of parents thrashing at each other over a few worthless trophies for a bunch of eight year olds.

There are records of me playing for Sadleir at four. I played for Dayments after that for two years. After my fifth birthday, well, I was pretty much a veteran. Then Mount Pritchard, Ashcroft and Cambridge Park. Mum's kept most of the records from those very early games, when I was a boney, freckle-faced kid. I'm looking through them now as I recall how my life was guided towards league from an early age. For the Mount Pritchard under-eights I made five tries in a 30–0 scoreline against Busby, seven tries in a 44–0 win against my old team Dayments — eighty-nine tries in a season. By the time I joined the under-nines a year later I'd tallied 1000 points, and we hadn't lost a match in seventy-six appearances. There's a picture of me aged nine with my right arm being raised by Steve Ella, the Zip Zip man in Parramatta's great back line of the early eighties. I'd knocked off his old district record with 267 points in a season.

By the time I reached my tenth birthday, I was playing three times a week — for the school and for the district. And at home at Ashcroft, life wasn't too bad. Mum had a boyfriend, John, who was my football coach. I liked him, and he was very good to me. He became the father of my sister, Kate.

I'd sit on John's lap and play euchre with the grown-ups. He'd go off to indoor cricket and let me play as well. It wasn't a bad life. The best part of it, apart from football, was cracker night and the annual bonfire. There's never been a better one anywhere, I reckon, than the one at our local oval at Ashcroft. A bloke called Lindsay Holmes organised it each year. Why did they have to ban cracker night? Was there ever any more fun for a child? Except for the ones who had a finger blown off, or copped a bunger in the bugle ...

I was doing well at school. In my last year at Ashcroft Public I was beaten by one point for dux of the school. But they made me up a special prize for academic and sporting achievement, and I'm not sure that prize has been given out before or since. Even now, I look back on that with immense pride. I've said before that this was a hard area to grow up in, but I would never complain about that little school at Ashcroft. The sports teachers were great. Most of the other teachers — Jim and Mark to name a couple (I'll leave out their surnames, but they'll know who they are) — were especially kind and caring to me. They'd pull you into line if you got too cheeky, but always with understanding and compassion.

I started playing junior representative football in zone competitions for Liverpool. The 'gun' side was Metropolitan

East, which included Jimmy Dymock, 'Tricky' Trindall and
Terry Hill, who would all become premiership players of high
calibre later in their lives. I often came up against kids I'd meet
years later in first grade. Anyway, when we played Metropolitan
East the match ended in a 5–all draw. In the last game of that
competition we played a team from the Hunter region at a
ground adjoining Long Bay Jail. It was the first time I'd ever
seen a jail.

In order to win the inter-zone competition we had to beat
Hunter by more than 20, and it all came down to a kick by me
from the sideline. The ball landed on the crossbar and bounced
over. I can just imagine how dirty those blokes at Metropolitan
East must have felt when they heard the news. I was swelled up
with pride for days. Winning felt damned good to me, even at
that age. I suppose it was also the first time in my life I realised
there was a gulf between west and east in Sydney. Us upstarts
from out west beating the big shots from Metro East — now
that was something very special, everybody told us. Times don't
change much, do they?

I played in the Harold Matthews competition for Penrith, and
came up against players like Ryan Girdler and David Riolo in
the final, two years running. They were playing with Illawarra,
and they beat us in the final on both occasions. In one of those
finals Riolo poked me in the eye, and I had to go off. But the
best thing about playing in the Harold Matthews for Penrith
happened at training. They'd leave the Streets ice cream van at
Penrith Park instead of taking it away and bringing it back for
weekend matches. I can't tell you how tough it was to train on a
gutfull of stolen Golden Gaytimes.

Having moved on from Ashcroft to Werrington, and with
league never a big priority for St Marys High School, which I
was attending at the time, I played footy at weekends only, with
Cambridge Park. When I was fifteen I found myself playing
rugby union by accident. They'd canned our A-grade
competition in league, and the only option to stay with that
code was to drop down to second division. We weren't about to

do that. So Cambridge Park moved over to rugby union. None of us, including the coach, Barry Scanlon, had much idea about this strange new code, but we made a pretty good fist of it. And 'fist' is the operative word — a few of my team-mates at Cambridge Park loved a blue. Several games had to be abandoned because of the fights. I'd just sit back and watch; I never saw any point in getting involved.

Our opponents in rugby league hadn't seemed to mind the wild action. But when we played rugby union, which was often against teams like Hurstville, from outside our area, they weren't used to violence. It was a pretty one-sided brawl when my team put one on against the rugby union boys. They didn't want any part of it. So for a while we played 'foot-brawl' — our version of rugby union — on Saturdays and league on Sundays, 2nd Division with Cambridge Park.

Football took me from ordinary schools to very good ones like St Dominic's and McCarthy Catholic College. I moved from one school to the next looking for a better education and more of an outlet for my football skills. McCarthy was my fourth and last high school — after six months at Ashcroft High, then St Marys and St Dom's, always upgrading for a better education and the promise of a better football environment and better coaching. St Marys, where I transferred to when we moved to Werrington, was a very rugged school. I just remember the fighting and the brawling. Every lunchtime there was a stink in the playground. The teachers were never game enough to break them up. I can't blame them: I wouldn't want to step in between some of that lot. You'd have put your life on the line.

I was never a fighter; I never saw the sense in it. Well, only once: at the bus stop, when I was a bit half-smart to a big bloke named Darren. 'What did you say, you pipsqueak?' he said. Of course, stupid me just repeated whatever cheeky crack I'd made, and he was into me. I remember thinking, 'What have you got yourself into this time?' I stood there, dooks up, and shaking like a leaf. My only fighting experience was shadow-boxing, hyped up after a *Rocky* movie. I must have done all right for myself, because after a few well-placed jabs he put his hands up in surrender. But I'm not proud of it. That was my one and only experience of schoolyard fisticuffs. I see it now as a very unpleasant experience, and one I'd do absolutely anything to avoid again.

I'll never forget my first day at St Marys, my brand new school far removed from Ashcroft, where I'd felt so comfortable and so respected. Halfway through Year 7, it was. Everyone eyes you off like a weirdo. Who's this stranger, what's his story, where's he from? They had no idea I could play football. I had a pair of new long King Gees on — way too big for me — and a terrible green jumper, St Marys' school colours. I must have looked like such a dag. A bloke in my class called Geoff saw me, sad and lonely, in the corridor, and said, 'How about you come up to the library with me?' I thought, *Well, I have to do something*, so here I was at the first recess in the new school, trotting on up to the library with my new mate, Geoff. I was rescued by a bloke called Michael Fitzsimmons, who's since become a lifelong friend. 'You don't want to be going to no library,' he said. 'Come over with us.' I remember looking at Geoff, then at Fitzy, and choosing Fitzy's group. A good choice. I was told Geoff went a bit alternative, became a gothic and dressed head to toe in black. I could've been a goth, I guess. I could've gone down that path just as easily. Black Brad. Funny how a simple situation like that can shape your life.

It was also my first experience of multiculturalism at work. Ashcroft had been full of Caucasians. In my group of mates at St Marys was an Aboriginal boy, Marcus; a couple of Croatians named Joe and Eddie; a Pakistani named Julius; 'Shippo' (Glenn Shipley) the Pom; Fitzy, who was of Irish background; and 'Boppa' was Maltese. To a curious young bloke like me, it was an experience to treasure.

I learned a valuable lesson there at St Marys about how straightforward and brutally honest kids can be. They can cut you down to size just as easily with their tongues as with their fists. At that age, I suppose, you haven't figured out how to go behind people's backs to gossip about them. You just tell them straight to their faces if you've got something to say. Anyway, I was telling fibs. Huge, bare-faced porkies. And lots of them. Mostly about my alleged prowess as a runner or a jumper or a climber. I guess I was trying to impress my new-found schoolmates. They just started ridiculing me, taking the piss. No one had ever done that to me at Ashcroft. I can tell you it worked — I gave up the big-noting and lies very quickly.

I felt that in a new school — especially a tough school like St Marys — I had to mark out my territory; I just went about it the wrong way. At Ashcroft I'd made my mark on the football field, but there was no outlet for me at St Marys. It was more of a soccer school. There wasn't much there for me by way of football, so I substituted lies for tries to get back my reputation. Looking back on it, I enjoyed the anonymity of that short time at St Marys. It was good to walk around with no one knowing who I was. For those few months — and for one of the last times in my life — I didn't have to live up to other people's expectations.

Fitzy and I were involved in a pretty serious train derailment later on. We were on our way home from school in Emu Plains to Werrington on a stinking hot day. The line must have buckled in the heat, and we were flung around the carriage something terrible. Some passengers were dazed and bleeding. I grabbed Fitzy and we headed for a door as the train wobbled ahead. We were in the last carriage. I remember looking back and seeing the line undulating like a snake. No one died, but I did think about the bridge coming up ahead and what had happened in the Granville disaster ten years earlier.

Next school stop for me was St Dominic's College in Penrith. This was a school with a much stronger tradition in rugby league than St Marys, and it's where I met Ben Alexander — we were in the same year.

There was an oval adjoining the school. We weren't allowed to play tackle football on it during school time, but you can't imagine keeping such a football-crazy group of kids as Ben and me and others off it.

I remember the day twenty-four of us were called out for disciplinary action after Brother Damian caught us on the field when we weren't supposed to be there, playing tackle. He lined us all up on the halfway line, facing the main school buildings. Ben was pretty much the star of the school then, and more than a bit cheeky. He whispered to me, 'Don't worry, mate, he can't hit all of us with that strap of his.' Except Ben's whispering was a bit louder than most people's normal conversation. Certainly loud enough for the sharp-eared Brother Damian not to miss it. To him it was almost like a dare. He accepted the challenge, and then some! He belted all twenty-four of us with a rock-hard leather strap, four strokes each: ninety-six strokes in one go. I couldn't believe he didn't fall over with all that effort. You could hardly wave your hand to say goodbye ninety-six times. But Brother Damian did a devil of a job and didn't miss a beat. I've often thought that the judiciary committee of the Rugby League might adopt a similar method of punishing a player who tackles high or throws a punch. I can tell you it worked on us. Four savage lashes with the strap on a cold winter's morning in Penrith at about zero degrees and with a layer of frost on the ground beats the hell out of a one-match suspension, believe me!

Going from St Marys — a coeducational school — to an all-boys domain like St Dominic's was an interesting exercise. A lot of distraction was removed, I know that much. And you took considerably less interest in the way you came to class for the period immediately after lunch. If your shirt was hanging out and you were covered in perspiration, you didn't care. At St Marys, sharing the class with some girl who took your fancy, you'd always spend a few minutes tidying yourself up and making sure you smelled sweet before going back to class.

Richard Quinn was the football coach at St Dom's, and he was a dedicated man with a lot of very enthusiastic students. The school had a proud scholastic record too, but there were some very hot young guns being loaded and aimed at some future football field. It was at this time that I made my first

Australian side, an under-fifteen merit team that sadly played in name only — there was no actual match. Looking back, it was a decent old team, including the likes of Terry Hill, Jimmy Dymock and Tricky Trindall. In the NSW team of the same age I got to play against Queensland, and I came up against another young would-be who'd later become a team-mate and friend: Jason Smith. We weren't friends then, though. He smashed me across the face and broke my nose. There was no way I was going to let him get away with that, so I lined him up and nailed him shortly afterwards, breaking his nose too. We were high-spirited, competitive kids, ripping in, not giving an inch, and wearing our bloodied noses as badges of honour.

on the launch pad

It was at about this time that I had to make a life choice: I'd come to a fork in the road. It was either football as a serious, all-consuming career or life as a party boy, student and then worker in a mundane job somewhere. It might seem a little thing for a fifteen year old to sit alone in his room and decide whether football as a career was a genuine option, but it was a very serious matter. I can't imagine how many potential champions had their dreams and schemes snuffed out by evading that choice and continuing on an ill-disciplined path, simply choosing another career and life route. We've all been to school with someone — boy or girl — who had the world at his or her feet at fifteen and somehow fell by the wayside in the years that followed. You wonder, don't you, whatever happened to them. There was, in every school, someone who could run like Cathy Freeman, or play football like Wally Lewis, or soccer like Harry Kewell, and didn't quite go on with it. How many great sporting careers have been lost that way?

I remember making that decision; I remember it very clearly. I sat on my bed at the Werrington house, thumbed through some old stories written about me that Mum had pasted in a scrapbook, and thought what it might be like to play for Australia for real, instead of for a merit team of under-fifteens on a piece of paper. When I rose from the bed I'd convinced myself where I was headed. I knew what I wanted to be. I didn't race outside and blurt it out to Mum, or my brother or sister or a friend. I just knew it, that was all. It was fixed in my head at that moment, and I vowed never to let it go.

I'd be the best damned footballer I could possibly be.

I managed to make the senior Australian Schoolboys team when I was just sixteen. All the others in the team were seventeen and eighteen. That age difference, just a year or so, might not sound like all that much, but it was particularly daunting because I'd never tested myself against older opponents at that level. I was as nervous as I'd ever been coming into a series of games. But in the end I proved to myself that I could do it. We played two Tests in New Zealand, won them both, and after the last game found ourselves at a party in the suburban outskirts of Auckland. As far as we knew, the invitation to attend was an act of kindness and hospitality. In fact, it was an act of revenge. We could feel the tension as we arrived in four taxis. I held back a bit — I knew something wasn't quite right. This giant Kiwi walked up to one of the cabs, reached through the window and smacked one of our team in the mouth. I've told you before that I'm no fighter; I just yelled out, 'Go, go, go! Get out of here!' All four taxis were off like a shot. It was very scary. And that was my first experience of the Land of the Long White Cloud. I must say, I wasn't in a hurry to get back there. Land of the Long White Clods, if you'd asked me then.

The following year I was back in the Australian Schoolboys team, playing alongside Jason Taylor, my old friend from Ashcroft days. We played Great Britain Schoolboys in a curtain-raiser to a Knights match in Newcastle in front of 20 000 spectators, and boy, was that a buzz. We kicked their Pommy butts and I had a blinder, and on the trip back to Sydney I couldn't help thinking, 'Brad, you made the right decision. Football's your go, mate. Make or break.'

I guess it was a natural progression that I'd end up playing at Penrith. I started very young in the SG Ball junior competition, and signed a scholarship with the club when I was in my third year at high school. South Sydney showed some interest in me; so did Norths and Parramatta. You wonder how they could find out so much about a kid who's just fourteen years old — Mum went to visit Tim Sheens at the Penrith club when I was that age, to sign a contract with the junior development program.

I was the youngest Panther cub ever on a contract. Mum wasn't sure I should be signed up so young, so she made a special trip out to see Tim, who told her, 'He can handle it.' I took the scholarship agreement home a couple of days later and Mum signed it. She had no idea what much of it meant, and I certainly didn't at that age. Who can understand what the lawyers write in contracts, and what you might be signing yourself up to? She sought some advice from a Penrith solicitor, Brian Tracey, who was the father of a school friend, and there I was, a Penrith Panther at fourteen, with a cheque for $1500 to prove it.

There were whispers as I grew older that Penrith wanted to cash in on their investment — the rumours said they wanted me to go up to play grade. But the senior ranks didn't appeal all that much. Well, they did, but I was gripped by a fear of failure. The temptation is always to stick with the devil you know, stay in your comfort zone, not stick your head out of the foxhole for fear it might be shot off — choose whichever cliché you like. It's just easier not to accept the challenge. I would've been content playing against guys my own age and size. I could've said, 'This is high-profile enough, playing Australian juniors and NSW juniors. Look, we even get to play in the curtain-raiser to State of Origin.'

I was always nervous and apprehensive about going to grade. Everyone I watched on TV seemed so much bigger, tougher and faster than me. I was a boy. These were men up there in the big league. But I had to overcome that feeling if I was to take the next step. What's life without challenging your limits?

I had some trailblazers to look up to. A number of guys my age were playing in the under-23s, and Tim Brasher was in first grade. I knew the call would come soon enough, and I went through weeks of soul-searching about it. Doubts flow into your head, and try as you might, you can't stop that. There's no easy solution. I just asked myself this: 'What's the worst that can happen?' The answer was, 'Not much'. You stuff up, so what? At least you had a go.

The call I'd been dreading came through to Mum: they wanted me to play reserve grade against Manly in Round 20 of the Winfield Cup, 13 August 1989. I was six months past my seventeenth birthday, and still at school at McCarthy Catholic College at Emu Plains for my final year; I only spent my last two years there. I start to feel old when I read through some of the names of people who lined up for their various clubs on that weekend of football. Try these for a bit of history and testing your memory: Brett Kenny, Mario Fenech, Trevor Gillmeister, Kerry Boustead, Peter Wynn, Wayne Pearce, Ben Elias, Sam Backo, Peter Tunks and Geoff Gerard. Peter Sterling was still playing that year. Gee, now, it does seem a long time ago. Souths were minor premiers, for God's sake!

Recently *Rugby League Week* looked back on my career by recalling what the world was like at the time of that first match. For instance, the *Exxon Valdez* was running aground in Alaska, spilling 240 000 barrels of oil; Chinese students were staging a seven-week protest in Tiananmen Square in Beijing, the rebellion ending in bloodshed; the Berlin Wall was coming down; and Kylie Minogue's singing career was being launched with the hit song 'Locomotion'. There will be people reading this who are too young to remember any of that — a very scary thought! All I know is, the old pictures show a kid with the worst haircut in history — the mullet from hell.

But I do remember the day extremely clearly. Manly had a red-hot reserve grade side, and would go on to win the Grand Final in September. We were coming second last. I had to mark Joe Ropati. He had legs the size of a sycamore tree trunk. But I did OK. I ran out onto Penrith Park with all my family there, plus my mates and my girlfriend, Sally. The last thing Mum said to me was, 'Go out there and show them how good you are.'

It was amazing. I scored two tries, one right in front of my mates on the hill. I wanted to run up there with them and shake everyone's hand, but couldn't, of course. There was no win for Manly that day. I remember floating back into the dressing room afterwards, and I don't think my feet touched the ground. It was like I was repeating to myself, 'Brad, what were you so worried about? It's not that hard after all.'

I did have one moment of blind panic, though. I roughed up a big bloke named John Jones in a tackle, and a moment later he stood over me and was about to knock me from one side of the ground to the other. I went white as a ghost. One of Penrith's visiting Pommy players, Tracy Lazenby, came across and saved my life. But I had nightmares about it for days.

It taught me to respect the older, more experienced players. That's one thing about the game today: young blokes run around the field with no respect. You can't give them a clip under the ear as was done to me — you'd get sent off, or put on report. Those days of belting and brawling are gone. And insolent young kids get away with showing no respect on the field.

For the first week in reserve grade, I turned up to training and no one spoke to me. These days, when a bright young player comes up into first grade for his debut, they welcome him with open arms and cuddle him all week. I think it's a better grounding for the young bloke to earn that respect on his own — to fight for his stripes. You get a player now who's like I was then, and there's more counsellors for him than coaches. Everyone has become so sensitive to his needs. It's not necessary, and you're not doing the young player much good. It's a tough game, and learning to fend for yourself, to establish your own mark, is part of that.

At training a few days later they read out the names of the first grade team to play Western Suburbs at Orana Park the following week. I was on the reserves bench. Ellery Hanley, the Black Pearl, was captain of Wests that day. I loved Ellery — he was just about my favourite player. And here I was ready to go on and take him on. This was the stuff of pure fantasy!

I'd been pacing up and down the sidelines for what seemed like hours before the coach, Ron Willey, sent me on. Again, it's all a bit of blur. But the next day's report in the *Sydney Morning Herald* said, 'A bolt of lightning hit Orana Park', and they meant me.

My first move in first grade football was to tackle Ellery Hanley. I didn't get hit back, so I figured everything was all right. In fact, it was more than all right — it was bloody terrific. I started to wonder what the heck I'd been so fearful about. My sidestep, which I prided myself on, didn't let me down. I ran at the defensive line without being scared. Then I laid on a couple of tries for Greg Alexander and Darren Willis. We won 37–0. And while the rest of the team went back to Penrith, I went back home to study for the Higher School Certificate (HSC) trial exams. Fact is, I wasn't yet old enough to get into a bar even if I wanted to.

There were some strange moments as schoolwork collided with instant footy fame. At one point a television network's helicopter landed in the school grounds to interview me. Now I've gotta tell you, *that's* good for your ego! Football was taking over my life, and my schoolwork started to take a back seat. I was falling a long way behind in lessons. So with the HSC looming, I had after-school coaching, along with my good friend Fitzy, tutored by Jan Davies, who was wonderful to us. You won't believe the coincidence, but there was another student in our group — Tim Brasher — whose career in rugby league would pretty much parallel mine.

I had some excellent teachers over the years, most of whom gave me invaluable advice. I can't say the same, though, for Miss Manners, the modern history teacher. She was a great teacher, but not much of a careers adviser. One day she told me, 'Bradley, you have to study more. You'll never make a living out of football.'

Along came the HSC, and I remember cramming for a biology exam with my mates Fitzy, Boppa, Barky, Shippo and Reddo.

We lay on the lounge room floor, filling ourselves with No-Doz and coffee to stay awake; we mucked around until nearly midnight and then studied until daybreak. We were trying to remember things by making them into rhymes, and every rhyme had a swear word or something filthy in it. We could barely stop laughing. The next day, poor Reddo was too sick from the No-Doz and caffeine and lack of sleep to take the exam. He missed out altogether, and my results were only average. Another valuable lessoned learned. As the Boy Scouts say, 'Be prepared'. But in the end I got my HSC without too much problem.

Anyway, back to the footy field. I must say it was really hard to keep my feet on the ground after that day at Orana Park. I was a 'teenage superstar' in the *Daily Mirror*, the 'mouse that roared' in the *Sunday Telegraph*, a 'rookie sensation' in the *Penrith City Star*, and a 'whiz-kid' or an 'ace' depending on what else you read or listened to. Another paper even said I had 'The biggest step since Gasnier'.

So then we came up against Balmain at Leichhardt Oval. These were pretty much the two toughest packs in the League locking horns — the Tigers' Wayne Pearce, Ben Elias, Paul Sironen and Bruce McGuire up against our lot of John Cartwright, Mark Geyer (MG), Geoff Gerard and Royce Simmons. 'Carty' got sent off for belting Benny Elias late. MG went for another shot at Benny and was sin-binned for it, and they stomped all over us to win 33–6. There was always going to be a brawl. Ron Willey said, 'I want a major, all-in stink in the first scrum.' Every tackle was a blue.

I knew Brad Izzard was pretty crook — you could see that — and I was sitting on the bench thinking to myself, 'Don't you come off. I don't want to be fed to the lions.' Compared with them I was skinny little pretzel, and they were all in a pretty mean mood. But Izzard did come off, and on I went. I've never been so scared in my life. I thought, *Well, here goes nothing*, and took the ball up just the way I'd done the previous week. Only this time Paul Sironen stood between me and the next step. I remember he was kind of blocking out the sun, he was so big, as I ran toward him. He sat me straight on my rear end, and I hit the ground so hard my backside was purple for weeks.

The next tackle, Bruce McGuire drove me just as hard into the turf. Just for good measure, he shoved his elbow in my face and I thought, *I'd better stand up for myself here or I'm going to get pulled limb from limb*, so I leaned forward with a tame headbutt. McGuire was pretty good about it. I mean, it was a flea biting an elephant; he wouldn't have felt much. But he looked down at me and said, 'Son, one more like that and you won't see your eighteenth birthday.' I got the message. It was a valuable and, thankfully, relatively pain-free lesson in retrospect. It was the first, and the last, time I tried something so stupid.

In the first semi-final against Balmain, Willey came under plenty of criticism for preferring me to Chris Mortimer in the starting line-up. But when I arrived at the ground the word was that Mortimer had had a pin in his thumb removed with some pretty rudimentary tools, and was in no condition to play. I did score a try, but Balmain beat us again. And then Canberra ended our year. But I remember thinking that this was right where I wanted to be ... that I belonged in first grade rugby league ... that this was where my future lay. And the man who would be there with me for most of it was about to walk into my life.

gus gould arrives

The man who was to play such a big role in my life, Phil 'Gus' Gould, replaced Ron Willey as coach for the start of the 1990 season. I was on a new three-year contract after there'd been a lot of speculation that I'd join Parramatta. Truth is, I was always going to play at Penrith, no doubt about it in my mind. But I tried to instil some element of doubt in the minds of club officials, hoping to snag a few extra dollars. No harm in that, I didn't think — you couldn't blame a bloke for trying to boost his income. Just standard to-and-fro, as in any job application or renewed agreement in any field of endeavour. As it turned out, though, the contract was not for huge money — $30 000 for the first year, going up by just $10 000 a year for the next two years.

The negotiations made headlines. On Sydney radio station 2UE, broadcaster Alan Jones said I was 'greedy' for wanting more money, and my Aunty Marcy rang him up on the talkback, introduced herself and set him right. 'He's a wonderful young man,' she told him. It was very, very sweet of her to do that. Family's a wonderful thing.

Basically, I stayed with Penrith because I had such great faith in the new coach. I'm not sure how much faith he had in me at the start, though, because he kept me in reserve grade for a few matches. I think maybe he was just blooding me, giving me some extra experience. He pulled me aside and said, 'You're better off in reserve grade for a while.' But I'll let Gus tell the story; he's better at telling stories than me:

There were a couple of things about his game I wanted him to work on. That big left foot step and the right foot step he had … well, he was doing it too far away from the line. 'You've got to run straight occasionally,' I told him. 'It's OK against schoolboys, but these are men you're playing against now, and they'll work you out very quickly.' So the second game was against Balmain. We were going to win it, but the game wasn't quite over and I sent Brad on for the last few minutes, and told him to go out there and 'Run straight, don't step.' He says, 'Good as gold', and out he goes full of enthusiasm, claps his hands and demands the ball straightaway.

He remembers not to step, runs straight into the Balmain forwards, and they absolutely smash him … they pick him up, drive him back, upend him in the dirt, and when he staggers up, every bone in his body aching, he looks across at me on the bench with utter bewilderment as if to say 'You betrayed me.' So I yell back, 'Good run, mate, get up, show 'em you're not hurt, get the ball and run it straight at 'em again.' A couple of minutes later he's dusted himself off, calls for the ball and goes for it, teeth clenched, arms pumping, full of determination. He looks up, and there standing in front of him is the massive form of Paul Sironen. Now I figure he's going to run at him like I told him, which would be like driving into a brick wall at 80 kilometres an hour. Instead his head wobbles and he puts on this huge left foot step, and Paul Sironen doesn't lay a hand on him. For good measure, Brad steps off his right foot to get past the fullback, and he scores underneath the posts. The game's won, and I'm waiting for him in the tunnel. I say, 'What happened? I told you not to step. What did you learn?' He says, 'I learned you're mad, they're big, and I'm steppin' from now on!'

So I was back in reserve grade, but I guess I just copped it on the chin. It wasn't until Round 5 against the Broncos that I actually started a first grade game that year: at five-eighth, at Lang Park, in front of 30 000 people and up against none other than Wally Lewis. We knocked them over, too, and I bagged a try. My role as a pivot, though, was never guaranteed. I played fullback and centre too, as the season continued; I don't think Gus was ever sure what to do with me. Maybe he had a plan, but if he did he kept it well disguised.

As it turned out, whatever Gus did was exactly the right thing. I'd go on to play State of Origin for the first time that year — the youngest player ever — score a try in a Grand Final, even though we lost it, and then make the Kangaroo squad as the youngest ever tourist. But, as Gus says, I was ever the 'problem child'.

I have to tell you one story about that year which Gus Gould loves to tell against me. We were heading off to play Illawarra at Wollongong in Round 13. The Steelers were a team we always had trouble with. Gus figured we'd take a team bus down there for a change, and if we had a win we could all stop for a few beers on the way home. We left Penrith just after midday, and stopped halfway, at the Appin fruit market, for a toilet break and a snack. It was about 1 p.m., less than two hours before the game. I'll let Gus explain what happened next:

We get back on the bus and there, up the front, is His Lordship munching on a packet of Cheezels, washing them down with a litre of chocolate Moove. He's got another packet under his arm, and an empty one on the floor. I say, 'What the hell do you think you're doing?' He says, 'I'm havin' lunch.' I tell him, 'Why do you think I stopped at a fruit market? Not for you to fill your guts with Cheezels. The bloody game's on soon.' He says to me, spitting Cheezel crumbs, 'Don't worry, Gus. I do it all the time.' Well, come game time we're down 24–6 at half-time and I'm seething. I'm composed at first, then get louder and louder. Suddenly, my tirade is broken by the sounds of loud throwing up in the corner. It's Brad, of course. He's got his head between his knees, with three packets of Cheezels and a litre of chocolate milk splashed all over his boots. Brad looks up and says, 'I feel better now.' We didn't. In the end we got beat, but we got back to within two points of them and Brad was the star of the show. He played absolutely sensationally.

I couldn't really say it was a technicolour yawn — there were only two colours: chocolate brown and orange.

With such a vast nursery of talent in the Penrith area, it was only a matter of time before something — or someone — brought a premiership home to the area. Phil Gould was the right man for the club at exactly the right time. The preceding seasons had created hardened and experienced semi-final footballers. These weren't rookies he was working with — they were tough men, with a smattering of Greg Alexander-style brilliance, who would provide a sound platform for Gus's vision.

The first thing that struck me about Gus, and I remember this very well, was that he was the first person I'd come across who could explain a football game in terms you could understand. He was a great talker with a huge passion for the game. And that passion was infectious. Ron Willey was an old-style coach, and that's how the game was in those days; Gus represented the new. Under Ron Willey you'd come to training Thursday, and bring your going-out gear with you. You'd leave it on the hanger in the dressing room, go out and train, then come back and get ready to get on the beer. By today's standards it was kids' stuff. By Phil Gould's standards, it was something to be consigned to a museum.

I'm probably not the best one to comment on the old style of coaching, because I played only three games under the late Ron Willey, who passed away just a few days before my last ever game. But it was enough to get an idea of the approach that preceded today's standards of full-time professionalism. In

Ron's day we'd never leave the dressing rooms to prepare for a game. There was a lot of boxing pads and ripping into each other. We'd be revved for a fight, not a football game, by the time we ran on. I can only imagine how much energy we wasted with all of that.

It brings a wry smile to my face, thinking back on a typical pre-match preparation then compared with what it's like these days. I'd be transfixed in a corner watching big, rugged men like Peter Kelly, Matt Goodwin and Royce Simmons smashing their fists into boxing pads. It was very much the whole 'gladiator' thing, as if there were lives about to go on the line. In a very real sense these men were my protectors, and watching them thumping into those pads left me with a feeling of 100 per cent faith in them. In those few games I got more than my share of accolades. But there was no way I could've been the same cocky, super-confident kid chancing my arm on the football field without a forward pack to control the lions coming at me. I learned very early to be respectful of, and thankful for, the work a strong forward pack does for those at the rear.

If I did get a touch too half-smart, I was quickly pulled into line. How's this — I thought I was way too sexy for my own good and went out to get my ear pierced so I could whack in an earring. Even in the big smoke, not too many guys wore earrings back then. Out Penrith way, it was considered, well ... How will I put it? Unmanly. After a game I slipped in the earring and felt a few eyes on me. It didn't faze me much. But word spread pretty quickly about this prissy wanker with a bauble in his ear, and as I skipped merrily down the steps of Penrith Park to meet up with the rest of the team for a post-game beer, I was ambushed. My team-mates Royce Simmons, 'Louie' Mortimer and Graeme Bradley tore it straight out of the lobe. I'm rubbing my ear now as I write this, recalling the sharp pain as two blokes held me down and the other ripped the earring out. No questions asked. No beg-pardons. I suppose that's another lesson learned. Not sure what the lesson was, mind you, but the earring wasn't seen again.

Phil Gould led us down the path to modern and professional methods; he was the first to do it. He brought in dedicated fitness conditioners to whip us into shape. One was a bloke called Terry Mogg, and I'll never forget the day he was introduced to us. He had these Stubbies shorts on with a penguin shirt tucked inside. You had to think this fellow was an easy mark, a pushover for anyone who wanted to cut a corner at training. Little did we know his background. He'd been a bareknuckle Thai boxer — absolutely brutal stuff in which pain had become second nature to him.

For his first session he put markers at the four corners of Penrith Park and told us to run around the perimeter for half an hour. Before not very long at all, the square had become a tight circle for most players, who cut the corners and took it easy. After the time was up, we all gathered around, quite pleased with ourselves, until Terry walked into the middle of the group and started screaming obscenities, using words that not even a larrikin like me had ever heard before, let alone uttered. Basically, he said we were soft, but that word was embedded in a few dozen others, all starting with an F or a C. He ended the spray with the order, 'Go do it again.' Needless to say, no one cut a corner again under any of Phil Gould's staff.

That evening, a precedent was set for the way we'd train for the rest of the season. Through Terry Mogg, Gus had raised the bar. We knew where we stood. It seems a small moment in my long career, but it's stuck with me, jammed in my head, all these years later. Premierships would never come easily — on that one Penrith evening, I learned that lesson.

Gus Gould called it 'line mentality'. I'll devote a later chapter to his methods, and their influence on me, but this was a very early and lasting impression of him. His philosophy was that if there's a marker there, you run around it, and if you're told to run up and touch a line at the end of the field, you run all the way and you touch that line. Cut corners in training and you'll cut corners in a game. These are little things that make a side into an outfit that wins big matches. Penrith had that toughness, and the Roosters had it too in my time there.

Gus was also big into 'body language', another Gouldism the Roosters inherited. No hands on hips at training. If you look tired, you'll act tired. It took me a few training penalties to wake up to all that sage advice, but I can honestly say that I have lived and breathed it ever since. Under Gus, suddenly, you had to be up for the physical contact *and* the game, and know your role. You were also told the strengths and shortcomings of every member of the opposition. Under old Ron you had to be up mostly for the physical contact, and that was about all.

They were wonderful times, during the off season and the season proper. We were young and fit and had access to what seemed like unlimited cash. I can't tell you how excited I was training on Saturday morning, in the off season particularly.

It'd be back to my place at South Penrith, a few beers by the pool, then showering, putting gel in my hair, hitting the pubs and bars and the club, feeling like I owned the joint. It was the greatest time of my life to that point. I was nineteen when I bought that house for $132 000 in Ikin Street, on the boundary between South Penrith and Jamisontown. Honestly, I have no idea how I paid for it. I was earning $30 000 a year when I bought it, and money went in one pocket and straight out the other. I had an accountant, but I just spent money that I didn't have. Penrith was always good for a loan. You could go up to the club and get an advance on your contract money; I was getting it every week. I owed tens of thousands of dollars which were just written off in the end. Maybe hundreds of thousands. I guess you can get away with anything when your employers feel they need you under any circumstances. Sometimes I think the club was happier to have us in debt to it, so they could take advantage of that situation. It put the player who continually borrowed from the club in a position where he needed the club, more than the other way around.

I bought anything and everything, and had nothing. I had three of my school mates sharing that house. I have to say, it was a pretty wild joint — party central. I had a terrible alarm clock, and missed a few training sessions. 'You had post-traumatic amnesia most of the time,' Gus Gould tells me now. 'No wonder you couldn't find training. You forgot where you lived half the time.' Every night of the week there was something going on. My housemates were party boys on Fridays and Saturdays. I used to wait up for them to come home just so I could hear about the night's activities, even though I knew I had to play the next day. Early-to-bed comes hard for a fit young bloke. Then other mates and team-mates and I would take over the social roster from Sundays to Tuesdays. Not sure what happened on Wednesdays and Thursdays. Usually something did. There was never a dull moment at Ikin Street.

I don't know how the neighbours ever got a moment's sleep, though. Ben Alexander lived there on and off; so did Mark Geyer and sundry other Penrith and local area football players. There was a pinball machine, a pool table and a swimming pool. People would climb in the windows to be part of the activities. Sometimes I'd come home and there'd be twenty people in there. I had no idea who they belonged to, or who had invited them. It was like the public house of Penrith, and they were just going berserk. Well, you would, wouldn't you, when it wasn't your house to destroy? I lived there for a year. That was all. I reckon property values in the street shot up the moment I left.

I have to tell you about one night at Ikin Street. Well, it was more like morning, about 6 a.m. The usual party had moved out onto the front lawn. The music was blaring. A bloke from across the road came over in his underpants. I can only imagine he hadn't enjoyed a minute's sleep all night because of the racket, and now it was practically happening under his bedroom window. He was spoiling for a fight, and he shaped up to all twelve of us. As it turned out, he was the boss of one of the guys at the party. This won't surprise you, but the bloke lost his job the next day.

Penrith police — I'm not kidding here — had a file on the place. It was as thick as your thigh. I think they thought it was a drug distribution centre or something, because there were always so many people coming and going. They had the house under surveillance for months, recording the car registrations and taking photos of people going in and out. I was shocked out of my socks when I went down to the police station on some matter and they showed me all of this.

At that time, though, there was a culture of train hard, play hard and drink hard. I suppose, looking back, and comparing it with my relatively monastic family life these days, that it seems pretty juvenile. But a lot of winning teams live by that culture, and do well because of it — on the field and off it. Girls were part of it for the single guys; getting lucky wasn't all that difficult for most of us. It was basically a case of teenagers being curious and enjoying themselves. In short, every aspect was covered. I felt my life could not have been more rewarding or fulfilling.

I know the way league players and footballers in general deal with women and alcohol is a huge issue at the moment. There was nude swimming in our pool. But it was fun. Everyone had fun — the guys *and* the girls. And they all wanted to be there. The swimming pool was pretty significant to me. When we'd lived at Werrington the neighbours had had a pool, but the Fittlers weren't allowed in. I had to sneak in over the fence when no one was there. When I bought that first house at South Penrith, the number one requirement was a pool, so that I could invite absolutely everybody to enjoy it.

It was 1990, too, when I became 'Freddy'. It was Jack Gibson, supercoach, who bestowed that name on me. Greg 'Brandy' Alexander introduced me to 'Gibbo' under the grandstand at the Sydney Football Stadium (SFS). I'd been selected for my debut State of Origin game against Queensland, Game 2, at Olympic Park in Melbourne. The Rugby League was eager to expand the code beyond New South Wales and Queensland, eight years before Melbourne Storm entered the competition. I was eighteen years and 114 days old, the youngest ever person to play State of Origin. By that time footy had become my entire life. More than a job, more than a passion, it was, quite simply, an obsession.

Life without it would have been unthinkable. The selectors showed enormous faith in me as a rookie to give me a shot at State of Origin, which had been a childhood dream, naturally. The only one it didn't seem to please was Gus Gould. He was quoted in the newspaper as saying, 'It's too early to thrust Brad into State of Origin football'. But the chairman of NSW selectors, Don Furner, countered: 'We've got no worries about him'. As it turned out, we won 12–6 and I was on as a replacement.

But back to Gibbo and his bestowing me with a nickname that's stuck for life. It went like this ...

We'd gathered at the SFS for the team medical. It was just a standard introduction. 'Brad, meet Jack Gibson,' Brandy said. 'Jack, this is Brad Fittler.' In reply Gibbo said, 'Hi, Fred.' To this day I don't know if he was trying to put me in my place, or meaning to be funny, or if he'd actually thought about it and deliberately given me that nickname. Or if he simply didn't know who I was. You never knew with Jack Gibson.

Greg thought it sounded good, though, and just about everywhere after that I became 'Freddy'. Paul Langmack heard it too and, well, there's only one better form of public communication than the telephone and that's the tell-Langmack. He'd spread anything around the world in a flash.

There are those who think I'm named after Fred Flintstone, and those who think it's after Blind Freddy, because I used to have a beer occasionally. But the truth is much less exotic. It was a simple greeting from Jack Gibson that did it. For a while when I dyed my hair jet black they called me Adolf, and that was clever, if nothing else. (You know ... Adolf Fittler!) But it didn't stick like Freddy, and I suppose I have to be thankful for that, given the connotations.

I did learn something valuable about the media that year. I'd come home from the Kangaroo tour 8 kilograms overweight. A photographer asked if he could take a picture of me alongside a half-eaten pizza, a hamburger container and a can of VB. And he got me posing in an uncomplimentary fashion. It was a totally set-up shot. And I was totally set up as well. He brought in the pizza, the burger and the beer, not me. I was still very naive, particularly about the media. I thought they were my friends and could be totally trusted. Instead, the picture was splashed all over the next day's paper, under the headline FAT FREDDY. I've never lived that down, and it hurt me. I've been wary ever since.

Greg Alexander's favourite story of our appearance in the Grand Final that year revolves around me. Why don't I let Brandy tell it himself:

> We all came in to stay at the Regent Hotel at the Rocks for a night in Grand Final week so we could attend the traditional Grand Final breakfast the next day. For quite a few members of the Penrith squad, it was their first time staying in the big city. I mean, seriously, we were pretty raw. And Brad was the youngest and the most unworldly. We all got on the drink. Way too much. And someone started ordering seafood and alcohol on the hotel bill. Nothing but the best, of course. Trays of lobster coming in and out. The bill ran to about $3500. The name signed on the bill happened to be that of one of our players rooming with Freddy that night. It was Col Bentley. There's no way Col was responsible — we all know that. His name had been forged. Now I wouldn't accuse Brad Fittler of being the culprit. You make up your own mind.

It was me all right. Of course I forged Col's name. We ordered up the best and the most expensive: Dom Perignon champagne, oysters, prawns, lobsters. There was a knock on the door at one time and it was Phil Gould. We all hid behind the curtains and switched the lights off. Well, what do they say? You can take the boy out of Penrith, but you can't take Penrith out of the boy!

That Grand Final would be the clash of the country bumpkins: Canberra and Penrith. Canberra players — only slightly more accustomed to staying in classy establishments like the Regent — found it hugely amusing when they heard about the great seafood rip-off. Canberra's Ricky Stuart recalls, 'It was the talk of the hotel when we got up the next morning. I was very pleased to hear they'd been on the drink all night with the big game only a few days away. Problem is, I think it worked the other way. It brought them all close together. That Brad — he was a larrikin back then.'

We stayed in a small hotel at Randwick the night before the Grand Final, and people said I looked like I was handling the big occasion fairly well. But I was as nervous as a kitten on the inside. I'd been a wreck all week but I tried not to let it show.

We travelled down to Randwick in the team bus, and Gus followed behind in his own car with his mate Ross Seymour in the passenger seat. I thought I'd break the tension by dropping my pants, sticking my big fat bare bum up against the back window of the bus and chucking a brown-eye at Gus and Ross. And at everyone else on the freeway, too, I suppose. What I didn't know was that, at that very moment, Ross was saying to Gus, 'It's their first Grand Final. Do you think nerves might be a worry? Do you think they might be too tense?' And then they looked up ahead to see my bare arse, and others looking down from the back window pissing themselves laughing. 'No,' says Gus to his mate, 'I don't think nerves are a problem.'

I can only imagine that it must have been a tense time for the older players like Brandy, who had to shoulder most of the responsibility. We knew we had to face a red-hot Canberra side, but we believed in ourselves, and played right up to our very best. We also knew we'd had our best year ever, despite a terrible run of injuries.

The Grand Final against Canberra could have gone either way. The Green Machine beat us 18–14, but it was three tries apiece. I scored one of those to get us back into the match at half-time.

At the club later on, the mood was subdued. But there was one amazing moment. My name had been bandied around as a possible bolter for the Kangaroo tour of Great Britain. Personally, I'd never believed it for a moment. Amid the noise and the distractions at Memories restaurant in the club, someone grabbed the microphone and called for quiet. 'I've got the Kangaroo team here,' he said. 'And there's four from Penrith.' Well, the place erupted, and I suddenly started to shake. 'Carty's in,' he yelled. 'So's MG and Brandy. And what about this: Brad Fittler, too.'

I can't print in these pages what I said at that moment, but enough to say it was three words yelled very loudly. The first was 'You', the third was 'beauty' and the middle one ... well, you work it out!

So in the midst of this deflated feeling of losing the Grand Final, suddenly there was the elation of a schoolboy's dream realised: I was going to be wearing the green and gold of Australia. I had everything to look forward to — a Kangaroo tour as the youngest ever tourist at eighteen years and 247 days when I played my first match. And when that tour was done, I knew Penrith would be heading for far bigger and better things in 1991. We had a bloody great side at the Panthers. Disappointed as we all were that night, we knew that 1991 would be our championship season.

kangaroos and emus

Before I left for the Kangaroo tour, Phil Gould pulled me aside for some fatherly advice. He said: 'This is a terrific honour. You're the youngest Kangaroo tourist ever. It's a great opportunity to play alongside the best the game has to offer, and under a great coach. Be good, look after yourself, and don't get into any trouble.' I said: 'Good as gold.' Apparently he kept calling Brandy to check up on me. Brandy's answer was, 'Gus, you don't want to know. He's eating everything in England, drinking everything in England and dancing with every sheila in England.' Well, I was a big kid on the holiday of a lifetime.

I was rooming with Chris Johns. He was a terrific bloke and we got on like a house on fire. That was a good thing — and a bad thing. 'Johnsy' loved a beer, and since we were both in the second team, the Emus, playing only once a week, there was ample time to indulge that passion for an ale. What could I do but tag along? Did I have a choice? Of course the answer is 'yes', but I wasn't about to refuse.

The principal venue was a wonderful English pub called Henry J Beans, across the road from where we were staying. Johnsy would pour half a dozen beers down his throat then retire across the road and go to bed. For me, that was just an entrée. I'd get back to the room hours later, desperate for a smoke but anxious for my roommate not to find out I was on the durries — he was supposed to keep an eye on me, and make sure I avoided such unhealthy activities. My ruse was pretty pathetic, when I think about it now: I'd close the bathroom door, put a towel down to cover the crack between the door and the bathroom floor, start the shower and remove a panel from the ceiling. Then I'd stretch up on tiptoe and blow the smoke into the roof. It's a wonder the fire engines didn't come racing. I certainly wasn't fooling anyone except myself.

I think Bob Fulton knew my reputation for being a little bit slack, so he brought the great boxing trainer Johnny Lewis on the tour. Sometimes I thought it was only for my benefit. Every morning, in the freezing cold of a northern English winter, Johnny would get me up out of bed and onto the roads. When we weren't on the roads, he'd have me boxing in the hallways. He thought he had Jeff Fenech or Kostya Tszyu, I think, not a footballer. He absolutely killed me. Some days I was too buggered to raise a glass.

Johnny had to go back to Australia early to attend to one of his boxers. Honestly, I've never been so happy to see the back of a bloke in my life. But I shook his hand, promised him I'd be up early the next day and jogging on the road, and wished him a good and safe flight home. He didn't see the finger gesture I gave him when he turned his back. He's nature's gentleman, Johnny Lewis, a truly lovely bloke, but I was thinking to myself, 'If I never see you again, mate, it'll be too soon.' And let me tell you, I didn't get out of bed early the next morning.

I was just on a huge adventure that whole trip. It started with a bang, so to speak. A few of us bought some cars very cheaply from the local car yard. The cars cost a hundred quid or so each. They were bombs. Greg Alexander, MG, Carty and I shared one, and that car met a very early end when we rammed it headlong into a car bought by Martin Bella, another Kangaroo player. It happened in a car park in Leeds. We just ploughed into the other car when we found it parked there, then left both the wrecks and hightailed it back to the team hotel.

We were staying in the Marriott in Manchester, a classy hotel where my behaviour didn't quite match the surroundings. I got hold of a couple of huge firecrackers and lit them in the room. I was holding one in my hand, with the pretty bits showering all over me until it got so hot I had to let it go over the balcony. It speared like a Titan rocket into the footpath outside the hotel entrance and put a hole in the cement. The other cracker finished up halfway across town. I hope it didn't land on someone's roof — it would've gone off like the blitzkrieg all over again.

The next morning we were all down at breakfast and the hotel manager came in holding the remnants of the cracker and bits of cement. I just buried my head in the cereal bowl and hoped I wouldn't have the finger pointed at me. He said to the team manager, Keith Barnes, 'One of your chums let this off.' I can't imagine why, but Keith looked straight at me. I guess that, face-first in the cornflakes, I looked as guilty as sin. Or maybe, because of my past behaviour on the tour, I was the most likely culprit.

Once I'd found out I wasn't going to make the Test team, that I'd be in the Emus instead, I'd pretty much decided to just enjoy myself. I don't know why Keith Barnes bothered, but every Monday we'd gather on the mezzanine floor of the hotel and he'd go through the list of misdemeanours for the past week. They were mostly down to the same people, and my name was always mentioned. Bob Fulton would sit there with this huge grin, shaking his head.

Before the Kangaroo team was chosen, Fulton had phoned Gus Gould for final words of advice on the Penrith players. Carty and Brandy were automatic selections. As for MG, Gus reckoned, 'You've got to take him. He'll come back the world's best forward.' Fulton replied, 'But he's mad.' And Gus said, 'Yes, but take him anyway.' Then it came to me. Fulton was wavering. Gus said, 'He'll be OK. I'll have a word in his ear.' True to that word, Gus spoke to me before we left, but it didn't make much of an impression, I'm afraid.

Before the Test match at Old Trafford in Manchester, there was an intra-code goal-kicking competition. Out of the second team — the Emus — I was the only one who could kick goals. So they put me in against the Irish rugby union goal-kicker, a bloke called Frano Botica from New Zealand, and an English rugby union wizard kicker. There were four of us. They were all gun kickers; I was hopeless compared with them, not in their class.

The competition's sponsor gave us each 200 quid to take part, with 2000 quid to the winner. Prior to the competition I gathered all the kickers in the dressing room. I got one of my team-mates to gee them up by telling them all, quietly on the side, that I was an outstanding kicker.

Then I came in and suggested that we all just split the money between us before the competition, so we got 700 quid each. I stood up on the seat and said, 'Now, guys, I'm a guest here. I'd feel really bad if I walked away with all your money. How about we just agree to share it now and don't worry about who wins?' And they couldn't agree quickly enough. So it came to the goal-kicking competition, and my first kick ... well ... it was in front and it scrambled over by a sheer miracle. I got one out of nine. The rugby guys got all nine. Frano Botica missed only one. But I got them where it counted: in the hip pocket.

The last kick of the tie was a dropout, from the sideline. There I was right next to the crowd, and they were giving me heaps. Well, I topped it, didn't I, and it dribbled 5 metres in front of me. You've never heard a roar like it. I got the cash, though, and I don't think any sportsman in Australian history has ever performed so poorly in an Australian outfit.

The tours used to last three months, a heck of a long time to be away. The first two months were in Britain, and the last few weeks in France. So it was December when we got to France, and it was absolutely bloody freezing. I've never felt cold like that in my life. It was three weeks before Christmas and minus 10 degrees. We had tracksuit pants on under our shorts, surely a fashion statement that should never be repeated anywhere. Chris Johns's solution to the extreme cold was to wear these big red motorbike gloves, another fashion faux pas, but effective in the conditions. Even I had done away with my beloved thongs. And we had beanies on our beanies in training.

Well, we're in Carcassonne playing Languedoc on a Wednesday, which is when we usually played. MG is geeing up 'Spud' Carroll to hit this big French bloke: 'Weak as ... he's weak as ... just hit him hard.' And that's what Spud did. Only, MG had done the form on this bloke, and knew he wasn't weak at all. As Spud went in hard the bloke turned his hip, and knocked Spud colder than the weather — and that was saying something. Spud came to just before half-time, and he was calling MG every name under the sun — or snow — as we walked into the dressing rooms. And who's in there but Kevin Costner. Spud must've thought he was still unconscious and dreaming he was in Hollywood. We brushed Bob Fulton and went over to Costner. He was huge at that time — it was the year of *Dances with Wolves* — Lt John Dunbar as the Civil War military man befriending Indians and wolves and all that. 'Bozo' Fulton wasn't happy at all: he was trying to deliver a half-time rant, but no one was listening. Costner hung around and went out for a beer with us later.

A few members of the team had bumped into him earlier that week while he was filming *Robin Hood* nearby. If you thought *our* fashion sense was odd — what with trackies under our shorts and Chris Johns's motorbike gloves — we were at least a step ahead of poor Kevin, who had to stand out in the snow in his green Robin Hood tights, freezing his nuts off while the cameras rolled. Anyway, some team members were bold enough to invite him to watch us play, and that's how Robin Hood came to meet up with our bunch of merry men in Carcassonne. I was sure he didn't want to waste his evening talking to us about *Dances with Wolves* or *Bull Durham*, so I shook his hand, thanked him for joining us, and then left him to the others. Well, to one in particular: John Cartwright. Carty hammered him. Wouldn't leave him alone. I really don't think Kevin Costner wanted to hear all about life in Penrith, but

Carty told him anyway. Endlessly. I think Carty figured there might be a career in Hollywood for him. 'You know,' he told Costner, 'they say I'm a dead ringer for you.'

So as you can see it was quite a trip, well summed up by MG when he told *Rugby League Week*, 'Freddy treated it like a Contiki tour. He was always the first up and last to go to bed. He was like a kid in a candy store. We got 400 quid a week expenses, and mine and Freddy's would be gone on the first night.'

ABOVE A babe in the arms of my brother, Nathan.

ABOVE Just 18 months old, and already a smiling grub.

BELOW Off to nippers, but still time to pose for the paparazzi.

ABOVE 'Something's choking me — I think it must be these shorts.'

LEFT My first game of footy, and it was serious stuff even then.

LEFT In holiday mode, aged eight.

LEFT In Year 12 at McCarthy Senior Catholic College. Studying hard with mates (L to R) Marcus, Shippo and Rob.

© NEWSPIX

RIGHT That damn 'Fat Freddy' photo.

© NEWSPIX

FROM THE COLLECTION OF BRAD FITTLER

ABOVE On the Australian under-16s tour of New Zealand. Who's a sexy boy, then?

LEFT My worst moment: carrying the coffin of Ben Alexander with his brothers, Greg and Peter.

© NEWSPIX

RIGHT Striding out for Penrith in 1990 with that black hair rinse gone horribly wrong.

LEFT Battered and bruised with Mal Meninga and the World Cup trophy in 1992. It was worth the pain of a shattered right cheekbone.

© NEWSPIX

ABOVE Holding the World Cup trophy at Wembley in 1995 with Prince Edward in the background.

BELOW On a Kangaroo tour of Papua New Guinea, arm in arm and treated like royalty.

© GETTY IMAGES

ABOVE Even disaster turns to smiles when Alfie Langer's around. After the State of Origin series in 2001.

© NEWSPIX

ABOVE To absent friends: the Anzac Test promotion I missed at the Kokoda Trail Walk in Sydney. Kiwi captain Jarrod McCracken is there, but not me.

BELOW Nothing beats the elation of winning in your country's colours. Another Kangaroo triumph.

ABOVE The spoils of a Blues victory — after the 2000 State of Origin series, possibly the best team I ever played in.

LEFT Looking apprehensive, with Kangaroo coach Chris Anderson, as controversy raged over whether the tour to Great Britain should go ahead after 9/11.

© GETTY IMAGES

RIGHT Walking to Aussie Stadium in 2001, to announce my retirement from international football.

BELOW Breaking out the champagne: time to celebrate an Aussie win, with Andrew 'Joey' Johns.

© NEWSPIX

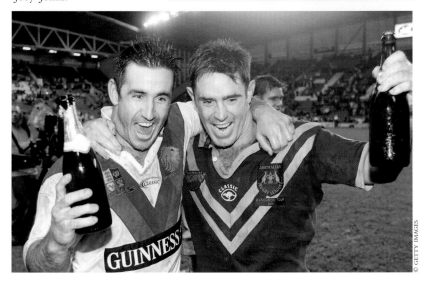

© GETTY IMAGES

ABOVE Getting the Blues downfield — it's always easier to defend at their end of the field than attack at ours.

BELOW Marie and I on our first trip away together, at the Twelve Apostles in Victoria. I love this picture of a couple getting to know each other on the verge of a wonderful romance.

our championship season

Let's get back to the Panthers' premiership-winning season in 1991. I returned from the Kangaroo tour keen as mustard, but way too full of myself. I was nineteen and carrying on like an idiot. And I was 12 kilograms overweight. Gus gave the Kangaroo tourists an extra week or two off, then told us we'd be training on the Australia Day long weekend, just a couple of weeks before the first trial game. We were to train on the Saturday and again on the Monday. That was no good for me: I had a long-standing agreement to join my former schoolmates on a holiday on the Gold Coast. I asked Gus for more time off and he agreed, reluctantly, muttering something about my life being 'one big holiday'. But I had to be back for training on Tuesday afternoon, ready and raring to go. I was enjoying the holiday, though, and didn't make it back. Tuesday: no appearance. Wednesday: no appearance either. Thursday and Friday: no appearance. Friday night I rang Gus, and asked him what time we were training the next day. He said, 'The boys are training at eight o'clock. You be there at seven.'

I'll admit, I did make something of a spectacular arrival for my meeting with Gus the next morning. I'd borrowed a mate's motorbike, a Yamaha 250cc, and roared down Mulgoa Road next to Penrith Park, mounted the gutter, blasted across a canal and flew out the other side, raced across a car park and footy field, and screeched to a halt in a cloud of dust and gravel in front of him. I was wearing a red headband, shorts and thongs. No training gear. I thought he'd be impressed. I thought he'd see me as another Evel Knievel.

I said, 'Hey dude, what's happenin'?'

Gus said, simply, 'Get inside.' He locked me in the tiny coaches' room at Penrith Park and proceeded to blast me. I've never heard a spray like it before or since. He just gave it to me, telling me exactly what he thought of the way I was acting. 'You're a f---ing bighead. You look like something they just dragged up from the beach. Wake up to yourself! You're a f---ing goose and you're heading downhill.' And he was right. I could only hang my head and say nothing in response. I started to sob and sniffle. Neither of us will ever forget his parting words: 'Jump back on your f---ing motorbike and come back with a different f---ing attitude. If I ever see that bike, or that attitude, again, I'll shove them up your arse.'

I left that meeting a shattered but better person — and in tears, I don't mind saying. No one had ever spoken to me like that before. Ever. Gus says now he thought at the time he might have been too harsh and broken my spirit. He says 'even the motorbike sounded sad' as I left. But I turned up for training later in my mother's car, with my hair combed, a crisply pressed white shirt, football shorts, runners, and all my footy gear in a brand new sports bag.

'How do I look, coach?' I asked.

'Fine,' Gus replied, 'now let's just get on with it.' It was the first of many bitter arguments and, later, happy resolutions with Phil Gould, with whom my career has been such a parallel over the past fifteen years.

I knew it would be our year at Penrith in 1991. Everything went our way most of the year. As the big one — the Grand Final, again versus the Raiders — drew near I found myself much more nervous than I had been for the 1989 finals series, or the decider in the previous year. I was shaking like a bloody leaf and I had no idea why. Our form going in was fine. We'd beaten Norths to get into the big one when dead-eye Daryl Halligan, the best goal-kicker I ever saw, missed with four shots at goal out of five. An off day with the boot for Daryl was unheard of, and I always figured the gods were with us after that.

Gus saved up one of his special speeches for us before the game. He said he'd seen a story on CNN earlier in the year about a career soldier heading off to the Gulf War for the US. A reporter asked the soldier if he was nervous, and he replied that for twenty-three years the United States government had paid him and made it possible for him to raise a family, and that he was ready to defend his country. The soldier said, 'I got the knock on the door and I knew it was time.' Gus told us we'd be getting a knock on the door at 3 p.m. and that was going to be our time. Gus loved those stories about patriotism and duty and serving your country, and added to them the idea of devotion to your team-mates. He spoke often of Australians going into battle, and particularly of the conscripts who also got the 'knock on the door' and put their lives on the line without question.

To steal a phrase from Phil Gould: when the wind blows away the balloons and the smoke from the fireworks, 'it gets down to the players'. And there's nothing to match that moment. One instant does stick in my head, though, and it was a trigger for me on that memorable day. The gear steward gave us our jerseys and socks, and when I pulled the jumper out of the bag there on the sleeve was the red Winfield Cup badge that said '1991 Grand Final'. The importance of the day was crystallised for me then and there.

The last words I remember before going onto the arena were those of my team-mate Royce Simmons: 'No one ever died on a football field'. He yelled those words with the same passion he delivered during the game. It pretty much summed up the way he played. To him, football was as good as life got. And this, a

Grand Final, was the ultimate stage. The first of his two tries that day symbolised his style, and such courage and determination as I've never seen before or since. He'd already bounced off a few players, and then 120-kilogram Glenn Lazarus stood between Royce and the try line. I reckon Goliath himself would not have stopped Royce at that moment; certainly 'Lazzo' wasn't going to stand in the way of Royce's undeniable path to the line.

Very early in the Grand Final I was tackled by Lazarus, and he hit me so hard I did a somersault backwards like an Olympic gymnast. It would've scored a perfect ten, I'm sure, but all it got me was a seriously corked thigh. The Raiders led us 12–6 at the break, and another bone-rattling speech from Gus had us fired up for the return. Gus verbally smashed us. He didn't miss a beat, and his voice never fell below the decibel level of a jumbo jet. He was red in the face, and screaming blue murder.

'Do it for Roycey!' Those were his last words as we ran back down the tunnel. Royce Simmons was so stunned into action by that, and an incident involving MG, that he made four tackles in a row soon after the game resumed. It was inspirational stuff. MG had been sent to the sin bin just before it on a touch judge's report after the judge ruled 'no try' when it appeared to one and all that we'd scored. MG went off his head, and then off the field to the sin bin. I think that turned the game.

When he came back from the sin bin, he threw a ripper of a pass to me. Somehow I jumped over the fullback's head and got it to Brad Izzard for the try. Brandy got the conversion and suddenly it was 12–all, with Penrith coming home the stronger.

I think one of my most memorable moments out of that whole game was a tackle on Mal Meninga. I'd always enjoyed playing against Mal because he was the world's best centre, and that was a challenge in itself. But sometimes I found it a less complicated task than coming up against some of the smaller, faster and less predictable centres.

Anyway, for one glorious moment in that Grand Final it came down to him or me. He'd taken an intercept on his quarter line and was in full flight up the sideline, powering downfield like a runaway Mack truck. I was the last line, angling across in cover defence. There's no more frightening sight for a defender than Mal Meninga coming at you at full pace. Never was, and never will be. I just launched myself, got my arms wrapped around those massive legs somehow and hoped for the best. It felt sensational as he toppled to the ground like part of an old growth forest. I'd played my part.

Brandy was always going to be the bloke we looked to for victory. For the previous two seasons he'd steered the Penrith ship, and there was no way he was going to let this chance slip away. In such a grim situation, Brandy was as good as they got. He kicked an unbelievable field goal from about 30 metres to get us the lead by a point, and then Canberra's Scotty Gale tried a short dropout and Mark Geyer snapped it up to put Royce over in the corner for his second try. At 17–12 we were still vulnerable, which is why Brandy's sideline conversion was so precious. When it sailed over I was overwhelmed by this feeling of total relief. We took it 19–12 in the end, and after 25 seasons of trying, a premiership finally went the way of the Panthers. No more the chocolate soldiers, melting under the pressure; now we were champions of the game.

The post-match scenes on the ground were amazing. I felt this massive sense of relief — it was over and we'd done it. All around me grown men in football boots, grubby and smelly from the game, were bawling their eyes out and hugging each other. One of the best sights of all was Ben Alexander sharing the excitement with the same sense of exhilaration as everyone else. Ben had been a first grade player all year, and must have been shattered when Gus chose Royce Simmons instead of him for the Grand Final. A lot of players — most, I'd venture to say — would've been disgusted. Yet here was Ben, first onto the field, just happy to be a part of the celebrations, with a grin on his face like a split watermelon. What a terrific attitude he had.

We piled onto the team bus and headed back to the club. From 10 kilometres away the highway was chock-a-block. Even that far from the club, traffic was at a standstill. There were flags and streamers hanging out of car windows. They couldn't wait to get back there to greet us. And our bus was marooned in all the activity.

When we finally got to the club it was chaos. Thousands and thousands of people inside the club and out. Looking down at them all from the stage, they seemed to be swaying as one creature, back and forth. One gigantic, euphoric animal. It was like the tides of an ocean, ebbing and flowing. I know now how pop stars or politicians feel when they have a crowd of thousands in the palm of their hand. If we raised our arms, they'd all do the same. If we jumped, or smiled, or did anything, they'd cheer so loudly I thought the roof was going to fall in. I couldn't believe you could make so many people so blissfully, so deliriously happy just by winning a footy game. I could make out my schoolmates and my family in the crowd. And I'd never seen such looks on their faces before.

They were in another world. It was surreal. A fantasy world. Brandy was absolutely beside himself. Our whole game in those early days revolved around Greg Alexander. It was very structured play. Brandy called the numbers and we all followed. I could've played the winger's role, the prop's role, any of them. It was football by the numbers, so much more so than it is these days. I never worked out why Brandy was ignored as the Australian halfback. He was just so dominant. I suppose it didn't help his cause that Alfie Langer and Ricky Stuart were also around, and that they too were wonderful players.

Night soon merged into morning, and a few of us ended up in one of the local restaurants when a TV cameraman came in to shoot some amazing vision of some of the happiest blokes in the world. Thirty schooners or not, we couldn't keep the smiles off our faces. After what passed for breakfast we headed up to one of the old favourite haunts, the Pioneer Tavern, and continued on with more of the same. I didn't believe it was humanly possible to feel that good.

It may have been the end of a long wait for a Penrith

premiership, but it was not the end of the football year. Four days later there was a medical for the tour of Papua New Guinea (PNG). Brandy, John Cartwright, MG and I were chosen. Everyone was trying to get out of the tour. In the car on the way down to Sydney the other guys were coming up with excuses about how they might fail the medical, when in fact I was the only one with a genuine injury. I had a massive bruise on my hip after the Grand Final — Lazzo had knocked me on my backside. But Bob Fulton insisted I go to PNG. He pulled me aside at the medical and said that at least one of us ought to go, and he thought it was in my best interests to make the trip. It was terrific advice, very much appreciated. The others withdrew, I went, and they were the losers.

I had a great time. When our plane landed it was greeted by thousands upon thousands of locals, and they lined the streets ten deep all the way from the airport to the hotel. It was rough as guts, though, and very hot, so training was less often and less intense. Most of the time was spent lying in a deckchair, reading a book or playing golf. I've never experienced anything like the superstar status in which they held us all, but none more so than Mal Meninga.

I played golf one morning with Mal and it was unbelievable. Anything up to a hundred people followed him around, and if his ball went into a hazard they'd launch themselves after it. There might've been crocodiles or anything where his ball was, but it didn't worry them. It was just fanatical. Extraordinary.

I played my first Test match on that tour, in the highland town of Goroka, and we won 58–2. I played lock, with Brad Clyde and Ian Roberts in the second row, Glenn Lazarus at prop, Kerrod Walters hooking, and blokes like Mal and Andrew Ettingshausen and Cliff Lyons in the backs. I just felt unbelievably honoured. Some of those people were my schoolboy heroes. I scored two tries, and from then on, rarely missed a Test, only once through personal tragedy — more of that shortly — and once through injury. Above all, it was the players who made it so special.

But those games were pretty violent. The Kumuls would try to rip your head off, then ask for a photo with you after the game. They definitely lived by the old rules of footy. Though they idolised us, the locals did show their appreciation in strange ways. All they wanted to do was touch us, and cram in alongside, and that was a bit frightening at times when there were hundreds pushing and shoving to get at us. We managed to sneak away one night for a quiet beer in our Port Moresby hotel, then people started shooting up the streets outside. That's when we knew it was time for bed. No need for some bloke to tell you it's 'last drinks please' when the sounds of gunshots are ringing in your ears.

Mostly, though, it was a tropical paradise for the Australian team. Our second game on that tour was against Islands Zone in Rabaul, on the island of New Britain, and conditions were as severe as they were at any stage. The heat was so intense that we struggled to win just 42–25, but the off-field activities more than made up for it. Five of us and a couple of the locals went deep sea fishing, and hooked onto a marlin but lost it after a short fight. Then one of the rods sizzled into action, and something massive took off at about a hundred miles an hour. It took all five of us heaving on the rod in turns to gain any line on this creature. But the Papuan crew comprised a couple of skinny blokes with the strength of an ox, and they managed to pull this thing alongside the boat. Well, more accurately, we pulled the boat alongside it — because what turned out to be a giant shark was longer than the boat.

The crew were screaming instructions at me to help get it on board. There was no way in the world I was having any part of that. If I was on the boat, that creature was staying in the water. Simple as that. If it was coming on board, I was jumping over the side. They gave me the gaff and told me to hook it in the mouth. Since its mouth was roughly the size of Sydney Heads I should never have missed, but I did, and cut the line by mistake. The shark was off and gone in a few seconds — and after a fight that had lasted an hour. I did honestly try to get the shark. But somehow I think it was the smartest mistake I ever made. I suppose it would've fed all of Rabaul for a month, but I'm glad it never got the chance to taste-test me first.

It was such a terrible shame to see those images years later, in September 1994, of the town of Rabaul and the island consumed by the eruptions, an hour apart, of the two volcanoes Tavurvur and Vulcan. Rabaul and surrounding villages were buried under tonnes of volcanic ash. Rabaul was such a stunningly beautiful place, built inside the active volcano caldera and blessed with one of the world's great harbours. But that natural beauty carried with it the threat of devastation at any time. Thousands lost their homes and their livelihoods, and many hundreds their lives. I wept when I saw the destruction on the TV news.

In 1991, though, we were treated like rock stars in PNG. We were huge heroes to them, even if the grounds were either like playing on a beach or playing on concrete; there was nothing in between. The tour was topped off by an unforgettable day aboard two boats. One was a big, old, uncomfortable-looking barge, the other a multimillion-dollar cruiser. Most of the boys went for the cruiser, of course, while Chris Johns, Kevin Walters and I were left with the barge, which didn't faze us much, because it had heaps of character. Sometimes I think I must be blessed, because I opened up the fish storage unit on board and there were thousands of beers on ice. It was like winning the lottery, and with the skipper playing Jimmy Barnes at full bore we headed off to a secluded island for an absolutely magic day.

It had been a wonderful, unbelievable year — the Kangaroo tour at the start of it, then the premiership. Then Papua New Guinea. Who could've known that such a free fall into defeat and shattering grief would follow so soon afterwards?

to the depths
of despair

So we arrived at 1992, and we were the premiers. People across the city and state treated us differently; we weren't country hicks any more. We were the pride of the Rugby League — the premiers! And how sweet it sounded. The hard thing was, it was difficult to get that sudden rise to prominence out of our heads.

It's not easy to put my finger on where it all started to unravel. Was it that some of the players started taking notice of the wraps, getting too much money, getting more intense, partying more than they had in the past? Were we believing our own publicity? Were we as focused as in previous years? Did we train as hard as the year before? Or were other teams simply lifting to meet and then surpass our own high standards? Certainly there was an added pressure of expectation that I'd never felt before at Penrith. Whatever the reason, or combination of reasons, the whole club handled that season atrociously. With every loss there was a crisis meeting; we stumbled from one crisis meeting to the next, and nothing ever changed. Football became a chore, training a nightmare.

There were drugs used at Penrith — one in particular, the common sinus medication Sudafed. In my time at Penrith, these were hugely popular. They were banned in the Olympics up until the start of 2004 because they contain pseudoephedrine. But they are not illegal in the game of rugby league and they never have been. Their use is monitored by the Australian Sports Drug Agency, which has statistical data to back up my claim of how widely Sudafed is used for a pre-game boost or simply to help with a flu. I was still having a pre-game Sudafed right up to the day I retired. I took Sudafed because it cleared my nasal passages, not for the lift — but there's no doubt that it did give me a boost.

Anyone walking into the Penrith dressing room before a game around that time might have got the wrong impression, as there was a merry-go-round of players getting needles about thirty minutes before run-on. They were vitamin B shots, I'm sure; at least, that's what they told us. I just got on the end of the queue like everybody else.

I am, however, sure that steroids were uncommon then, and now. It's a subject I feel very strongly about. If steroids were made legal, or testing dropped off, it would destroy our sport. There's just too much body contact. Players would get seriously injured in every tackle if the blokes hitting them were full of steroids. I've been tested plenty of times by the Australian Sports Drug Agency. We all have. And more power to them.

The one thing that kept me sane during that woeful Penrith season was State of Origin. I was fortunate enough to be part of an awesome team captained by Laurie Daley and containing the likes of John Cartwright, Benny Elias, Ricky Stuart, Andrew Ettingshausen, David Gillespie, Paul Harragon, Paul Sironen, Glenn Lazarus, Paul McGregor and Rod Wishart. It was a different era, too, and State of Origin was not yet the legend it has become. When asked to train until we dropped, we did it. When asked to appear at various promotions, we did it without question. When it came time to enjoying ourselves, we did it with the best of them. I suppose it helped that the Tooheys brewery company was the sponsor. Laurie was such a terrific leader, too. Blokes were so keen to be a part of that squad that there was literally a race to get to the medical first. 'Cement' Gillespie, a truly damaging forward, used to camp outside the team hotel the night before selection just in case he was named, which he always was, as run-on player or reserve.

No sooner had the team's medical officers, Dr Nathan Gibbs and physiotherapist Liz Steet, given the go-ahead than we put on our jeans and compulsory State of Origin shirt and headed down to the team hotel bar. A couple of hours later we'd be sitting around the piano with John Rowles turning out requests from the boys, gathered around three and four deep and singing our lungs out. We only knew it was stumps when Gus Gould did his perfect rendition of Frank Sinatra's 'New York, New York' — time to board the bus from the Holiday Inn, armed with a few more beers each for the trip.

The drinking served a twofold purpose. It was fun, of course, but it was also accompanied by serious assessment and analysis of the upcoming game. Match tactics were often formulated at Studebakers nightclub in Kings Cross, the next stop after the team hotel, and then at the old standby, the Bourbon and Beefsteak bar. You paired up with someone who had similar drinking habits, a team-mate who drank his beer and/or spirits at about the same pace. Paul 'Mary' McGregor heard about my reputation and thought we'd make a good pair. We went drink for drink. (As I said, this was a different era.) It would've been a lot smarter and cheaper and quicker if we'd just compared shoe sizes and been done with it. Not as much fun, mind you — just more sensible. It was a win for Freddy at the end of a very liquid evening and early morning. I was still standing. Mary McGregor was flat on his back, dead to the world, sleeping it off in a back alley of the Cross.

You couldn't do that these days, and I feel considerable sympathy for today's sports stars, with so much intense scrutiny of their actions on and off the field. To some of you, a night such as I've just described will no doubt sound like juvenile, boorish and loutish behaviour. I make no apology for that. Life isn't meant to be taken seriously all the time. I'm a massive believer in doing what makes you happy, as long as you don't hurt anyone along the way. There's no reason in the world why you can't do that from time to time and still be seen as a responsible, upstanding citizen. It certainly didn't do any harm to the Blues in 1992, winning the first game 14–6 at the SFS, losing the second 5–4 at Lang Park, and then taking back the series at the SFS 16–4.

It was nights like that one at the Bourbon and Beefsteak with Mary, and playing in great Blues squads, that kept me going in that season, and the next two. State of Origin was more to me than just a wonderful challenge and a great footy series; it was a reprieve from something I could never get used to, and that was losing week in and week out in club matches. In the end it just became easier to lose. But however hard it was to lose games, it was nothing compared with losing one of my closest mates.

goodbye, mate

When Ben Alexander died in a car crash on Sunday night, 21 June 1992, it ripped the heart out of the Penrith club and the Penrith area. And it sure ripped the heart out of me!

We were young. Bulletproof. We weren't supposed to die — that was something that happened to old people, not people like Ben and me. So when he died it was a weird feeling, an out-of-body experience in which I seemed to be watching it all unfold from a distance. When I say it was weird, I mean it was like a dream — a nightmare, of course — but right up until the burial, it *was* a dream scene. Not quite real.

Ben was pretty much my best mate at that time. We were rarely ever apart. We went to school together. He shared my house. I remember expecting that he'd turn up the next day, and all would be well again. Ben dead? Impossible!

I was in the Australian team, getting ready for the second Test against Great Britain at Princes Park in Melbourne. We were in a training camp in Coogee. I'd been up to Penrith to watch the first grade match against Eastern Suburbs at Penrith Park. Ben's reserve grade team won easily 25–6 and he played well, kicking a field goal. Everyone was in good spirits. Later that night I was having a beer with a few of the Test players at a bar in Bondi Junction, in Sydney's eastern suburbs. Mal Meninga was the Australian captain at the time. A call from him came through for me; I guess he was the one that team manager Geoff Carr and coach Bob Fulton asked to pass on the bad news. Mal used to be a policeman, so part of that job was probably giving bad news to relatives who'd lost loved ones.

That time is a bit of a blur. I'm sure I've deliberately shut it out of my mind. I ended up pretty drunk, too, hoping it would all just go away. As I said, I'd been up to Penrith Park and enjoyed a beer or two with my pals because I wasn't playing, and then, as it was a Sunday night, we'd had a few more at the Australian team session in Bondi Junction. When Mal passed on the news I shook my head and went and sat in a corner and cried. I do remember that. I bawled and bawled. I felt very bewildered and very alone. I was twenty years old, for God's sake. This was one of my very best mates. His family was like a second family to me — I'd been in and out of the Alexanders' house from the time I was fifteen.

When I received the news, the first thing I wanted to do was to call someone close to Ben and close to me. I was feeling so alone in this room full of some of the most famous faces in Australian sport. I didn't want to be there. I wanted to be with close friends from the west. I wanted to hug someone, cry on a friend's shoulder. Instead I cried myself silly in a lonely corner of a Bondi Junction bar all by myself, 50 kilometres from home and lifelong loved ones. There were no mobile phones, of course. It wasn't so easy to get people on the phone. I did ring the Alexanders' house, but couldn't get through. I don't think I slept a wink that night. If I nodded off, it was just so much worse to wake up and realise that Ben's death wasn't some odd nightmare but a reality.

The next day I drove up to Greg Alexander's house in Penrith. I drove west along the freeway, filled with dread about the scene I was about to confront. Again I say it was weird, but I didn't know how I was supposed to feel. I was questioning everything about myself. What would I do when I got there? Was I feeling the way you should at a time like that? I pulled up in the driveway of Greg's place. He had a big block with lots of open grassy space at the front. It was packed with people. They were crying. It was horrible. Absolutely horrible. Brandy met me as I pulled in and we just hugged and cried on each other's shoulders. What else could we do?

Even now I think about Ben most days. Usually I wonder what he'd be doing now. Would he live near me? Would he still be playing football? Would he have kids? Would we still be as close as we were then? We first met when I was thirteen, playing for Cambridge Park. He was a year above me. I started dating his sister Linda when I was in Year 10 at school. Mark Geyer was dating Greg and Ben's other sister, Megan. Ben loved MG more than anyone in the world, I'm sure. It was such a fun-filled household, such a warm and loving environment. The Alexanders' house was a home to one and all. Their mother, Leonie, stepfather Gerard, the brothers Greg, Peter and Ben, and the girls were the most beautiful family I knew. Ben was the glue that held it all together. He had such a great spirit and love of life and family.

Ben and I were kids, then, exploring things. You never forget people you found out those things with. He was a tubby thing, and they called him 'Buddha', which was shortened to 'Boods'. That's the name that Mark Geyer, his brother Greg and the other coffin bearers, including me, have tattooed on our shoulders.

The service at St Nicholas' Church, and carrying his casket to the funeral car, are lost in a haze to me. They are. There were a couple of thousand mourners, most of them outside listening to the service on loudspeakers. I think the church's capacity was only about 700, and half of that was taken up with family and Penrith club players and officials. The worst thing of all was the burial at King's Lawn cemetery, right behind St Dominic's College in Parker Street, where we'd gone to school together. There's a car wrecker's yard right opposite the cemetery.

Can I say this? Burial's inhumane. That's my opinion, anyway. It should be banned. Outlaw it, I reckon. I can't believe they allow people to be buried in the ground and, worse still, have people stand around and watch. It's like looking at an execution, putting death on public display. It's barbaric. I definitely think I managed to separate my mind and my body that day in the cemetery. It was like I was standing in one place, there by the grave site, and my mind — me — I — was a few metres away, thinking, *This can't be right.*

Sometimes I go to the scene of the accident on the corner of Desborough Street and Bennett Street, Colyton, where his little Honda Integra ran a red light and collided with another car, going into a wild spin. Ben, not wearing a seatbelt, was killed instantly when the car slammed into a traffic light. There were three passengers in his car — Glenn Liddiard, Luke Goodwin and Scott Murray — who got out of it without life-threatening injuries.

Ben had come from the club where, only hours earlier, he'd received his premiership blazer from 1991 the night after playing reserve grade against Easts. He then moved on to the Pioneer Tavern at South Penrith, where he picked up his three friends to kick on further at the Temptation nightclub in Mt Druitt. They never made it that far, of course. It was just a dreadful, dreadful accident.

And for weeks and months after it, I thought there was a serious problem with the way I was coping with Ben's death. It was as if I believed life had to change because of it. But it didn't. It just went on. Here was this momentous thing — my best friend's sudden, horrible death — but people were still playing footy, the sun still came up the next day.

I went to King's Lawn recently. I pulled up alongside the cemetery. Stopped the car. Got out. But for the life of me, I couldn't go through those gates. I couldn't. Does that make me a bad person? I don't think so. You don't have to visit someone's grave to remember them well. Ben's in my mind and in my heart, not in that place in the ground. Whatever part of him is in that grave is nothing compared with the memories I carry in my heart. Maybe I should have gone in there to visit him. I did try. But I just couldn't do it. Boods, I loved you then, and I love you now. I just couldn't bring myself to go to the grave with you again.

The coroner reported that Ben was over the legal alcohol limit at the time of the accident. But the truth is, he wasn't a heavy drinker. His world didn't revolve around alcohol and good times the way it did for some others. On occasions I drove around Penrith with alcohol in me, too. I guess I was protected; someone was looking down on me. It wasn't accepted as a smart thing to do, and I knew it was wrong, but I did it nonetheless. How I didn't get killed — how I didn't kill a mate — is way beyond me.

In hindsight, looking back at my early twenties, I can't believe there weren't more tragedies. With some apprehension, and no pride, I'll tell a couple of stories of close calls in the hope that someone will read about them and learn a lesson about safe, sober driving. It took the loss of Ben for me to learn.

I had a sponsor's car, which was a small four-wheel drive vehicle with a soft-top roof. We'd been to Penrith Leagues Club, then to the Kingswood pizza shop, and to a friend's unit to chill out for a while. All in all, a pretty standard night on the social scene, such as it was, in Penrith. I figured I was probably fine to drive by then, and after all, it was only a couple of kilometres to my place. What sort of trouble could I get into? That was the thought that always prompted me to jump behind the wheel. I very rarely travelled far from home in those days.

I came around a corner way too fast and there was loose gravel on the curb, which sent the car out of control. The car went into a roll and was still tumbling over and over 50 metres down the road ... until it came to a stop, appropriately, at a stop sign. The car was flattened to about waist height. We didn't have the roof on, and my mate Shorty, in the back seat, was thrown clear, dislocating his shoulder. John Cartwright's brother Mick was in the car as well and lost most of the skin off his knuckles. I had a broken nose. It happened not far from the Pioneer Tavern, Ben's last stop before his fatal crash. When I snapped out of the shock, I checked where everyone was. There was no sign of Shorty at first, and then I saw him in the darkness, still 30 metres away, walking towards us. I didn't know whether to laugh or cry. We just left the car and started wandering the streets. I was spinning out, dazed I guess, maybe in shock. We headed home.

When Ben was killed my days of drink-driving were dead as well. There hasn't been a time since when I've had more than three beers and got in the car. The thing is, it could have been any of us buried in that plot. I'm not obsessed with that thought, but it has crossed my mind, absolutely. Between cars and motorbikes, it's a miracle I'm alive and out of jail.

I bought a Harley-Davidson motorbike, and got done three times for riding it without a licence. I had Greg Alexander doubled on the back once and the police crossed three lanes of traffic to book me. I think it got around at the local station that I'd been let off on more than one occasion, and a couple of them were out to get me. But let's face it, you didn't have to be Sherlock Holmes to catch me out.

There was another motor vehicle incident with Brandy and I which involved the presentation of the Rothmans Medal in 1990. Only the two of us from the Penrith team travelled down to Sydney with the team doctor, Norm Southern. We borrowed a brand new corporate car belonging to the club's chief executive, Don Feltis. Only because Don wouldn't give us a Cabcharge. Bad move, because we, or rather I, had to drive all the way home to Penrith.

We made it safely, and without being pulled over, which was quite an achievement in itself, and by way of celebration we figured we should try some good, old-style 'paddock-bashing' in Don's new car. I remember the club doc being tossed around in the back seat, banging his head on one back window and then the other as we put the car through its paces in a field meant for cows, not cars. We'd stopped off at McDonald's on the way home, so the car, which had been spotless when we picked it up, was strewn with bits of cheeseburger and gherkin and rubbish.

The good news is that all of us — Brandy, me, the doc *and* Don's car — got home in one piece. The next day, though, Norm Southern had a heart attack; thankfully, one from which he recovered.

So I've never really had much luck in cars. Like the time I was driving in my two-seater red sports car on the M4 motorway from St Marys to Penrith. I drove up behind a car that was travelling slowly, hogging the right-hand lane. Is there anything more frustrating? It took ages to angle over into the left-hand lane, which allowed me to get by.

I flew past him, maybe just nudging over the speed limit — but nothing dangerous or excessive. I didn't gesture toward him. No road rage on my part. Nothing. That night I had a phone call from a police officer. He wanted me to come and see him. I had no idea what it was about. It turned out that he was the driver of the car that had been holding me up in the right-hand lane; he was off duty, and had his wife in the vehicle. 'I'm charging you with speeding and driving recklessly,' he told me. And because he was a highway patrol officer, he could do just that. It was absolutely bloody ridiculous.

I appealed the charges and, as usual, got nowhere. I was told that no matter whether he was in his little Astra or the police highway patrol vehicle, he'd have known exactly how fast I was going and whether or not I was driving recklessly. I was fined and almost lost my licence over it. Here's the crunch, though: a couple of weeks later I was playing footy, and who was there as the first grade touch judge? You guessed it. The same policeman. I can only imagine I must have upset him in a game sometime beforehand, and he got square with a trumped-up driving charge. I wanted to give him a gobfull during the game, but then he could've done just as much damage to me with a linesman's flag in the air and a dud report to the referee, so I kept quiet. Once bitten, twice shy.

Then there was the tour of England when I left my sponsored car with my fiancée, Marie. She got caught twice by the speed cameras on Spit Hill in Mosman. I needed to get the points transferred where they belonged — to Marie. I wrote to the police infringements bureau, explaining that I had been captaining Australia in far-off lands at the time and obviously could not have been driving in Mosman. I supplied a couple of statutory declarations, witness statements, everything they needed. I thought it was open and shut in my favour. 'Sorry,' they said, 'can't do anything about it. Put up and shut up.' Now that was pretty poor.

So I've had my problems with cars, and I'll certainly admit that, around the time of Ben's death, I was no angel. But in those days — at that time — you did whatever you wanted, without thinking of the consequences. Anything and everything.

After Ben's death it just wasn't the same at Penrith; certainly not in the few months that followed it. In fact, things went from bad to worse. However, the club did step out a week later and beat Wests 18–10 at Campbelltown. Captain John Cartwright told the players before the game, 'You remember some wins more than others. But if you win today, you'll remember *this* win for the rest of your lives.' The Panthers played on emotion, and carried the day on heart.

For me, playing football was the best way to deal with Ben's death. I played on each week because it was the best way for me to deal with what had happened. There's no textbook on how to get over the loss of a close friend. Anyway, all the players wanted was for the season to end. We were the 1991 premiers, and here's a statistic for you: we scored fewer tries in the 1992 season than any other team in the competition.

Both John Cartwright and I made the World Cup squad to go to England, and he was our best and fairest club player. There were no lead-up games to the World Cup final on 24 October that year; teams made the final based on points over the preceding years. I was chosen as five-eighth (Laurie Daley was unavailable through injury), to play at Wembley in front of 73 000 people, a world record for an international game. We'd had a long run of outs at London's most famous ground.

Only one try really sealed the game for us — a ripper from the Broncos combination of Kevin Walters and Steve Renouf.

Renouf scored in the corner and Mal landed the conversion to put us in front for the first time in the match just a few minutes from the end.

I played OK, but I got whacked really badly. I stepped off my left foot, and the English hooker Martin Dermott elbowed me straight across the cheekbone. I thought to myself, *F--- that hurt*. He got cautioned. I went to the sideline for a while and asked our doctor, Nathan Gibbs, if it was broken. He said, 'No — get back on.' So I did. It was one of the toughest games I've ever played in. We were down 6–4 with twelve minutes remaining. Then Kevin Walters put Steve Renouf through for that try, and Mal converted. We won 10–6, and afterwards I went up to John Cartwright and asked him if he thought my cheek was broken. Carty had started on the reserves bench and came on as a replacement for Mark Sargent. He said, 'Hold your nose and blow out, and if it's broken the cheek will fill with air.' So I did that, and the side of my face blew up like a parachute. It was broken for sure.

I went to see the doctor: 'You lied to me, didn't you?' Nathan Gibbs replied, 'If I'd said it was broken, you wouldn't have gone back on.' I followed Mal Meninga up to get the trophy, and there's a photo of us holding up the World Cup, me looking like the Elephant Man. I love that photo.

It was earlier in that year that I came to realise what an amazing captain Mal was. I was always very lucky with captains. Royce Simmons was a very good captain, very tough. Brandy used to lead from the front. Laurie Daley was great. I came to learn that captains need to be very selective about how they lead the team, on and off the field. I think a captain needs to be divorced from his players off the field, to a certain extent. Perhaps 'divorced' is not the perfect word. But you do have to be more of a role model. The captain should not necessarily be leading the way to the bar. The captain has to be a little remote in order to be able to issue orders and have those orders followed and respected. Mal was a great leader on the field, but it was his leadership off the paddock that really left a mark on me. He was always extremely respectful of his players. He was there, around, but never in the thick of it. He enjoyed a beer, sure, but never to the point of falling over, and he knew just when the time was right to let himself go a bit.

As captain, one Mal Meninga game really stood out. We played a match for Australia against Papua New Guinea in Townsville. It was on 15 July 1992. It was cold by North Queensland standards, and a no-account match. No one wanted to be there. And Mal said, 'Stuff you lot, don't you know you're wearing the Australian jersey?' He took on that PNG team single-handedly. And they were a dirty bunch of players — kicking, gouging, head-high tackles. Nothing was barred. Mal just bowled them over like tenpins. The rest of us looked at each other and thought, well, if that's the way he feels, we'd better follow him. We went on to win that game 36–14.

Before Mal did his bit I'd been keen to hang back and shirk it like everybody else. Suddenly, though, I was looking for the ball. I got a try out of it too. We played together in more important games — World Cups, Tests against Great Britain — but that one game stands out most in my mind as the testament to Mal Meninga's greatness as a captain and player.

Unfortunately, in that same game, while Mal fired me up to go looking for the ball, one mad Kumul went looking for mine: he headbutted me in the testicles. It was so bad that they were swollen up black and blue, and I feared some serious damage had been done. I was ordered to have a CAT scan in Townsville Hospital. I have to tell you it's pretty embarrassing to have a succession of nurses and doctors examining your crown jewels. And for once, they didn't need a microscope — my bits were blown up to the size of a cucumber and a couple of watermelons.

By the end of 1992, after I'd been on a premiership-winning side and toured with the Kangaroos and a World Cup side, and I was approaching my twenty-first birthday, I'd come to realise that football was a career, not a game. And I wasn't a silly little kid any more. I'd been through so much, and lost my closest friend along the way. I just thought, *Brad, you can't keep going on like this*. So I sold that madhouse in Ikin Street, South Penrith, and bought a beautiful house in Glenmore Park, a new development.

To make sure I settled down a little, I moved my family in there. Mum, Kate and Nathan. It was a gorgeous house. There was never any thought of trashing it like the previous one — not that we didn't have fun. Quite a few young Penrith players cut their teeth in that house. I remember Craig Gower, still in school, arriving there one night, meek and mild and too nervous to approach some of the senior players. By the end of the night he was walking up to the likes of John Cartwright and saying, 'Hey Carty, you old bastard.' Craig didn't make it to school the next day, so we all signed a note and gave it to McCarthy Catholic College: 'Craig can't make it today because he's drinking and partying with his mates.' We signed the note, 'His mates'. Boy, was he in trouble with the principal.

Quite a few players came of age in that house, but mostly we had an everyday family existence in a very comfortable home which Mum decorated and furnished and cared for. Until I moved into that house, I'd never understood that football could build me a life, and make me a very good living. The trappings of success were about to come my way.

money, money, money

There wasn't much to keep me at Penrith, especially given that the club was in turmoil. My contract was up, and I suppose I was hot property. It was Phil Gould who kept me there.

Gus was instrumental in organising extras that tipped the scales in favour of staying put at the Panthers. He got me a number of bonuses in that last contract, taking in seasons 1993, '94, '95 and '96. No one knew then, of course, about Super League's impending arrival on the scene, which would cut short the length of that deal.

One of the extras Gus organised was a club credit card with $10 000 per year to spend on it. I still had no sense of money. How could someone like me, who'd had nothing for so long, understand how to manage his cash? I spent all three years' credit in the first three months. Really, I had no idea about money. If I stayed in a hotel room, Penrith would pay my hotel room bill. On the 1994 Kangaroo tour I spent tens of thousands of dollars, making calls and ordering room service, with the bill going back to Penrith. At the end of the tour, we'd just beaten England and had arrived in France. Laurie Daley, Steve Menzies and I sat up in our Paris bar and ran up a $1000 bill. I got a letter from Penrith asking me if it was my signature on the account. Of course it was. But I don't think I told them so. Not for the first time, Penrith paid a giant price for my generosity with their money. Not sure if it helps to say it now, but I'm sorry. I really am.

I can't begin to tell you how much of Penrith's money I spent on phone calls to overseas and interstate. No matter what time zone I was in, there was usually at least one mate still up in the Penrith area. Shorty took most of the calls. He was a night trader on the futures market. I'd speak to him for hours on end, and it was the beginning of a terrific friendship. A decade later we still talk for hours, only now I have to pay for the calls.

The less said about the 1993 and 1994 seasons at Penrith the better. As a Test player, and a State of Origin regular, I should have been taking on a leadership role, trying to motivate others to get out of the doldrums. I regret that I didn't, very much. My only excuse is that I was still young and immature. We were a shadow of the team that did so extraordinarily well in 1989, '90 and '91. I had the 1994 Kangaroo tour to look forward to, and this time I wouldn't be just a passenger in the reserves side, as I had been four years earlier. I was a Kangaroo for real.

There was a new breed in that touring side. People like David Furner and Jason Smith. I roomed with Furnsie and, as I'd done with Chris Johns four years earlier, I drove him mad. I thought I was going to be rooming with Kevin Walters. But we got on too well. I asked if I could get out of rooming with him because I thought we would be distracted. He still has a go at me about that.

One thing Gus Gould taught me was that you have to grab an opportunity when it comes along because it might not come your way again. By way of an example. he'd use the case of Paul Langmack, who was the logical next Australian lock after Ray Price retired. Only problem was, Brad Clyde came along and never looked back.

One of my proudest moments came when just such an opportunity arose for me for the first Test. I was offered the spot at lock. I could have said no, but Gus's words kept ringing in my ears. 'Take the opportunity, son, when it comes your way.' It's actually one of the high points of my life. To think that they moved a wonderful lock forward like Brad Clyde out of his favoured position and into the second row, just to accommodate me in the team, makes me swell with pride. Brad Clyde was the finest lock forward I've seen. He was a terrific workhorse, fast and furious, and able to take a knock and come back even stronger. I just loved playing with him. I couldn't help but have my game lifted by his presence on the field. They moved Brad Clyde to the second row with Paul Sironen, and put me in at lock. To me, that was the greatest compliment. For Bob Fulton to have such faith in me, I was just so proud. I played lock right through that tour.

We lost the first Test at Wembley 8–4 when Clydey got smashed up in an appalling head-high tackle by the Great Britain captain, Shaun Edwards, who was sent from the field in the twenty-fifth minute. The rain continued to tumble down after half-time, and with it our chances were washed away. We just failed to adapt our game to Great Britain being a man down. You can imagine how the Poms reacted to a win like that, gained with such bulldog British spirit. Writing in the *Daily Mail*, much-respected columnist Ian Wooldridge said, 'It was heart, absolute commitment, blood and guts, skill and strategy, spectacle and remorseless tension. I have enjoyed nothing within those walls of Wembley more hugely since the World Cup soccer final in 1966.' How's that for praise? I was happy enough with my game but naturally disappointed in the result, and terribly disappointed for Mal Meninga, playing his record-breaking fifteenth Test against Great Britain.

Mum was in the stands at Wembley, too. As part of my contract, Penrith shouted her the trip over for all three Tests, so she became a seasoned traveller. Not like the first time she followed me to Queensland for a State of Origin match. Penrith paid for her plane fare to Brisbane, and it was Mum's first time ever in a plane. She thought you'd have to get dressed up to the nines to be allowed on board. Everyone was in tracksuits and slacks and joggers. Mum got all dolled up, dripping fake gold. She sat next to Gus Gould on the flight. Gus told her, in his typical straightforward fashion, 'Christine, I think you might be a bit overdressed.'

We went to Old Trafford for the second Test, and won 38–8. I was much more relaxed with my own game, setting up a try for Brett Mullins after Rod Wishart burst away. I was officially awarded man of the match, although Glenn Lazarus got the nod from all of us as the best in green and gold. So it was 1–all, and off to Elland Road in Leeds and a 23–4 victory to us for a series triumph. It wasn't as easy a win as the score indicated. Laurie Daley was probably the difference between the sides: he was absolutely magnificent that day. And just to top it off, we flogged the Frogs 74–0 on the way home. We were that pumped up, France was lucky to get to nil. I had a terrific trip. I was one of the players of the tour. I'd played lock throughout the tour. Laurie Daley was five-eighth. He and Ricky Stuart at halfback had a wonderful understanding; they were just magic together. Glenn Lazarus and I were voted players of the tour — it was all such a stark contrast to my first Kangaroo tour. I might have had a lot of fun on that first tour, but no amount of enjoyment could match the satisfaction of knowing I'd learned discipline and had contributed and played my part in a successful venture.

I didn't play up much on that tour, though everyone knows the story of how I made love to a Christmas tree in the foyer of the Dragonara Hotel in Leeds. I thought it was a good sort. I don't remember this, obviously, but I'm told it's true: I invited the Christmas tree up to my hotel room. I was absolutely deflated when I got a knockback.

When we cleaned up the Ashes at Elland Road, the celebration was huge. And you have to understand that by my standards this was a very quiet social tour. During my first tour, in 1990, once I knew I'd never make the Test team, I went out on the drink every night. I didn't look after myself at all. But I was all business on that 1994 tour. Until the Ashes series was done and dusted, anyway. So there we were, beating the Poms 23–4, and

I'm carrying on this conversation with the Christmas tree as dawn breaks the next day. I can only imagine it was a one-sided conversation. And that the one side making the conversation was not making any sense.

So then it was back home for what seemed like an uneventful 1995. It would be just another season back with the Panthers. I'd be at home in Glenmore Park, and that's where I'd stay with Mum, Nathan and Kate. Nothing could have prepared me for the earthquake that was about to rock the game I loved to its very foundations, and provide a platform to help set me up for life.

super league

The first I heard of Super League and the grand global vision for rugby league was at the home of Royce Simmons. The first meeting I had with the organisers was at Royce's home in Penrith. John Ribot was there, doing most of the talking. It was just before the day the lid was publicly lifted off the greatest drama in the game's history, on April Fool's Day, 1995. The madness that led to endless courtroom battles, a divided competition in 1997, some of the finest talent around not considered for representative selection for two years, the rise and sudden death of teams like the Hunter Mariners, Western Reds, Adelaide Rams and Gold Coast Chargers, the amalgamation of Saints and Illawarra, the passing of Norths, and the hullabaloo over Souths, was to last one thousand days. It seems so long ago now, doesn't it? And Lord only knows how much money was burned up and whistled away. Billions. The lawyers got rich. So did quite a few good players. Some ordinary ones did too. And some ordinary agents. But lifelong friendships were shattered. It was obvious from that very first meeting at Royce's home that money was being thrown around like confetti. This was to be a civil war fought not with guns but with $100 bills as bullets. They told me that evening that half a dozen players had already signed. And they said, 'We'll give you $100 000 up front and $500 000 a season.' It was three times what I was getting at Penrith. I mention the figures not to big-note, but to show how ludicrous it was, how out of all proportion, and to indicate how it would change people's lives. They said they already had players like Steve Renouf, Laurie Daley, Ricky Stuart and Alfie Langer signed, and it was only a matter of time before they had many, many others. They outlined their plans for a grand-scale Super League: TV rights; international matches; everyone paid a fortune; the global vision — the players with much greater control over their fates and futures than they ever had previously.

The news broke, as I said, on 1 April 1995. I'd never been one to stand up and make a statement. I'd always preferred to remain in the background, letting others make the running on any bold new plan. So I was initially reluctant to sign. The money was a great temptation, but it wasn't about that in the end. I just didn't want to be paraded as the champion of some daring scheme, that's all. They wanted my signature then and there. On the spot. On the dotted line. It was a bit of a dilemma.

I'm a shy person, and I don't like making a scene in public. I get nervous if I have to stand out in a crowd. I can go from feeling calm to being in a muck lather of perspiration within a few minutes. Honestly, I go into a full-body sweat from anxiety very quickly. And nothing does it for me quite like standing out in a crowd, feeling the eyes of the world on me. That's how I felt it would've been if Super League got my signature at that first meeting. Funny how they started, these major anxiety attacks I suffer from on a regular basis. I was never that way growing up, only when I began to make a serious name for myself at the age of eighteen or nineteen. I can recall a number of occasions when I've had these massive attacks.

There was a sponsor's charity function at the Sheraton on the Park hotel. It was a super-swank affair. They asked me to stand at the front of the room to help with the charity auction. I suppose there were 200 people in the function room. And I had one of these attacks. In less than a minute I was in a full sweat;

it was literally dripping off me. I backed away slowly, ever so slowly, feeling everyone looking at me. I eased my way out of a side door, ducked through the kitchen, out into the car park, jumped in my car and was home on my lounge within fifteen minutes. It's very scary, very embarrassing, and there's nothing I can do about it. It's happened a couple times on *The Footy Show* as well. The first time, the host, Fatty Vautin, bagged the crap out of me for it. They put the camera on me, and it got worse and worse. Other times on that show I've had minor attacks, but I've managed to dab myself down and get composed.

People say to me, 'How can you take centre stage in a big football match with 80 000 in the crowd, and millions watching on TV, and then unravel at something as minor as a TV show or a sponsor's function?' Well, the truth is that I can't answer that. I've never sought medical or psychological treatment for it. I don't want to take any medication for it. Never have. Anything I took would be mood-altering. And I'm a happy enough person as it is. If I took something to make me even happier, my jaw would break from smiling. I don't know what sets it off. More often than not it comes with a severe skin rash as well. Oddly enough, the earliest incidents I recall happened to me in church. Maybe because I was wearing a suit when I was there, or because it was claustrophobic and lacking air conditioning. While I'm on that subject, why can't churches afford air conditioning? It can't be lack of money. Maybe they need people to suffer for their religion. Mind you, I'm Catholic.

Anyway, the point is I loathe standing out, or standing up, in a crowd. I hate the spotlight on me. And that was the principal reason I chose to knock back all that money and not sign right away with Super League. I had no desire to be a stand-out crusader. Basically, I'm a bloke who loves footy and loves fun. This wasn't about football or fun, only about business. That was obvious from the very outset.

So I held off signing. I rang my manager, Wayne Beavis, and told him about the first meeting at Royce's house. I told him there'd been an approach. But our strategy was to wait and see what both sides had to offer, and where the game itself might be headed. Between then and when the story broke a few weeks later, no one from Super League approached me again. A day after the story broke that a number of players — led by Alfie Langer — had signed, the Australian Rugby League swept into action to fight a rearguard defence of its game. Wayne Beavis and I fronted a galaxy of business and sporting heavyweights at League headquarters in Phillip Street, Sydney, on a Sunday night. The front entrance was awash with media. Inside we were ushered to a back office. James Packer was there; so were Bob Fulton, Phil Gould and League boss John Quayle. My old mate Tim Brasher was there, as was Paul Harragon. I guess we represented the troika that would be the spearhead of the ARL fightback. It was an extraordinary day, etched into my memory for ever.

Wayne and I went into the meeting with James Packer, Gus, Bob Fulton and John Quayle. I reckon it must've been that way for Churchill in the British war room, settling into a bunker for a fight to the death. They were grim-faced and defiant. They said, 'The ARL competition will stay alive. Channel Nine and OptusVision are backing us all the way. We won't give in to the rebels.' It was hard to know whether we were talking rugby league or revolution in the streets. I was expecting trumpets and a drum roll any minute, flags dropping from the ceiling and a band of angels blowing trumpets descending from the heavens. No angels, as it turned out, just one Santa Claus.

James Packer took the running. He was calm, and spoke at length about saving the game. Then he started on the figures. And it was all that Wayne Beavis and I could do to keep a straight face. 'I'll give you $200 000 up front,' James Packer said. 'And I'll guarantee you $600 000 a season.' At the time I was on $160 000 a season at Penrith — Packer was offering five times what I was getting. I wanted to burst out laughing and rub my hands together. But I couldn't do that. So I just sat there, dumbstruck, spinning out, really. These were figures from fantasyland.

I didn't sign there and then, but I was pretty sure I would. In my heart I felt the game had done me a lot of favours, and I owed it something in return. I didn't care to be part of splitting it off into a new direction. Bob Fulton was the current Australian coach, and that played a part in my decision as well. Some ill-informed people have suggested that I was promised the Australian captaincy and that's why I agreed to stand by the ARL. The meeting was about nothing more than saving the game, and how much cash it would take to do so. The Australian captaincy was never mentioned.

Paul Harragon was the next in, and then Tim Brasher, with his manager. After half an hour they called me back in.

'Well, here's the deal,' said Packer. 'Brasher wasn't happy with the up-front payment. He wanted $300 000, not $200 000. So $300 000 it is, and for you as well.' So in the space of ten minutes Tim Brasher had made me $100 000. That was the total amount of my football earnings in my whole first three years at Penrith. I'd slogged my guts out for three years for less than 'Brash' had just won for me. To me, that summed up the madness of Super League versus ARL and the madcap rush to sign players before the other lot got them first. Whichever way you look at it, $100 000 is a lot of money. I couldn't even get my head around the rest of it. I hadn't seen so many noughts since my days playing knee cricket in the front yard at Ashcroft. You could've bought the whole suburb for that, with change left over for parts of Werrington. I have no idea why I said it, but I piped up, 'How about some cash for a drink?' James Packer signed a cheque for $20 000 right there and then, and handed it to me.

So I went outside and threw my arms around Tim Brasher and said, 'Thanks, mate, I owe you a beer. Mind if I repay that debt right away?' And off we went to a club in Drummoyne and got thoroughly pissed. I mean, who wouldn't? I was twenty-five years old and made for life. And why? Simply because I was in the right place at the right time. I can never understand why I was so blessed to be always in the right place when I needed to be. Most people, when their ship comes in, are waiting at the airport and miss out. I'm the luckiest bloke alive. I'm always *where* I need to be *when* I need to be. Always! My contract with Penrith was to be up at the end of the following year. I was at the peak of my form. And here I was caught in a tug of war between Rupert Murdoch and Kerry Packer, each with an unlimited supply of cash. Wake me up, I must be dreaming!

I may have been rich beyond my wildest dreams, but the smarts didn't come with it. The next day I cashed James Packer's cheque over the bar at the Pioneer Tavern in Penrith. I used to put some cheques from the club into the office at the Pioneer and use it as a bank to have a drink, have a play on the pokies and a few bets.

I'll tell you how well things were going for me. I had a couple of hundred dollars on a horse, and watched the race on the television in the office of Buck, the boss at the Pioneer Tavern. The horse was narrowly beaten and in disgust I threw a pen at the TV. Miraculously it hit the on/off switch and turned off the power on the TV. You could try it a million times and it wouldn't happen again. Buck and the others just looked at me and said, 'You're blessed, Freddy, you tinny prick.' And I felt I was, too.

Not surprisingly, the $20 000 was gone in a month. What the heck? There was plenty more where that came from. I wasn't going to be so stupid, though, with the rest of it. Wayne Beavis pretty much took care of it all, and that's the best thing that could've happened.

The only problem for me in siding with the ARL was leaving behind my life and friends in Penrith. The Panthers had already signed with Super League, so there was no turning back for me. But again, I say it was right place, right time. I was ready to leave. It wasn't as if the ARL was asking me to move away in 1990, when Penrith was firing and I was just a kid on the way up with stage fright every time I went east of Strathfield. Penrith was now ordinary, and I no longer saw the eastern suburbs or the northern beaches as a foreign land. In fact, I couldn't think of anything better than moving out of Glenmore Park and settling in a house on the beach.

When I signed, I signed only with the ARL, not with a club. I had no idea where I'd finish up, but I didn't much care. It was my choice. I could've played where I liked. I figured it would be either with Manly or the Roosters, and either was fine by me — Manly because of my connection with Kangaroo coach Bob Fulton, and I'd fallen in love with the peninsula area, or the Roosters because of the connection with Phil Gould. Late in the piece Parramatta weighed in with a large bid for me. I went to the Roosters on a five-year deal. I sold the Glenmore Park house and started looking at properties on the northern beaches. Again — right place, right time. It's just amazing how it happens to me.

I turned up at an auction at Sydney's northern beaches, but missed out on the house. Someone read in the paper that I'd been bidding on the place and called up to ask if I'd be interested in looking at a beachside block of land in Collaroy. The bloke had adjoining blocks, one vacant, and he lived on the other. I went down to inspect it and bought it right away. I paid a high price for the block, which has the beach on one side and Pittwater Road on the other. It was the talk of real estate in the area. A lot of people told me I'd paid way too much. Not lucky Freddy! Within a year the real estate boom had hit, and now you couldn't buy a block like that for five times the amount. And how often do they come up for sale anyway?

Selling Glenmore Park left Mum with nowhere to go. She said she wanted to live near her family at Sussex Inlet, and I told her to go house-hunting. She chose a place and I bought it for her, a magnificent home on the water with its own boat and private jetty. So within a couple of months I'd spent almost two years' worth of James Packer's money, and I hadn't played a game yet. But I was set up for life, and so was the mother who had sacrificed so much for me in Ashcroft and Werrington. Super League may not have helped the game of rugby league all that much, but it made me for life.

At Christmas time in 1995 I moved into Highgate, an ultra-modern, ultra-swank high rise apartment building next to the Observatory Hotel in The Rocks in Sydney. I moved in with my best mate, Shorty (Michael Shortland), the futures trader. There I was on the twenty-second floor, looking out to the west, where I'd come from. There was a brand new BMW in the garage below, courtesy of a sponsor, Trivett Classic. I'd change to a new one every six months, and the dealer principal, Greg Duncan, would become a firm friend. Talk about a rat with a gold tooth.

Penrith didn't want to let me go. They went all the way to the Supreme Court, trying to prove that my contract was with Penrith, not with the ARL; that Penrith had first dibs on me for 1996, not the ARL; that I was still signed to Penrith when I signed what they deemed an illegal agreement with the ARL. Penrith sued both Matt Sing, who'd also signed with the ARL, and me. The case went to the NSW Supreme Court in February 1996. It was our belief, and certainly the belief of our barrister, that the final year of our contracts with Penrith had become null and void when the club signed with Super League.

As I said, I'm a very nervous person. I can break out in a full body sweat in a matter of minutes. So I went to the Supreme Court in a full sweat. I was scared out of my wits. I'd never been in a court before; I thought I'd be in the witness box for ages. But it descended into nothing but hours of legal argument. I was bored to death. The judge, Justice Santow, reserved his decision but came to the only conclusion he could after a short while. And that was that Matt Sing and I had been contracted to the League, not the club, all the while, and when the club quit the ARL they left us behind too.

I didn't have one bit of animosity towards anyone who signed with Super League. I never even talked about it with other players. I never met Lachlan Murdoch or News Limited's John Hartigan. I had nothing to do with the Super League competition, not because of animosity but simply because I never crossed paths with it. It was a funny thing with the players — we never had a cross word. I'm aware that officials who'd been mates all their lives fell out over the footy wars. I know journalists and the TV people took sides and, on occasions, came to blows. On talkback radio, and in the letters pages of newspapers, the war of words was bitter and angry and full of bile. It consumed people's lives.

You were either a traditionalist who loved the game or a believer in the vision for the future. You loved Rupert Murdoch or you loathed him; he was either a visionary or the devil incarnate. Take your pick. Take sides. That's what it was all about. But as far as the players were concerned, it was all a nonsense. All it was to me was like winning Lotto. We were playing the game we loved, and with a lot of very ordinary players getting a whole lot of money, every one of us was earning more than the prime minister. Who cared to come to blows or swap angry words over that? Not bloody me, that's for sure. I just figured it would sort itself out, and if it didn't I'd be living in the lap of luxury anyway, and still doing what I always loved: playing footy.

The first major drama was the dumping of Super League players from the representative sides. In the 1995 NSW State of Origin team, I took over the captaincy. I wasn't ready for it, but Gus Gould advised me that I, along with a couple of other players, was the face of the ARL and I'd just have to live with it. Says Gus now, 'You didn't need that at the time, and it wasn't fair to you. But you stood up to it.' I guess it was down to a choice between me and Paul Harragon.

The loss of those great players took a lot of shine off the game, no doubt about that. No Laurie Daley ... no Ricky Stuart ... no Alfie Langer for Queensland. We lost that Origin series 3–0. We had a pretty good side, but without the old hard-heads I've just mentioned there was a lot of inexperience. With so many new faces, the enormity of the annual interstate competition was lost in many ways, for spectators and some of the players. Queensland was in the same boat, but handled the incoming rookies a lot better. Previously, NSW State of Origin had always been about a team of seventeen leaders, everyone on the same wavelength, all men on a mission, and that mission was to win at all costs.

I guess I was the same way on that first Kangaroo tour in 1990 — out for a good time, not a tough time. During Origin our blokes spent too much time in casinos and not enough time in each other's company, living the Origin experience. I suppose, as captain, I should've taken it upon myself to lay down the law. Certainly the person I blame most is myself. I was new to the captaincy. I was lost, confused and frustrated. I had no idea what to do to shape that side.

We did tell the blokes to wake up, but it was a case of going in one ear and out the other. We were staying in the Park Royal Hotel in Brisbane, having lost the first two games of that series, 2–0 at Sydney Football Stadium and then 20–12 at the Melbourne Cricket Ground. We were to play the last game at Suncorp.

On match eve 'Chief' Harragon came into my room and said, 'We've got Buckley's tonight with this lot. What's going on with them? Don't they know this is State of Origin?' At that moment, a number of the NSW players were at the casino. We just threw up our hands and awaited our fate, which was certain defeat. That was the moment when I realised what a swathe Super League had cut through the game. We had such a tremendous NSW unit in 1992, '93 and '94, winning the series in each of those years. We bonded brilliantly. Not a slacker among us. You could have trusted any other person on those squads with your life. And now here were Chief and I in this mess.

Predictably, we went under in that match, 24–16. We were basically a disconnected rabble running around for the sake of it. Don't get me wrong — we had some terrific players, some of them on a launching pad to greatness. Andrew Johns, for one. But there was no cohesion, no teamwork. We deserved to be whitewashed.

I was captain, too, for the internationals. We played New Zealand in a three-Test series, winning the first 26–8 at Suncorp, the second 20–10 at Sydney Football Stadium and then 46–10 at Suncorp again. I only kicked one field goal and it was in that second match as captain. And the *Rugby League Week* match report rated my performance at 10 out of 10. That happens very rarely and made me extremely proud. I had every right to stand up and say, 'This is my proudest moment, leading my country to victory.' But in fact it wasn't like that at all. Super League not only stole State of Origin, it stole from me that magic moment of captaining Australia for the first time. I could never really revel in something that would normally have been Laurie Daley's and was not truly mine. Australia's wins did prove one old adage, though: if you had 25 injured Test players, you could still field an Australian side that would beat any other in the world.

World Cup games were designated as Test matches in that year. We went down to England at Wembley in a lead-up game, then walloped Fiji. We met New Zealand in the semi-final at Huddersfield and the match went into extra time. Matthew Ridge could have won it for the Kiwis except that he missed a conversion right near full time. It was perhaps the worst kick I've ever seen, an absolute shocker. Then he had a shot at a field goal. I tried to charge it down, and he neatly shifted from a right foot dropped goal to a left footer. I turned around, and with Dean Pay watched it sailing towards the posts. I remember very clearly that time seemed to stand still, and all I could think was, 'Brad, mate, you're going home tomorrow. It's been fun, but this kick is going over, and you're out of the final, and heading home.' Right at the last second it slewed away, thank God. We cleaned them up in extra time 30–20. 'Joey' Johns was absolutely brilliant in that extra period.

Maybe I came of age as a Test captain on that tour, maybe even in that moment before extra time began. We gathered the blokes around and rallied them to get on top. I even led by example, scoring a try in extra time. It was my sixth time as captain of Australia — and the first time I realised the awesome responsibility that goes with that title.

We were still pumped up six days later when we beat England 16–8 in the decider at Wembley Stadium in front of more than 66 000 spectators. Even cut about by Super League signings, we had a hot side. Andrew Johns, Steve Menzies, Terry Hill, Geoff Toovey ... too good, too fast for the Poms, even with talented players like Denis Betts and Martin Offiah and Bobbie Goulding and Jason Robinson in their side. We weren't expected to win, so I was delighted with the result. Still, though, it never felt like I deserved the Australian captaincy. I always felt I was number two, really, to Laurie Daley. I couldn't get it out of my head. But I'll tell you this much: the side Australia put on the field prior to Super League was no better a team than we had to play New Zealand that year, or in the World Cup. We were mostly young, enthusiastic, and just happy to be there.

The next day we had the wildest victory party of any Australian touring team ever, I think, in a place called The Church. It was basically a giant beer hall in a warehouse in London, full of drunk Aussies, Kiwis and South Africans. I finished up on a gantry that traversed the length of the building and overlooked all the drinkers. I was pouring beer down their throats from a great height, and they didn't let a drop hit the ground. The team made its way onto the stage, and everyone was diving off it into the crowd. You'd finally get back on stage with half your clothes torn off. It was a very spontaneous thing, and that's what sticks in my mind about it. We were a mostly youthful team, untried and inexperienced, and against the odds we'd won the World Cup. That was worth celebrating and we did it in spades.

While all that was going on, I'd become a Rooster. I saw going to the Roosters as the best thing for me. And most probably the right thing to do, as Manly had a red-hot side and didn't really need my services. I liked the officials and the players and the coach, of course, at the Roosters. But a funny thing happened before I made the final decision. I rang Gus for advice. Years earlier he'd told me that if I was ever to leave Penrith, there were only three clubs a player of my stature should think of joining: one was the Bulldogs, and the others were the Broncos and Manly. Now here he was telling me I should sign with the Roosters. He said, 'Yeah, I did say that, but I think the Roosters are going to be better than the lot of them. You gotta trust me on that.' So I put pen to paper. And a whole new chapter in my life was about to kick off.

cock-a-hoop

The day I signed with the Roosters to start the 1996 season, I went to a restaurant near Parramatta with Wayne Beavis and Nick Politis. The first time I met Nick Politis I thought he was Al Pacino — no offence, Nick. I was terribly intimidated by the exalted company I was in. I tried very hard to behave myself. In the years ahead I would come to learn that Nick is a fabulous, loyal and down-to-earth bloke whose company I relish. But at that first meeting I was shaking in my westie desert boots. It was like I was a kid fresh out of school applying for my very first job. I kept checking to see that my shirt was tucked in, that I was using the right piece of cutlery, and keeping my elbows off the table. Nick talked about his dreams for the club. There'd been only nightmares over the previous three seasons. Before I joined they'd finished eighth, fourteenth and ninth.

The Roosters made me extremely comfortable and contented from the first day I arrived at training. It was hand-in-glove stuff for me. My old mentor, Gus Gould, was into his second season as coach. I knew a few members of the team, and within the first twenty minutes I felt as if everyone was an old friend. I've never had such a warm welcome before or since. I knew right then that red, white and blue were the colours for me. It was pretty much a young team: blokes like Andrew Walker, Nigel Gaffey, Sean Garlick, Jim Smith, Luke Ricketson.

I had a great year, but I was knocked over by a bad groin injury. It was the worst injury I've had, apart from damage to my shoulder in later seasons at the Roosters. I did the groin pretty early in the season, and played on with the help of painkilling analgesics. No junkie could have had more needles in those few months. I had an operation on it mid-year at a hospital in Merrylands, and a manipulation under full anaesthetic — they pulled my feet up over my head and then the other way, up behind my back.

It was a hugely exciting time for me to be taking a hand in a finals series again — and for the first time in a number of seasons. We made the finals in that first year at the Roosters, and came up against St George in the semis. The groin was suspect, and I hurt it again in the first half. Despite the needles, I could still feel it — the pain was unbelievable. Naturally I went off the field, and that was end of my season, and the Roosters' season too. Except for three more tackles.

Our team doctor, Neil Halpin, said to me at half-time, 'Brad, there are three tendons that keep your leg attached to the hip. You've snapped one of them clean off. But there's some good news: you can't do any more damage to it. So you may as well get back on the field for the second half. It's up to you if you return.' I replied, 'I'll go back on but I need a painkiller for confidence.' They hit me with more painkilling injections, as if I hadn't had enough already. I counted them going in. By about the third I was numb. I was running out of fingers to count on. I think that's the only reason the doctor stopped.

I suddenly thought that the pay rise wasn't coming so easy after all. Out I went onto the field for the second half. I thought I'd best test the injury early. St George kicked off, we fielded the ball, and I moved into position to take the ball up on the third tackle. Wayne Bartrim hit me with a perfectly legitimate tackle, and I screamed out in agony. Even now I can remember Wayne sitting on top of me with this really concerned look on his face, like he might be charged with murder. He thought I was dead. And I wished I *was* dead, I can tell you. They carried me off. I made it home that night, but couldn't get out of bed the next day when the painkillers wore off.

Team-mate Nathan Wood and his brother Garth 'borrowed' a wheelchair from a local hospital — apparently they smuggled it out by putting Garth in the chair and wrapping a blanket over his lap — and arrived at my house in a handicapped taxi. They carried me out into the cab and off we went to the Watson's Bay Hotel for Mad Monday end-of-season celebrations. I was wheeled into the Watto Bay to rapturous applause from my team-mates. At least I didn't have to get up and shout a beer — they kept bringing them to me. A few hours later, and feeling no pain, from amber fluid painkillers this time, I was wheeled into hospital.

Surgeons couldn't operate for a week because so much blood had congealed around the site of the damage. No wonder it hurt so much! My leg was just dangling free. I was jet black and purple from hip to knee, including my crown jewels. For the second time — the first was after I was headbutted in the groin in Townsville — I had a black penis. And the only thing big about it was the surgery and recovery. It took six months of rehabilitation before I was ready to go again.

Then came the strangest year in the game's history: the split competitions of 1997, Super League and ARL. I just found it very odd. You'd play your own games and go home and watch Super League on pay TV or free-to-air.

We were pretty much the best ARL side all year apart from Manly, and we came up against them in the semi-finals. We'd won eight games straight. Manly had won all but one of their seven finals games in the previous three seasons. All the talk, justifiably, was that whichever team won on that day would have no trouble coping with the winner of the Newcastle Knights–North Sydney game.

We had a 6–4 lead at half-time. Then Manly dominated, putting on a 16–6 lead with 18 minutes to go. We fought back to get it to 16–16 as the seconds ticked away. In the end it was Craig Field who sealed our fate for that season with a dropped goal in the seventy-eighth minute. And history shows us that the Newcastle Knights, with the Johns brothers and Chief showing the way, upset Manly in the grand final.

It was the Roosters' best year in a decade, but an up-and-down year in the sense that we lost six in a row in a mid-season slump. And an up-and-down year for me as well: a broken thumb kept me from leading New South Wales to a State of Origin win that year. But I was the ARL's official player of the year, taking the Provan-Summons medal. A mixed year, but a very successful one for the club.

No one was gladder than me when peace reigned the following year, when a brokered deal gave birth to the National Rugby League (NRL) of twenty teams. Two tribes had gone to war, and the end result was a whole new tribe. The Roosters played extremely well all year, but in the finals we suffered under the home-game rule. We had to journey to Melbourne for the first of our qualifiers, winning 26–12. Then it was off to Newcastle for the next qualifier. I don't recall playing in a more amazing game. They belted us in the first half and went to the break leading 15–0. But in the end it was the Roosters, 26–15. Put Gus Gould's half-time address down as one of the most stirring I've ever heard: 'I don't care about the scoreline,' he screamed at us. 'And you shouldn't either. They're just numbers, that's all. Do you believe in yourselves? DO YOU BELIEVE IN YOURSELVES?' It was like a revival meeting in the Baptist American south. We all shouted back that we believed, and out we went.

It was an incredible turnaround. But the gospel of victory as preached by Saint Gus didn't help me get to heaven that day. I was sent to purgatory thanks to one of the most painful injuries I've ever suffered. Billy Peden hit me in a tackle that popped my ribcage. Boy, that was painful. More so, even, than the groin injury. Once more, I screamed out.

Then we went to ANZ Stadium in Brisbane for the Grand Final qualifier against the Broncos. I went to the hospital the night before the game to see if another painkiller might ease the discomfort, which was verging on agony at times. The doctor hit me with heaps more painkillers. When game time came, it was so painful I couldn't even kick the ball. It's been said to me that painkillers are morally wrong, as well as creating a risk of more physical damage. The argument goes that painkillers are no better than performance-enhancing drugs — they get you onto the field and performing at your best when you should not be there at all. I hear the argument — isn't that the same effect that banned drugs like steroids or even cocaine have? I hear it, and I understand it, but I don't hold to that argument at all.

Painkillers in rugby league are an absolute necessity. Simple as that. It's a heavy body-contact game. Until the salary cap is extended to unlimited tens of millions of dollars and the playing roster is equally unlimited, painkillers are a necessity to keep a team on the paddock each week. That's the reality of it. For me, it's about reality, not morality, when it comes to shooting you full of analgesics. Without painkilling injections I would've played at least fifty fewer games. Many is the time you have a minor injury which would heal in a day or two anyway, and taking a shot simply ensures that you're on the field a little bit earlier.

Anyway, history shows we lost 46–18 to Brisbane, and I was no better than a passenger. I did score an intercept try and ran 40 metres to put the ball down. It must have seemed like I was training for the hop, step and jump. I looked like I was smiling when I put the ball down, but I was actually wincing in pain. All I could think about was getting the ball over the line and running all the way home. For most of that match the look on my face was one of being disheartened. I was thoroughly embarrassed by my performance. Maybe it wouldn't have mattered. The Broncos were at their awesome best that day: 'Boys against men', that's how I described it to the press later.

By 1998 I had a two-storey house built on the block at Collaroy, and I was on top of the world. I'd be rocked to sleep by the sound of waves lapping at the back garden and wake up to the sight of the surf and sometimes a pod of dolphins or a whale. I'd walk on the beach, ride the surf ski and watch the

fishermen. It was a wonderful time, and a long, long way from
Ashcroft, I can tell you. And while I was single, well, it wasn't
difficult to find some company from a willing beachgoer.

This was the first year that the maxim 'the Roosters can't win
without Brad Fittler' became firmly entrenched. And it's never
gone away. Statistics seem to indicate that it's true, I know. But
there were many factors to consider on days when I wasn't in
the run-on side. It was much like that with Greg Alexander in
the early days at Penrith. By season 1998, though, I was hearing
it all the time.

It must have been frustrating and annoying and belittling for
the other blokes in the team. I just got sick of it. It would go on
year after year. Only in later years, when the Roosters had such
a terrific halfback and organiser in Brett Finch, and I could take
a back seat, did the thought start to wane. I'll get to the final
season later, but it's appropriate to say now that when you have
two organisers in a side it's possible for one to miss a game and
the team to not be too disadvantaged.

I did play a dominant role in the team. And if you take a
dominant player out, the team has to lose something. You take
a prominent swimmer out of the Olympic relay team and you
must lose something. Obviously. It's logical. I like to play with
the ball in my hands. I do a lot of the kicking. Run the plays as
well. And you can't ask someone to step in and do all that when
they haven't practised it much at training. It's not fair to expect
a fill-in, however good a player, to adopt the role of the
dominant man. That's why when you lose a halfback, or a five-
eighth, or a prop, it's almost impossible to put a bloke in to fill
that role, no matter how strong your reserves bench might be.
And it's a massive psychological boost to the other side. If I
wasn't there, the opposition felt just that little bit stronger and
more confident, and they often played accordingly. I've been in
that position myself in the early days. Your mindset is different.
You think, 'Let's just stick it to them early, and they might give
up without so-and-so in the side.' And so often that's exactly
what would happen.

Anyway, it was another great year for the Roosters. By then we'd become a permanent fixture in the finals.

So to 1999, my fourth year with the Roosters, and we had to think it was our year. We'd gone so close in the past three seasons. Halfway through the competition it looked to be just a matter of how far we'd win by. I could almost taste that champagne out of the championship trophy. We won ten out of our first twelve games. Then came the representative season and more injuries to kick the life out of us, and we ended up only fourth of the top eight. It had become all too much for Gus Gould. He had another couple of years to go on his coaching contract, but he was just about out on his feet with exhaustion by the end of the 1999 season, after all those desperate battles with Super League, then bolstering the Roosters' role in the rationalised competition, taking us to the qualifiers each season.

But the question so many Roosters supporters were asking was a perfectly valid one: when would we ever bring home a premiership to Bondi Junction? In the first qualifying final, Canterbury, led by Ricky Stuart and Brad Clyde, knocked us over 12–8. In the semi-final, St George-Illawarra put us out of our misery 28–18. Although I scored two tries and had a hand in another, it didn't mean squat, as it signalled the end of another year.

With perfectly good reason, given the results, the critics and some of the fans were saying we were too soft to ever win a premiership. The knives were well and truly out. Maybe they were right. We should've won at least one finals game. I remember thinking to myself that we would prove them wrong. I had an unshakeable self-belief, and belief in my team-mates. I knew a win wasn't far off. But that 1999 season came to a premature end. And it was an end, too, to something much bigger than any of us: the millennium. What came next was perhaps the greatest year of my life.

the new
millennium

I saw in the new millennium in at my home on the beach at Collaroy, complete with our own massive fireworks display at my expense. It was a fancy dress party. I went as Hugh Hefner, king of the Playboy empire. And that was me to a tee. Well, in my own head, at least, if no one else's. I thought I had the world at my feet. Big house, lots of money, booming investments, a team that couldn't keep out of the finals, captain of Australia. All of that. I didn't see how life could get any better, but it was about to. Gee, it was a terrific year. Where do I start to tell you about it?

I'll start away from footy. At the Olympics. I hadn't thought much at all about the Games in my home city until the torch came to town. I think a lot of us were like that. We knew the Games were coming, and there was lots of controversy and drama about tickets and traffic and security. But until the Olympic flame arrived, and people started to get swept up en masse in the spirit of it all, we didn't worry much about it.

I was due to carry the torch at Parramatta a couple of days before the Olympics. It was day 97 of the torch relay, starting at Kurnell. I was given the honour of lighting the cauldron at the end of the day. I was on the bus travelling to my destination with Olympic decathlon champion Daley Thompson, and that was the first time I really felt the importance of the Olympics. Here was one of the finest athletes the world had ever produced, sitting next to me on the bus, singing the praises of the Olympic ideal. How right he was! I always remembered the story about Daley saving his hardest training session for Christmas day. From that Christmas on I did the same, and in a strange way I did feel it gave me an edge.

I had to run towards that natural amphitheatre in Parramatta Park and light the cauldron at the end of the day's torch run. I came up towards a hill and couldn't see anyone, then I went over the hill — and the scene that greeted me was just chaotic. Tens of thousands of people, all screaming and yelling and clapping.

It was amazing and, I have to say, I lost it at that point. I did. I've heard people say they were 'in the zone'. I suppose that's where I was. I was pumping the air, and dancing and skipping and throwing my arms about like a stupid kid. My limbs were behaving with no sensible direction from my brain. It was just absolutely and totally spontaneous. It was such a magical time to be in Sydney, and here I was, a kid from the backblocks, suddenly at the centre of it all. From the top of that hill in the park I could have looked across to Ashcroft and Werrington, where it all began. But that would have meant acting consciously, and I was incapable of that at that point. I got lost in the emotion of it. And whatever zone I was in, the crowd was right there with me. All my family was there — my mum, my girlfriend Marie, everyone. It was one of the most overwhelming moments of my life.

I had another magical experience during the Games. At a charity auction some months before I'd bought a day out on an old coal-fed cruising boat on Sydney Harbour. I never thought they'd let me use it during the Olympics, but they did. Again, all my family and friends were present. There were thirty of us. We cruised around Darling Harbour, past this huge ship which housed the NBC television team from the US. They filmed us for several minutes, and I was told later we all made it onto prime-time TV in the US in the lead-up to the Olympics.

I went to the opening ceremony and a number of other events. It was just so inspirational.

I sat with Greg Alexander in the stands to watch Cathy Freeman win the 400 metres final, and that was a rare privilege that will remain in the minds of all who were there to see it. Brandy and I tried to imagine the pressure Cathy must have been under and how much advantage you have in a team sport where others around you can help out. Cathy looked so alone and frail on the starting blocks. You don't need me to tell you what a fantastic job she did that night, and when she finished, with waves of relief washing over her, she was just as humble as ever, the way Aussies love their champions to be. I was on my feet, cheering madly like everyone else.

The NRL Grand Final had been brought forward to allow the Olympics to open on 13 September, so footy was over by then. I guess I'd better tell you about the 2000 premiership season.

It was Graham Murray's first year as coach, and the Roosters' best season in twenty years, as we made the Grand Final. It was the reverse of our previous season, terribly inconsistent in the first half and then dominating in the second half. I'd have to say Graham did an extraordinary job. Sure, he had an established outfit which, under Gus Gould, had become a fixture in the finals series. But with a limited preparation time in the off-season, he did very well.

We had some of the club's biggest wins in the run home that year — 41–6 over Melbourne, 26–0 over Parramatta and a whopping 28–0 blot-out of Brisbane, who were leading the competition. The only stumble was the 32–8 loss to Parramatta at the start of the finals series. The critics again said we were 'finals chokers'. We were 'too soft'.

We gave them 'chokers' next time out, beating Canberra 38–10, and turning a 2–16 deficit against Newcastle into a 26–20 win, sparked by an incident in which Darren Albert, the Newcastle back, played up to the camera, indicating that he and his team were number one. Much was made of that at half-time. 'How do you feel about being mocked?' That was the gist of the half-time discussion in our rooms. Not very good, obviously. But it was all the motivation we needed for the second half.

Graham Murray sat back during the break while I let my team-mates have it with all guns blazing. All those insults about the Roosters being finals chokers, the dream of Nick Politis to win a premiership, all the crap about the Roosters being the new 'silvertails' ... well, I brought it all up in my half-time rant. And that's the best way to describe it: a rant. I let go with everything. I have a feeling that, up to that point, some of my team-mates didn't understand how much it would mean to me to captain a premiership-winning side. I have to tell you, I put an end to that theory in the dressing room that day. Out we came for the second half, and I got one on Joey Johns straight away, latching onto an intercept from him. It was as good as over after that.

We arrived at Stadium Australia for the Grand Final against Brisbane on 27 August. I was superconfident. Everything was going our way, I figured. I can't remember another big game where I've felt so supremely confident, especially after the terrific win we'd had over the scoreless Broncos a couple of weeks earlier. I was truly excited about the prospect of a premiership win. But I'm not sure that being excited and being focused are one and the same thing. I was thrilled to be there, sure. But did I truly know where I was and what I had to do? I learned a tremendous amount from the experience. Most people would not see reaching a Grand Final as a failure. But that's an observation you can only make if you've been in that position, and here's my take on it: for the Roosters, it was a fine achievement; for me, I failed.

We lost 14–6, clinically dissected by a super-efficient Broncos side. It could've been a lot worse but for a staggeringly good performance by our fullback Luke Phillips, who saved four tries at least. Darren Lockyer won the Clive Churchill Medal. There were plenty at the ground who thought Luke was just as good.

Apart from that defeat, it was my year of living fabulously. In State of Origin we won in a 3–0 whitewash with me as captain. Just to top it off, we shattered every scoring record in State of Origin history to that point with a 56–16 win in the final game at Stadium Australia. My close mate Ryan Girdler smashed all the point-scoring standards. That was a hot side, one of the best I've ever been associated with.

To the internationals — first up the Anzac Day Test against the Kiwis at Stadium Australia, and another 50-point slaughter. Australia won 52–0; I bagged a couple of tries. Australia beat Papua New Guinea by 80 in Townsville in an official Test match. Our next challenge was the World Cup in Britain. It was always going to be a great trip, given the side we had — and there was to be a personal and private surprise for Marie and me at the end of it, a secret I held all the way through that campaign. More of that in a moment.

The Australian team faced our old rivals New Zealand in the World Cup final, beating them 40–12 at Old Trafford. The match was tighter than the scores indicated, but once we put our foot down on the accelerator, the Kiwis couldn't match us. On the way to the final we'd accounted for England, Fiji, Russia, Samoa and Wales, amassing a total of 310 points in just those five games. It was, I think, the greatest side I've ever played in. Chris Anderson was national coach. He rated us better than the 1982 Kangaroo Invincibles, of which he'd been a part.

It was a great way to finish a great year, and at the end of that World Cup I was named the greatest player in the world. Geoff Carr was the team manager at the time. He came up to me and told me I'd just been named the world's number one player — the Golden Boot. It topped off the year. During your career there are always people who put you down, and others who praise you. That's the way it is. So there's nothing wrong with being proud of the accolades that come your way. You get enough kicks where it hurts, on and off the field, and when finally your achievements are recognised, there's no point in hiding your light under a bushel. I was absolutely rapt to get that award. I was at ease with the world.

I made a brief mention of the fact that my girlfriend, Marie Liarris, was there when I ran with the Olympic torch, and there again for the World Cup. She's now my life partner, and the mother of my beautiful daughter, Demi, and I can't let any discussion of the year 2000 pass without recalling how we met and fell in love.

Marie has quite a story of her own to tell. Her father, Harry, came to Australia from Greece on his own, with one suitcase, no money, just the clothes on his back. Back in Greece he'd grown olives, tended cows and ridden his horses bareback. He didn't know a word of English when he arrived. He worked for a while in a takeaway store, drove a Valiant, met his Greek-born wife, Christine, in Sydney and went on to do well for himself in business through a chain of flame-grill burger bars. It's the typical southern European migrant success story from the '50s and '60s.

Marie and I were set up on a blind date. Here's how Marie tells it:

> I told my brother John I was going out with some football player. I said, 'Do you know who Brad Fittler is?' He said, 'Do I ever. Come on the Internet — I'll show you who he is. He's really famous.' This was at the family home at St Clair.
>
> John was more excited than I was. He said he wasn't going out that day — he'd stay home to meet Brad when he came to pick me up. I knew nothing about Brad or rugby league; I followed the Panthers a little bit because I went to Colyton High School with Craig Gower. I saw a photo of Brad in the newspaper, that was it.
>
> We were set up on a blind date through a mutual friend, Barry Scanlon, who was Brad's coach when he was thirteen. I was sitting in Penrith Plaza having coffee with Barry when I saw Brad's picture in the paper. I said, 'He's nice', and Barry said, 'Oh, I know him.' So Barry called him and

asked, 'How are you? Are you single? I've got this nice girl for you to meet.' Brad said, 'Tell her to give me a call.' So I did that night. We spoke for about four hours on the phone.

It took me three attempts to call him again. The first time he was in a meeting and couldn't talk. The second time the same. Finally I tried again at night. We arranged to meet for coffee at his place in Collaroy on a Friday night. I told him the night before that I couldn't stay for long because I'd already organised a night out with my girlfriends. I hadn't really, but it was an escape clause in case he ended up being some kind of monster. As it turned out I had an amazing time just talking to him and laughing our heads off at stupid things. I didn't want to leave, but I had to. I'd put myself into this dead-end and couldn't get out of it. So two hours passed and I had to go. 'My girlfriends will be waiting,' I said sheepishly, all the time thinking to myself, 'What bloody girlfriends, you idiot?' On my way out he gave me a book called *The Alchemist*, a fantasy novel about a boy with a dream and the courage to follow it. He said he'd just finished reading it and I should give him a call when I finished it. I suppose it was his way of saying, 'Let's stay in touch'.

When I came home, Mum and everyone said, 'What was he like?' I said, 'He's beautiful ... really a beautiful man.' A week went by and I hadn't heard from him. I was playing hard to get. Finally he called and said, 'Let's go to a movie then have dinner with some friends.' He came to my house like a proper gentleman, picked me up, came in, met the family. That was March 2000.

Now here's my version. She sounded like good fun on the telephone, and having been told she looked all right, I was keen to make a good first impression. I decided to hit her with my best shot first up by inviting her to my house at the beach. That was my trump card ... in fact, my *only* card. The sound and sight and smell of the ocean does amazing things for romance.

I searched my wardrobe to find something to wear that would make the right impression. Jack Elsegood, a bit of an expert in these things, calls it 'casually dressing with purpose'. I finished up with a sarong and a daggy white T-shirt — can you believe that? Where was that mob from *Queer Eye for the Straight Guy* when I needed them? I should've been arrested by the style police. Maybe I was just in a fog because I had a feeling that Marie might be the one. When she knocked on the door that first night, and I opened it, I was smitten. Instantly. She was the one, all right. Talk about love at first sight. From that moment, I knew I would marry that girl.

Later that year, during the last two weeks of the World Cup, and after we'd been apart an agonising six weeks, Marie flew to Britain to join me, resting first in London for a couple of days to get over jet lag, then taking the train to meet me in Leeds. It was bloody cold. She arrived at the station in scarf, gloves, overcoat ... everything. I was standing there waiting in shorts and thongs and beanie. That's me: shorts and thongs, no matter what, no matter where, and no matter who you are waiting to meet.

After the tour, Marie, my mate Shippo and I went off to Amsterdam for a holiday, then took a ten-day bus tour of Italy. The bus was full of Americans who had no idea I was a football player of some notoriety. I bought a 1 metre-tall piece of Venetian glassware for Marie — a man and woman intertwined — for Christmas. It was so romantic. Except poor Shippo didn't think so. It was a secret, you see, and he had to carry it all the way around Europe and take it back for me as a surprise. After Shippo went home, Marie and I made our way to Paris, the south of France and then to Switzerland.

The only thing I had on my mind when we got to the Alps was that here was the woman I wanted to spend the rest of my life with. And here we were in just about the most romantic place on the planet. Proposing a life together was uppermost in my thoughts. Again, I'd best let Marie tell the story of what happened next.

Brad was strangely quiet for a few days. I said, 'Are you OK?' There was something on his mind, and I didn't know what. I said, 'Come on, snap out of it. We're on holidays. Just enjoy yourself.' He had it all planned. I must have had some inkling because on our way to the restaurant overlooking Lake Geneva we went past a jewellery store. I said, 'If you ever feel like proposing, I'll take that ring' — just as a joke. Little did I know! At dinner that night he produced a poem from his jacket pocket, and over the first course and a glass of wine, and with the candle flickering, he read the poem to me. He'd had a specialist in calligraphy write it in the most beautiful handwriting. It was a love poem, of course. It's framed now on our bedside table. I'm not telling you what's in it. There have to be some secrets. But it's unbelievably warm and beautiful and romantic and passionate. And he read it like Richard Burton reading a Shakespeare sonnet. It could've come from *Romeo and Juliet*. And then he proposed. Well, after that build-up, what was a girl to say?

So there it was, that most fantastic year, 2000. I can't believe how fabulous it was from get-go to whoa. A terrific fancy dress party at home in Collaroy, complete with Fittler's own fireworks to bring in the new millennium. I met Marie. Ran with the torch. Made the Grand Final. Won the World Cup and the Golden Boot as the world's best player. And finished it off with a trip through Europe with Marie and a proposal of marriage. As the New Year dawned to usher in 2001, I figured it'd just get better and better from there. How bloody wrong can you be!

the worst year of
my footy life

Over the Christmas–New Year period I came to a momentous decision in my football life. I thought it was time to hang up the boots as far as representative games were concerned. No more State of Origin at the end of the 2001 season. No more Test matches. No more World Cup.

It wasn't a spur-of-the-moment thing. I'd been thinking about it for quite a while. The wear and tear on my body was resulting in injuries. The responsibility and pressure as NSW and Australian captain was sapping more energy than it had previously. I'd loved it and lived for it for years. Now it was exacting a heavy toll, physically and mentally. I knew I had to do something.

And, even more importantly, I wanted to spend more time at home in Sydney with Marie and the rest of my family and mates. When I'd first moved into Highgate, in the city — at Christmas 1995 — I'd been a completely different person. I was scarcely ever at home. I was at the casino, or out at dinner, meeting friends somewhere. I often joked that we should have applied to Sydney City Council and the body corporate to erect a flying fox from the balcony on the twenty-second floor directly across Darling Harbour to the casino. All we needed was a strong wire and a basket, and it would have saved a lot of late-night booking of taxis and other transport hassles. Maybe it would've created some problems for helicopters and low-flying seagulls, but nothing more than that. Nothing that some flashing warning lights would not have overcome.

But by the start of 2001 I was ready for a more peaceful and fulfilling life, sitting out on my surf ski at Collaroy, or walking along the beach with Marie of an early morning or evening. Or strolling around The Rocks or the city with Mum, playing at being a tourist. These things were starting to appeal to me more and more. Really, my life had revolved around nothing but football since I was a tiny child, and now I wanted something more out of it. I found myself — and this is going to sound silly for a grown man not far off celebrating his thirtieth birthday, as I was then, but it's true — walking along the street or the beach observing simple things the way a child would when he'd never seen them before. I'm talking about the way seagulls walked and flew, or the colour of leaves on trees, and the way the waves rolled into Collaroy Beach or the ripples across Sydney Harbour. The fact is this: I had always been looking beyond those things to the next game of football or some way to get a laugh. So I talked it over with Marie and made the decision to pull the plug on representative league.

I made one mistake, though: I should just have let the season run its course and then made an announcement in the off-season, quietly and with no fanfare. As I've said a number of times, I hate being the centre of attention. Instead I told Phil Gould early in the year that I was going to retire from representative football at the end of the season. He was on radio then, on 2GB, doing sports round-ups with Graham Richardson on the drive program. And he called me up and spoke to me on air, and from that point on it was all official. The focus went onto me, and I hated it. The attention was overwhelming.

It was right on me as captain when we played the first match of that State of Origin series at Suncorp Stadium. Queensland just gave it to us, 34–16. Andrew Johns, Ryan Girdler and

David Peachey had withdrawn, but New South Wales was still the overwhelming favourite, particularly after the 40-point thrashing the Blues had handed out to Queensland in the final game of the 2000 series. There was talk even then that the State of Origin series was dead, and that New South Wales would dominate for years, if not decades. But Queensland had a hatful of new players — ten were making their Origin debut — and, inspired by Wayne Bennett as coach, they flogged us.

Then, in front of 70 000 fans at Stadium Australia, we came back to win 26–8 and square the series. Trent Barrett was halfback in place of Brett Kimmorley; we developed a terrific combination very quickly, and in the end I bagged two tries. Who would've ever thought that, three years down the track, we'd line up together again in my last State of Origin game with the spotlight on me again? But more of that game later. For now, the Stadium Australia match was to be the lone highlight of my worst year. As far as I knew at the time, it might have been my last game at Stadium Australia. I remember being perfectly focused the whole week. My head was in exactly the right place. Everything was planned, and everything went according to plan. It was my perfect game. It also started a preparation technique which I was to use in the future: I barred myself from reading a newspaper or watching the news — anything that could alter my focus.

So up comes the final Origin match, and back home from England comes Alfie Langer at the behest of Wayne Bennett. The Blues' whole approach to the game was wrong. There was all the crap about 'Let's do it for Brad'; I tried to turn the focus down, but it didn't work. The more I said, 'Hey fellas, give it a rest', the worse it got. In my hotel room just before we left for ANZ Stadium, I had a visit from an old mate, Ryan Girdler. I said to him, 'Girds, I'm drained.' There was no logical reason to feel that way. The bookies had us as favourites; we *deserved* to be pronounced favourites. On paper we had the game at our mercy. But I said: 'Girds, I gotta tell you — I'm scared out of my wits.' Not scared as in nervous — I was like that most of the time. Often I'd try to make myself vomit to overcome being so sick with nerves before a big game. And that's a good thing. It keeps you on your toes, and gets the adrenaline flowing. This was different. I mean, I was seriously dreading it, and expecting a thrashing.

I said, 'Mate, I feel like I'm empty. I'm in a deep hole and can't get out of it.' He said, 'I feel exactly the same.' We were a couple of condemned men on our way to an execution. He put his arm around me, I put my arm around him, and honestly we were just about crying on each other's shoulders. And in reality there was no rhyme or reason for it. Is it any wonder we lost?

I got on the bus feeling bloody awful. I felt inadequate. I kept saying to myself, 'Just do your best. It'll be all right', all the time acutely aware that it wouldn't be. I've never felt that way prior to a game before or since. Never. Not once. So why on this occasion? One that wasn't just a series decider but a huge cornerstone in my life — my last ever representative game? Here I was, supposedly at the pinnacle after a dozen years. And I felt like crap. The great motivators will say, 'Never think negative thoughts'. Or if you are having negative thoughts, replace them with positive ones. But I'm a human being like everybody else. Sometimes you can't help but feel that way.

So you know what happened. Everybody knows. Queensland won 40–14, and it should've been a lot worse. Eight tries to two, 28–8 down at half-time, and Queensland riding on the coat-tails of little Alfie Langer, back from Warrington on used tyres but with a reworked engine, pushed and prodded by a mechanic named Wayne Bennett. To make it worse, we had been leading 6–0 after less than a minute. And it was Ryan Girdler who scored the try and kicked the goal! At half-time we tried to tell each other we could come back.

I can't even tell you what I felt like after the match, or what I did. I've read that I was sobbing. One report says I had my head in my hands for twenty minutes, saying nothing to anybody. I honestly don't know. It was all so bloody embarrassing. That's the best word to describe it: embarrassing. I don't like to think about it, even now. I find myself singing out loud or whistling, the way you do when you don't want to hear something bad. Perhaps if I sing loudly or whistle, those thoughts and memories will go away. It's a psychological thing, but I've blotted that part of my life out of my memory bank. It's gone. Seriously. That hour or so after the game isn't there any more. I know someone tried to interview me for Channel Nine ... Gus Gould, I believe. He may as well have interviewed the statue of Wally Lewis. I was oblivious to everything. Dead in the head. My tank was totally empty. Sometimes, regardless of who you are, life seems to get too hard. That's the point where you need to make decisions about your future. And it was at that point that I first thought of retiring not just from representative matches, but from all of it. There was room for only one thought in my head: *I just want to go home.*

If I was looking for comfort, there was none back at the Roosters. Turmoil reigned there too, with coach Graham Murray under threat. I know he blamed the players for causing the unrest that led to his departure, and as captain I must have been in his sights. But his eventual sacking had nothing to do with me or any of the others, except that our role was to perform as players, and we didn't. I suppose the club felt it was Graham's job to ensure that we did, so the axe had to fall on his head. Coaching is such a cut-throat job. Often the results don't reflect the amount of work that's gone into it. But as Jack Gibson used to say, there are only two types of coaches: sacked ones, and those waiting to be. Better to sack one man than the whole team.

But I'll say this: at no stage did any official with the Roosters — anyone at all — ask me if I thought Graham Murray was a good or a bad coach. That goes for all the players. And a few seasons later, Graham Murray would prove his capabilities by coaching the Townsville Cowboys to the finals series, and all but knocking the Roosters out of the 2004 Grand Final.

We came sixth in the end in 2001. We went to Marathon Stadium to play the Knights, and went under 40–6. That's a decent thrashing, isn't it, in a qualifying final? But it was a fitting end to a truly miserable year of football.

To make it worse, I'd been hit high by Michael Vella the week before and had twenty stitches in my top lip. My lip was massive; it was purple, and the size and colour of an overripe plum. The doctor gave me a couple of needles in it before the game. Well, I was about to kick off, and Andrew Johns was standing opposite me for the Knights. He looked at me and almost fell over laughing. It was that sort of a game ... that sort of a season ... that sort of a year. It had gone on way too long for me. I couldn't help but laugh too. We were primed to get beaten.

As the team drove back to Sydney on the bus we were listening to the other qualifying final — between St George and Canterbury — on the radio. If St George won, that was it for us for the year. They got to the lead by a point, 23–22, and I tapped Bryan Fletcher on the shoulder and was about to say something like, 'Fletch, pray for the Saints. Please. I don't want to have to play again', but I didn't have to open my mouth. He just nodded. It was clear we were feeling exactly the same way without having to voice it.

All my life I'd been competitive. And here I was, glad our season would end there and then. It was a terrible feeling. Luckily for me, St George held on to beat Canterbury and put us out of the competition. When we got off the bus I said to Fletch, 'Our prayers were answered, mate.' We went down to the Coogee Bay Hotel for a beer, and that's about as comfortable as I'd felt all year.

It didn't help my wellbeing that a poll of 100 players published in *Rugby League Week* in August 2001 voted me as the game's most overrated player. Boy, did that cause some drama. Andrew Johns said he thought I'd be 'devastated and hurt'. Chris Anderson blamed jealousy for the way players cast their votes. Johnny Raper called for the players who voted that way to be publicly named and shamed. There was outrage everywhere. Except from me. Maybe it was a fair assessment, given the year I'd had. The truth is, I wasn't much bothered by it — and in fact, a week later against the Dragons, I had one of my best club games of the year.

Later, Ricky Stuart was confirmed as our coach for the following season. I was almost ready to call it quits from football at the end of that season. I considered requesting that my contract be cut short for a year. I was still contracted for the 2002 season, but I was in a foul frame of mind. I wanted out. You know what probably saved my career? A few lousy lines in a newspaper. Columnist Mike Gibson, who's always been crooked on the Roosters, wrote in the *Daily Telegraph* in September 2001, after we were knocked out of the premiership, 'Personally, I find something flaky about the Roosters. What they lack on a week-to-week basis is passion and commitment. They're like a flashy new car with all the fancy tricks, but when you push the pedal, there's no grunt. Like ordering the French champagne in the ice bucket, and finding it's flat. Like the guy in the Armani suit, except when he turns around, there's a hole in his trousers. The Roosters kept promising but the cheque was always in the mail.'

He ended by saying, 'I get the distinct feeling that the heavy hitters who call the shots at Bondi Junction will look a little deeper than simply blaming the coach'. There was a personal reference to me and the players' poll: 'It took an ego-bruising wake-up call from fellow players before skipper Brad Fittler finally produced the goods against the Dragons'. The essence of his column was that we were a bunch of perennial losers, Ferraris with a blown piston when put under pressure. He figured we'd never win as long as our Rooster tail feathers pointed to the ground. He had history backing him up, with more than a quarter of a century since the last title. But I knew, too, that it was a load of crap, not worth the paper it was written on. Someone once described newspaper articles as a 'burial shroud for yesterday's haddock'. In the case of that column, whoever said so was absolutely spot on!

But I didn't wrap the bones in it. I kept that column. I ripped it out of the paper, had it laminated, looked at it almost every day for the next twelve months — always before I ran onto the field for a game — and never forgot a word of it. I showed it to the new coach, and he distributed the column to every player. It was my motivation — and the team's motivation — to get back on top. The moment I read it, I thought to myself, *I'll give him 'flaky'*. At no stage have I ever raised it with the writer himself. I will now, with two words: 'Thanks, Gibbo.' He helped us win a premiership.

Over the years I've had an arm's-length relationship with the media. I never fully trusted journalists after that 'Fat Freddy' incident with the photographer back in my days at the South Penrith house. The beer and the pizza and the hamburger alongside me, and 'Fat Freddy' plastered all over the back page of the paper the next day. The guy asked if he could take a picture, and I said, 'Of course, mate', without questioning how it might be used. That taught me the lesson that journalists and photographers aren't always there to do you a favour. I learned another lesson, too, as I went on — it's no use getting upset about what's written or spoken about you in commentary, because they've got the space in the newspaper or the access to the microphone the next day, and you can never win.

I've found some journalists to be cynical. Whether they started that way, or the profession made them that way, I'm not sure. I often wonder what it would be like in that sort of job where you go to work each day and your role is to judge and comment. I'd find out later on. But not all journalists use their column space in that way.

I copped a hammering over the Glebe police station incident, which I'll talk more about later. And they gave it to me over the players' poll that said I was overrated, and again when I missed the gathering of captains before the 2004 finals. You have to rise above it, though, not strike out. Overall I think I've had a very good run from the media. I can't really complain.

I acknowledge that many journalists are hard-working, disciplined, eager reporters and that they're important for promoting the game. Some, though ... well, you have to question their research. I did an interview with Steve Price, the drive-time host on radio station 2UE in Sydney. He's from Adelaide via Melbourne, and knows a lot about Australian football, but little about league. He conducted a long radio interview with me, thinking I was Andrew Johns the whole time. 'And how's the neck injury, Brad?' he asked me. And kept on asking it. I was reluctant to say anything. I just said, 'Oh, it's OK thanks.' But eventually it got to the point where I just had to set him straight: 'It's Brad Fittler, not Andrew Johns, mate.' It was an honest mistake, and amusing at least, not something deliberately nasty. The bottom line is this: I appreciate the nice things they've said about me over my career, and have accepted the criticism.

After the failed premiership season that year, there was still the Kangaroo tour coming up — a six-weeker — which was something to look forward to at the end of my very own Year of Living Dreadfully. Little did I know, though, that it was only about to get a hell of a lot worse. September 11 brought those horrifying attacks on the twin towers in New York and the Pentagon in Washington. A wave of fear swept around the globe. Travel plans were being cancelled. And I was about to fly into a whole new mess.

a kangaroo with white feathers

I watched the terrorist attack on New York and Washington from my home in Collaroy. It happened nineteen days before the NRL Grand Final, with a Kangaroo team due to leave for Britain the following month. Doubts were being cast on that tour, and whether or not players' safety could be guaranteed, within days of the attacks. Those doubts were being expressed by officials, and I stress that point. ARL chief executive Geoff Carr made the first public statement, saying that the fate of the tour depended on future international developments.

Some players were debating among themselves about whether it was wise to be away from their families for so long while a world war, or at the very least further major attacks like the ones on New York and Washington, loomed as distinct possibilities. Front-row forward Shane Webcke came out in public and asked the ARL to think about changing the dates of the tour. So uncertainty reigned for several weeks.

The ARL went ahead with naming the Kangaroo squad, with me as captain, the day after the 30 September Grand Final, which was won by Newcastle. There were twenty-four of us in the squad. Of that group, eighteen travelled to Port Moresby for a one-off Test against a Papua New Guinea team coached by

Wayne Bennett's brother, Bob. I was the only one to have been there before; I'd made my Test debut against Papua New Guinea. Most of us were unfit, unprepared and shackled by the savage heat. We won by 40-odd points in the end, but it was far from impressive.

One thing, though, about going to Papua New Guinea: the trip was always a real buzz. People idolised us. It was totally amazing, and like nothing I've ever experienced elsewhere. It's a beautiful and scenic place, the sort of place I like to go to so I can get my feet back on the ground. A wake-up call, if you like, about how lucky I am to live in a privileged country like Australia. The thing that never ceased to blow me away was how much pleasure a simple game of football could give the locals. Or even just a smile and a handshake — it's as if they were getting blessed by the Pope. There are massive social problems up there, that's no secret. But I wish Australia was helping more with financial aid and assistance. I'm going to try to help where I can, now that my football career is over. The other players and I might have given them pleasure with our appearance, but I can tell you this much: I got more in return. Each time I went to Papua New Guinea, I came back a better person.

After that trip was over, it was back to this bitter debate over whether or not the tour of Great Britain — the first Kangaroo tour in seven years — would go ahead. We were due to leave in a week. It began to get very, very ugly. Just two days after our return from PNG, the ARL announced that the tour was cancelled because half the squad — twelve of us — were unwilling to go. The British were up in arms because they rely on tours like that to fill their financial coffers. And there was a huge public backlash as well against the ARL and the players in particular. In the newspapers, on TV and talkback radio, we were all widely condemned.

The *Daily Telegraph* in Sydney broke the story that I'd been sent white feathers anonymously in the post. I didn't know at the time what that meant. I was told later that white feathers were sent to men who refused to enlist in the two World Wars to let them know they were considered cowards.

The ARL gave in to the pressure and announced a new plan of three Test matches played over three weekends, with no lead-up games. A squad of twenty-one departed for England on 5 November. It was reported that 'Test captain Brad Fittler surrendered' by reversing my decision not to tour. The publicity was hugely emotive, and extremely stressful and demeaning to me.

Words like 'coward' and 'surrender' are powerful and hurtful, and they were being aimed and fired at me on a daily basis in the media, on the street and through the post. In short, as the team captain I bore the brunt of an angry and frightening public reaction — and I never said a word.

In fact, I was caught in the middle of a difficult situation, and became the fall guy. I was set up and back-doored by the ARL, and was the victim of a very deliberate act of vandalism by the person — he or she knows it too — who sent those white feathers. A representative from the ARL came to me when the squad was announced and said, 'The ARL does not want this tour to go ahead. The ARL does not think the tour is a good idea.' I didn't object at the time. He asked me what my views on it were, and I told him I would go along with what the administrators directed. I thought it was most probably the right thing to do for the captain to back his national team management and officials. Truth is, I had no fears about terrorism. It's a part of life and you deal with it. It's my earnest belief that you carry on your normal life in the face of terrorist threats, otherwise the terrorists win. I was happy to go to England. No problems at all. What I should've done, as the team leader, was to stand up for what I believed in. But in this case, on behalf of the ARL, I came out publicly in the media and said it was dangerous to go, and unfair to ask players to leave their families behind in troubled times. Unless the English League was able to guarantee our safety, I said, we should not go. I said it, but I didn't believe it.

When I started getting tidal waves of threats and abuse because of that stand, I expected the ARL to back me to the hilt.

Instead they left me high and dry. There was no support at all. I felt betrayed. The response from the League was that this was my private opinion, not theirs. I'd dreamed of wearing the green and gold, maybe even becoming captain of Australia one day. As a young boy I used to dream that some fairy godmother would wave the magic wand and suddenly I'd be Captain Kangaroo, leading the Australian rugby league team to Ashes victory on English soil. I'd made that dream come true. And here they were, shoving the magic wand fair up my rear end. I'm sorry if that's a vulgar way to put it. That tour was to be my last appearance for Australia. And they gave it to me big-time.

To be fair to the ARL, though, there were numerous times when they covered for me when I missed plane flights and training sessions. But in 2001 it felt like the bad was outweighing the good. That's politics.

Now to those feathers again. I know they were sent by a person looking to set me up. That's all I will say on it. It was not the act of a person outside the game angered by my decision to pull out. No, the culprit was a person from the inside who could benefit from the knowledge that I'd been sent such a thing. Someone close to the game. The feathers arrived in the mail at my home in Collaroy. How many people would know the address, for a start? As I said, at the time I didn't even know what they meant. But it made one heck of a story. And it made my life an absolute misery for weeks. I know it's a stupid way to be, but I've always worried what people think of me. It's one thing I wish I could change about my character. And here I was being called a coward by people who didn't know me, and didn't know the truth of it all. I suppose I should've made this public before now. I've kept it bottled up inside for years.

Anyway, off we go to England for my last appearance in an Australian jersey. With our campaign disrupted by all the controversy, and no preparatory games to work on our fitness, we were set up for defeat in that first game at Huddersfield. We were just about done and dusted at half-time, down 12–0. Joey Johns bounced back with a try, then Adam MacDougall scored, and for a brief moment we actually got within one point of the lead. It was only very brief. They got our cash 20–12 in the end. I was lock in that, and all three matches, with Trent Barrett and Joey Johns the halves.

Then to Bolton for the second Test. Chris Anderson made an inspired decison in the dressing room before that game: he brought Mal Meninga along. Mal was there as part of an Ashes Legends exhibition game. As I've said a number of times, there are few people in the game I respect more than big Mal. He spoke about what it meant to be a Kangaroo, mentioned some of the great names of the past who'd played under the same banner we now carried, and asked a very simple question: did we want to be the first team in thirty years to lose the Ashes? I was very greatly affected by what Mal said.

I certainly didn't want to end my Australian Test career as a losing captain. I'd had an ordinary game in the first Test. This time I came out like a man possessed, fired up to the max, and landed the first try after Joey put Robbie Kearns through a gap. Well, it was a cakewalk from there, and an amazing turnaround from the first game. We led 24–0 at the break, 40–0 after that, and took it out 40–12 at the finish. It could have been a record-breaking Ashes win except we slackened off a bit at the end and let the Poms in for a couple of late tries. When I look back on that now, I see a performance of which I'm hugely proud, and one I was very privileged to be a part of.

Coming to the decider at Wigan, there was no stopping us; we wrapped it up 28–8. That was the Test when Chris Anderson suffered chest pains and was taken off to hospital midway through the game. He'd had a mild heart attack and did exactly the right thing by leaving us to go to the hospital.

I had one last moment of glory in the green and gold. Trent Barrett scored near full-time, and I landed the conversion. It was a strange feeling in the dressing rooms later. I had a swirling mix of emotions — relief that we'd won the Ashes, worry about our coach's health, sadness that I'd never play for Australia again, and pride in all the things I'd done. I couldn't have been happier with the statistics of my career in Test matches: fifth on the list of appearances (with thirty-four), behind Mal Meninga, Reg Gasnier, Clive Churchill and Graeme Langlands; fourth on the list of captains with twenty Tests, behind Churchill, Wally Lewis and Meninga; and even up there in the top ten try-scorers with fourteen. In a way, looking at those figures, writing them down here like this, it makes me a bit sad. You play the game, reach the heights, but don't often get to grasp the importance and historical significance of what you're doing. That only happens when you look back.

crowing again
after 27 years

Back from the shortened Kangaroo tour, and shaping up with renewed enthusiasm for the 2002 season, I wanted to get everything off on the right footing. I thought about ways in which I could bounce back from the terrible year just past. I sat down in a quiet corner on my own and wrote down the things I could do to show the way. I'd never really thought much about the true qualities of leadership until that time, but I needed to work out a way that would shine a light to the rest of the team, and ease the way in for the new Roosters coach, Ricky Stuart.

What I came up with was this: get to training first, every session, and be waiting out there on the field, ready to go. And that's exactly what I did. I made sure I was the first out there, all set to warm up. Every time. I wrote down, 'It'll make me a better player, and a better leader.' And with a solution as simple as that, it turned my life and my footy around from a nightmare in 2001 to the dream result that would be 2002. I made a couple of other notes as well, little things like making sure I went that extra metre at training. You can't be chipping other players for pulling up short in warm-ups unless you are doing it all and more yourself.

Ricky Stuart was on board as the new coach and I knew he'd be a hard taskmaster, but I wasn't sure how tough he'd go on me, since we were close friends and team-mates. We'd had a long history as opponents, team-mates, and just mates. 'Sticky's' Raiders knocked Penrith out of the finals in 1989, beat us in the Grand Final a year later, and then we beat them in 1991. There were two Kangaroo tours, Test matches, State of Origin games and a whole lot of history between us. I was even a guest at his wedding. All that could have made for a difficult working relationship with me as team captain and Sticky as coach. He had to be seen not to be playing favourites with me. I couldn't be seen to be expecting favours. That would only breed contempt and disquiet in the team. There was a very fine line to be walked.

I was in two minds. One part of me thought, *This is OK — I can slacken off if I like, he's not going to say anything.* The other part said, *He'll be twice as hard on me to make an example.* I'm glad to say that it was a case of the latter. I got absolutely no latitude from Sticky. Not a scrap of it. In past seasons I'd take an extra two weeks' break in the off season. Sticky made sure that didn't happen. So even before training began I knew where I stood with the coach. We were mates, always. But I was not to shirk it for a moment. There'd be no beg-pardons, or 'sorry, mate'. It was just *do what I tell you, and put your body on the line.* From the moment when my leave was cut short, we formed an iron-clad partnership as coach and captain. I would come to thrive under his coaching, partly, I think, because we were such good mates. I never wanted to let him down. Ever.

Our agreement — the seed of the 2002 premiership triumph — was forged on the St Michael's golf course on the windswept southern shore of Sydney, at about the same time that coward was posting me the white feathers. Ricky called me up. 'Come and have a hit, mate,' he said. But there was more on his mind than just golf. Since it was his idea, I'll let Sticky tell the story:

I was worried about it. No doubt. I had to use our friendship to my and the team's advantage right from the start, not have it loom into view as a hurdle at some later stage. People instinctively follow Brad. I needed him as a leader, not a liability because of our longtime association.

I figured the best place to lay it all on the line with Brad was the seclusion of the golf course at St Michael's, just him and me. I told him I was young and inexperienced as a coach. I told him that anything I did was not for Brad Fittler's benefit or for Ricky Stuart's benefit — it was for the team. I insisted that if he had an opinion to state, or a problem with me, he should hold his tongue and air it in private with me, not in front of the team. I told him that he had to lead the team by getting his shorts dirty, not pointing and directing from the back. I told him that if he finished playing without doing a victory lap as a Grand Final winner again, the back-end of his career would be pure waste. I reminded him how much it meant to one of his idols, Mal Meninga, to go out with a premiership win. I knew Brad had finished the previous season on an uncomfortable note. His career was plateauing, I told him. He was simply treading water, waiting for things to turn around. He needed to make things turn around. I told him I'd give him no slack in getting fit. And it's his commitment to getting fit that caused his career to surge again, spiralling upwards all the way to retirement.

I got square for the tough talking-to — I won the golf game. I really won a lot more, though: a renewed passion to get back on top, and the fire in my belly again for the first time in a year. But Sticky had one more trick up his sleeve. He had me keen to get fit. But he needed me to lead from the front again. And here's how he did it, early in the new season. He got us all together and handed out a sheet of paper, one to each of us, and with another player's name on top of the piece of paper. Best I let Sticky explain again, since it was his brainchild:

I asked each player to write the answer to two questions about the team-mate whose name appeared at the top of the paper they held in their hands. The questions were: 'What do you like best about taking the field with this player?' And, 'What do you hate about taking the field with this player?' They thought it was anonymous, but I knew exactly who got which player to comment on. I gave Brad's name to Craig Wing. I did so quite deliberately, because 'Wingy' is very honest, blunt, and also very intelligent.

Then I collected all the sheets, and the next day I read out the responses to the gathered players without saying, of course, who'd made the comments. I was the only one who knew who got what. When Brad reads this, it'll be the first time he'll know that it was Wingy who got to write about him. Anyway, Craig wrote, 'The thing I like best about taking the field with Brad is when he leads from the front. I just love following him. When he takes on the line, the whole team wants to follow. The thing I hate about taking the field with Brad is when he stays at the back and just yells out directions and points. It irritates me and it irritates the team.' I added a little bit extra after that, I must admit. And it really hit home to Brad. It made him sit up and take notice. There was no hint of offence being taken, just a lesson to learn. I think that moment reshaped his season, and quite possibly the rest of his career. When Brad's up, it's like a virus that spreads through the team. He doesn't need to say, it's seen. When he's up for it, they're all up for it.

It was definitely a turning point, to realise what others thought about me. But I had more trouble keeping the old frame together, rather than my head, from the start of 2002. In a trial game against Manly I cracked a rib, and immediately thought, *Well, here you go, mate, another wonky year ahead*. It crossed my mind, as soon as it happened, that I would have been wiser to quit everything when the Kangaroo tour had ended. So the season that brought the Roosters their first premiership in twenty-seven years, and me my second in eleven years, began as miserably as any I can recall.

Our first game of the season had the spotlight right on it because the Roosters came up against South Sydney, back in the competition for the first time in three seasons. There were more than 35 000 fans at Aussie Stadium, and I'd be very surprised if more than 1000 of them were barracking for the Roosters. The Rabbitohs were back in football for about eight minutes when I put up a bomb and Shannon Hegarty scored. I'm not really the one to blame, though, for raining on Souths' parade. We were a red-hot team that day. It was 26–0 at half-time, 40–6 at the end, and suddenly all the romance of Souths' David and Goliath courtroom victory to get back in the premiership came thudding down to earth. You're back, bunnies, but this is your reward: a thrashing first up, and the likelihood of more to come.

That's the way it looked, at least. The only problem was that Souths won the following week, we got run over by Auckland, and I found myself on the sidelines for a month when I aggravated that broken rib. We lost to Auckland, Brisbane, the Northern Eagles and Newcastle, and at the end of Round 5 we shared the bottom of the ladder. At that point we had more chance of winning the wooden spoon than the premiership. And a number of our finest players were out injured. The Eagles game was a particularly low point — we had five blokes stretchered off and Ryan Cross broke his leg. The Eagles have always been a bit of a bogey team for the Roosters, and so it proved again.

Suddenly 2002 was shaping up as another nightmare, just like 2001. The big difference was that we were never stressed about it. We weren't that bad against the Broncos, just falling a bit short, and Newcastle were running hot at the time, so there were some positives for us. We were only on two competition points, but it belied our strengths.

Ricky Stuart was extremely calm at that point. 'Things will turn around,' he'd say at training. 'Don't worry.' It was a severe test for him — his first big one as a coach, coming in to take over a star-studded team and finding himself one-for-five — and he stood up to it brilliantly. That period, I think, laid the foundation for him as a great coach. There were injury worries — we used twenty-eight players in the first eight games — and a new defensive style to get used to in a bid to stem the flow of points against us, but there were signs of a real spirit developing at the club. Far from being a problem, the great bond between Sticky and me was proving a huge advantage.

We bounced back to flog North Queensland, and then got on the express train to the finals. But the bad start still left us with one crucial game at the end: the final round, against Cronulla at Toyota Park. The two teams would finish fourth and fifth — that much wasn't in doubt. But the winner would gain a massive advantage by staging the opening finals match on home soil. Gus told us — and I don't know if this is true or not or just a way Gus thought he could gee us up — that Cronulla had already organised the fireworks for a semi-final on home soil. The Sharks had already paid for the lot, he said. That's how confident they were of beating us. After all, they'd won eleven in a row.

The Roosters had to come from behind, but I managed to see their halfback Brett Kimmorley out of the corner of my eye as he prepared to throw a pass that didn't appear to have a ready receiver. I grabbed the intercept, ran 40 metres to plant it down, and from that point on it was never in doubt. I made the most of my moment in the spotlight, running all the way to the back of the in-goal area to ground the ball. Their David Peachey had done something similar to us a couple of weeks earlier, slamming the ball down at the back of the in-goal, and then waving the ball to the crowd in triumph. I saw that and said to myself, 'There'll be a get-square, mate.' I didn't realise it would come quite so quickly, but here was my chance for a payback and I made sure they knew it, too.

The Roosters won 30–18, and we couldn't have hoped for a better confidence booster with the finals coming up. You know how the sports psychologists get you to visualise yourself in a match-winning position? You imagine you're serving for the match at Wimbledon, fire down a bunch of aces and win it, and you picture yourself with the trophy held high over your head. That's supposed to make it come true. Well, I often visualise an intercept like that one against the Sharks, with a clear, uninterrupted run to the try line. There's nothing to beat that feeling. Especially in such a vital match.

So the finals arrived, and although some controversial refereeing decisions by Paul Simpkins took centre stage in post-match discussions, the truth is we were again too good for Cronulla. Newcastle presented a completely different challenge in the second semi-final. It was sudden death, us or them. They had Andrew Johns out. There'd be no excuses. And there we were at half-time locked up at 6–all.

Out we went, and with twenty minutes to go it was still 6–all. It could've been worse but for an amazing tackle by Anthony Minichiello, chasing the runaway Sean Rudder. Then Craig Fitzgibbon latched onto a stray pass from the Knights' Danny Buderus and ran 95 metres to score, chased all the way by Matt Gidley. It was one of the most inspirational events I've seen on a football field, and it turned the tide for us. But we had to wait a while before it counted — the video referee took an interminably long time to decide whether or not Fitzy was onside. Your stomach churns at a crucial moment like that, while your fate turns on a decision that's totally out of your hands, and out of sight as well. That was pretty much the turning point in the game — in our season, really— and we steamed home with a mighty period of play to win 38–12. Fitzy, you saved our year.

Suddenly only Brisbane stood between us and a Grand Final berth. I say 'only Brisbane' but it's a bit of a ridiculous way to put it when they had a side containing the likes of Lote Tuqiri, Allan Langer, Darren Lockyer, Gorden Tallis, Shane Webcke and Michael De Vere. It's some task to knock over that lot. But the Roosters did, extremely clinically. Brisbane led us at the break by 4, and at the end we had 4 on them, winning 12–8.

That was pretty much the Grand Final right there in those last gripping fifteen minutes. I believed that whichever team, Brisbane or the Roosters, won that preliminary final would have beaten either of the other two sides, the Warriors or the Sharks.

I don't have to tell you, I'm sure, that it was the Warriors we faced up to in the Grand Final on 6 October that year. I've never gone into a game so confident. I felt good. Only a minor ankle injury worried me. The bookies had us as overwhelming favourites, and there's just no way we were ever going to lose that game. Sometimes — and it's only happened to me very rarely — you reach this zone as a team where you feel unbeatable. You have total faith in every member of your team. That was the Sydney Roosters that day. I made sure I didn't read the papers that week. I didn't want to know that we were 'newspaper certainties'. I needed to stay focused. Totally focused, not distracted by a view that we only had to turn up and they'd hand us the premiership.

I had learned a lot from the 2000 Grand Final we lost. I'd been no less confident then. But I'd played like I had my head up my butt the whole time. There was a plan, but I didn't stick to it. I lost composure back then. Worse still, I led the team like a rookie. 'Choking' is a word that comes to mind. Those are bad memories. And there was no way I was going to have it happen again. I don't know what I would have done if the Roosters had lost in 2002. I can't even contemplate what might have happened. The Gap at Watson's Bay might have seen another suicide, I think.

The Warriors did hit the lead briefly with a try by Stacey Jones, but there was no need for concern. I suppose the crunch moment, the turning point, was my long 40–20 kick that put us on the attack and led to a Craig Wing try that sealed it for the Roosters. I booted that kick so sweetly, and turned it neatly to the left, like it was remote controlled. Ivan Cleary is one of the best positional fullbacks around, but it managed to beat him over the touch line. There have been so many times in big games when people have looked to me to make a match-winning play

and come up with something that changes a game. It happened
for me in that moment, with that simple kick. From the scrum I
ran to the line, hit Wingy with a pass, and he crashed through a
hole on the inside, a move we'd worked successfully five or six
times in a previous win over Auckland. From then on, it was
our Grand Final.

After that Fitzy scored, and later I put a grubber kick through
and Chris Flannery went over, putting the match way out of the
Warriors' reach. What happened next is one of those out-of-
body experiences I've spoken about previously. I looked up at
the Roosters fans in the crowd, in the far right-hand corner of
Telstra Stadium, and they were all on their feet, stamping and
cheering. They were going ballistic. I could sense all their eyes
on me, and I felt like I was king. There were probably 10 000 of
them, and I could feel them staring right at me. I thrust both
hands in the air without thinking. It was as if all their energy
and enthusiasm was invading my body. Honestly, for that split
second, I felt like a god. Like I'd delivered and they'd accepted.
That was our moment together: Freddy and a few thousand
Roosters die-hards. In all of my football career I don't think I've
ever had a moment to match that one. Thinking about it now
sends tingles up my spine. So thanks, guys and girls, for that —
you'll never know how good you made me feel at that moment.
I'd believed in something so strongly — that the Roosters would
win a premiership — and worked so hard to make it happen.
Thank you so much.

Problem is, I suppose, anyone up on a pedestal has to expect
to be a target, and I certainly was that afternoon. I got belted
twice — once as I shaped to kick the ball, changed my mind and
went to run it, and got smacked by an elbow or shoulder from
their interchange forward, Wairangi Koopu, and then later in a
flying headbutt from Richard Villasanti. I have no idea what
Villasanti thought he was doing. I've seen it on replay, and it
looks like he launched himself at me head-first and got me on
the left temple. I was in Disneyland after the first hit; I don't
remember the headbutt at all. I must have regained

consciousness a few minutes later, because the next thing I recall is trying to get up, and people all around me while I tried to play the ball. I looked at the referee, Bill Harrigan, as if to say, 'Come on, Bill, let me get on with the game', and everyone was holding onto me. I guess I would've fallen over if they'd let me go. I lost a minute of my life.

That crazy moment might've knocked the sense out of me, but it put even more starch and steam into my team-mates. What happened next is, I think, the proudest few minutes of football in my whole playing career. And it had absolutely nothing to do with anything I did. Villasanti tried to make a burst, and my team-mate Peter Cusack came off the line and smashed him, legitimately but savagely. Villasanti tried to do it again, and this time our Adrian Morley sized him up and knocked him arse over apex. It was as if all my team-mates were standing up to say, 'You mess with our captain and this is what'll happen to you.' Even now, thinking about that all over again, I'm getting a bit misty-eyed. Seriously — I am. I felt I'd led them well all season, and shown courage in the Grand Final. And now here they were showing me how much they appreciated it. You can't imagine how much that means to the leader of a team in a game as brutal as rugby league.

The blokes just gave it to the Warriors at the end, and eventually it was a cakewalk: 30–8. Walking back after Bryan Fletcher's final try — and I knew there were some big bets on him being the last try-scorer that day — I was floating on air.

I'd won a premiership before, of course, with the Panthers eleven years earlier, but there was a world of difference between the two experiences. Back then all I had to do was my job. I was only a kid, and as long as I did my job nothing more could've been expected of me. Others, like Greg Alexander, were there to win us the game. We won, and that was a premiership, and it was an awesome experience for a kid. In 2002, though, I had the weight of the world on my shoulders running onto the field as captain and playmaker. I felt that what I did would influence the game; I had to stand up. This time, *I* was the Greg

Alexander and other players were looking to me. I felt that pressure tremendously as the day developed. But oddly, by the time we'd run onto the field, heard the national anthem and kicked off, I felt calm and confident.

When the final siren went, and victory was ours, I had this extraordinary feeling of relief, like the whole world had been lifted off my shoulders. I hugged Luke Ricketson and felt tears welling up in my eyes. I couldn't speak. I couldn't move. I felt I was somewhere else looking down at this person who was trying to mumble words and they wouldn't come out, and trying to walk and his legs wouldn't move. It's very real to me, and perfectly clear in my memory. I don't know how to explain it other than by calling it 'another out-of-body experience', but the essence of whoever I am was not in that body for a while.

Paul Harragon came up to interview me, and someone was answering his questions, but it wasn't me. All I could say was, 'I love everybody for making me feel so good'. I wanted to thank everyone who enjoyed watching football, not just Roosters fans, but everyone. At that moment I didn't have an enemy in this world or any other. I don't even know which world I was in. I was just totally blown away. There could not possibly have been a happier person on the planet that day. Then my mate David Gyngell, who was out on the field, gave me a mobile phone and told me Marie was on the other end. I took the phone but I couldn't speak. My mouth was opening but the words wouldn't come. I was out there, looking down at myself, saying, 'Speak, you fool, tell her how much you love her', but no words came out. I was a blubbering idiot. Every time I tried to talk, I cried.

At that point I wouldn't have known who I saw or what I said. I scarcely remember holding up the trophy at the presentation, and that was ten or fifteen minutes later. I have no idea what I said. I hope I thanked the Warriors and the sponsors and the fans. If I missed anyone out that afternoon, please understand that I was lost in space.

I was still like that in the dressing room. All the officials and supporters were crushed in, and the look of satisfaction and joy on their faces was something to behold. Nick Politis hugged me and my blood was smeared over the side of his face. 'I'm never washing it off,' he said. We were slapping each other on the back, hugging and sobbing. But the strangest thing happened not long after that. We were on the bus leaving the ground, and that overwhelming feeling of elation was totally drained from me. I felt, suddenly, like I was on the way back from a no-account game at Campbelltown or somewhere remote. Go figure that one out. I don't know what it was. All I can say is that the wondrous feeling, the volcanic rush of emotion that had completely overcome me a little while earlier was gone. In its place was a feeling of calmness and contentedness. It wasn't the after-effects of celebratory alcohol — I was drinking only water. Those that know about such things tell me that the dazzling highs experienced by drug users result in a similar thud back to earth. I was high on the addictive drug of success, and I suppose I had to come down eventually, too.

A few of the boys were playing up at the back of the bus, but I was in no mood at all for skylarking. I just wanted to lie back, close my eyes and relax. I hardly said a word on the long trip back to our home ground, Aussie Stadium, on the bus. I just thought about how the expectations had finally been achieved, and how the words of our critics had been shoved down their throats. It was a childhood dream to lead a Grand Final–winning team. That's as good as it gets.

From there we transferred to an open-top bus, and were taken up Oxford Street towards Bondi Junction, and with music blaring and people shouting and waving from the streets, the blood and the adrenaline started pumping again. I don't know, maybe it was just the wind in my face from that open-top bus. Who knows? The fact is, I was ready to celebrate and share the joy again. I was feeling a million dollars. I wanted to see my old schoolmates, and Marie and my family and friends. I suppose it's a bit like when you're a kid and you do something good, you want to be praised for it by your mum and those you love. I couldn't wait to share the joy with them.

We arrived at the Leagues Club in Bronte Road and there was a mass of faces, everybody laughing and grinning, shouting and waving wildly. I only had to walk about 20 metres from the bus into the club, and I'd lost just about all my clothing by the time I made it. My jacket went, then my tie, then my shirt. I lost my suit, I know that. Someone gave me a Roosters T-shirt, and that went too. I was getting hit in the face and the head, smacked on the bum and belted on the back. If you think it was tough copping an elbow or a headbutt in the Grand Final, it was nothing compared with running the gauntlet to get into the Leagues Club that evening, I can assure you.

I fought my way onto the stage in the auditorium, clambered up the staircase and then crawled on my hands and knees towards the front of it. I had no idea what was out there until I scrambled back onto my feet, and as I rose it just blew me away. The auditorium was packed to the rafters. There was this massive ocean of heads. I had that feeling of déjà vu, going back to the Penrith club eleven years earlier on the night I was in my first premiership-winning team. This was very different, though: first, I was the captain and, second, I was old enough to take it all in and appreciate what a special moment in my life this was. I felt like I was in charge. It was our night. I was ready to settle in.

And there was no way I wasn't going to snap out a stage dive. I got away with it, too, unhurt. Anything I did, the whole crowd did as one. I'd stand there, thrust my fist in the air and scream, 'Yeah!' and as one person this crowd of thousands would do exactly the same. It's an extraordinary and overwhelming feeling of power and control. I suppose I should have said something deep and meaningful, but at that moment a single 'Yeah!' was more than enough. It's all-consuming when you have thousands of people in the palm of your hand the way I did at that moment.

The relationship between the players and their devoted club fans is an interesting one. These are mostly people who work hard during the week and then back up weekend after weekend, rain or shine, win or lose, to support you. That's a huge act of faith and deserves to be repaid. The problem is that you can't afford to walk too closely among them at times because they'll tear you to shreds, quite literally — I could've been crushed to death when I arrived at the club. Sometimes the support can be overwhelming, especially when I want some quiet time — a beer with a few close friends, or a dinner with Marie and my family. I see it as the least I can do to smile and shake their hands and sign autographs. It seems to make people happy. I find that intriguing. After all, I'm just a bloke who plays football. It's just a game. But the fans will stop asking one day, and I'm sure I'm going to miss it. Marie has often borne the brunt of the intrusions into our private time, and she has handled it with unbelievable patience and good humour. For that I thank her from the bottom of my heart.

However, when you come together as one to celebrate a Grand Final win it's a terrific feeling. At that time the player and the fan are absolutely at one. We're all there to join in celebrations of this great joy, of achieving some magical goal. At Penrith it was a first-ever premiership for the club. On that night at Easts, it was the first in more than a quarter of a century. A lot of the people in that auditorium had not seen their club win a premiership in their entire lives; others had lived through that fabled nightmare season in which the Roosters failed to win a game.

It didn't matter if you were an ordinary fan, on welfare, or a multimillionaire, the boss, or a star player — the feeling was exactly the same for everyone. Sheer, unadulterated joy. That's what it was. There are not many sports where, even for one brief moment of celebration, everybody is equal like that. It happens in rugby league, and the game and the players are the better for it.

I'd embraced Nick Politis. Then, as night merged into morning, I was in the street outside a local pub dancing with a fan's young daughter. He'd come into the pub and asked me if I'd go outside and say hello to his young girl. Not only that, we then shared a few dance steps, and although she was only about six years old, she'd had less to drink than me and her dance skills were vastly better than mine. The bloke asked if he could have the premiership T-shirt I was wearing. I would've given it to him, too, except I didn't have a singlet on underneath and they wouldn't let me back in the pub barechested.

It's those little moments that mean a lot to a player and, I suppose, much more to the fans. Men of means, or with no means at all, share the same joy with you the same way. It's what I love about the game. They say in horse racing that all men are equal on the turf, and under it. I feel the same way about footy. And I'd achieved the goal that Ricky Stuart had mapped out for me in that pre-season golf game at St Michael's. To set yourself a difficult target and make it is the best feeling in the world.

One last word on that Grand Final win and its aftermath, and it revolves around my mate 'Fletch'. I remember him well as a younger player, sitting on the bench for reserve grade. He couldn't even crack it for a spot in our reserves team then. But his attitude was not one of a grumbling, 'Why do they keep leaving me out?' It was more like, 'Well, I'll just train harder.' I don't think I've ever seen a player improve so much, and it was all down to dedication and self-belief. He helped make us into a premiership-winning team, and also won himself an Australian jumper. Bryan Fletcher provided an attacking option for us, and you knew that when you called on him, he'd back himself against anybody.

It was a wonderful couple of months for me after that, my first real break from football in almost fourteen years. The team took off to north Queensland for an end-of-season holiday, meeting at Sydney Airport all dressed like '70s tennis players in short shorts, whites and fake moustaches, and carrying racquets. The first few days were mostly business, attending some functions and signing autographs. Later, on the way to Airlie Beach, Bryan Fletcher called for a nude bus trip, and so it was that twenty naked blokes in a minibus zipped down the highway. At one point we stopped for a toilet break and stood in perfect formation, all in a line, all naked as the day we were born, taking a leak beside the highway. It must've looked very funny. Where was my camera then?

It was fabulous to be able to take a break without having end-of-season representative commitments. I knew then that I'd done the right thing in pulling the pin on representative games. Just being able to settle back with Marie, have a holiday, catch up with the family, generally live a regular life again, was indescribably good. I found myself walking down the street and noticing things I'd ignored all those years. I even took a greater interest in an old hobby, photography. In the past somebody would point out a glorious sunset and I'd look up briefly, and acknowledge that it looked interesting, and immediately get on with thinking about the next football game. There was training to worry about, or seeing the physiotherapist, or going to the gym. These are the things that had occupied my mind entirely from the time I started playing, 24 hours a day, seven days a week. I had lived footy every waking moment. It's a selfish way to be, consumed with thoughts about what you do and not about what appeals to others, but that's the way it was with me. I'm not joking — every hour I was awake, footy would occupy my thoughts.

Pretty soon, it was time to do it all again.

tricky ricky

When the 2003 season came around I was feeling on top of the world. I'd never gone into a season in such a rock-solid frame of mind and body. The first time the team gathered after all the premiership celebrations had been and gone was on the beach at Kurnell. Sticky had given me a couple of extra weeks' break and I appreciated that. I used it to work out in the gym at Highgate, but I think it got into Sticky's mind that working out with the old blokes in a posh boutique gym the size of a shoebox might not be enough for me. He sent me a text message saying he'd pick me up the next morning and we'd go for a beach run. What he really meant was, 'It's the dreaded sand hills for you, mate'. But he was keeping that as his little surprise. Here's Ricky Stuart's version:

> When I spoke to Brad a couple of days earlier he said he was working out and feeling good. I knew that was bullshit, if you'll pardon the expression. A few minutes on the treadmill and the stationary bike wasn't going to help you get fit for premiership rugby league. No quality there. He came to a skills session and really lifted the tempo, so I figured I could use this to lift the team's quality of training.
>
> I pencilled in a really arduous sand hills session, but told Brad we were just going for a run on the beach at

Cronulla. 'Not hills, mate, is it?' he said. 'Nah,' I said, 'Trust me ... just the beach.' It was the hills, of course, and he knew it the moment we pulled up at Kurnell. I won't tell you what he called me. Anyway, he figured he could do it, and by the second run, when it was starting to hurt all of them, he saw one of the young blokes with hands on hips, stopping halfway up for a bit of a blow. At the Roosters we hate hands on hips. It's bad body language. A sign of weakness. Brad stopped and yelled at the bloke to get his hands off his hips and get moving. He really gave it to him. The bloke was actually halfway through vomiting. After Brad blasted him, he continued to vomit with his hands dangling by his sides.

After the third one Brad, totally buggered, came up to me and said, 'Sticky, I'm in trouble.' I thought he meant that he was worried about doing another one. 'No,' Brad said, struggling for breath to get the words out, 'I need to put my hands on my hips and that young bloke keeps lookin' at me. Where can I put 'em?'

Later, Ricky and I sat down to work out the best way to get ourselves back to those great heights. 'What goals are we going to set?' we asked each other. He came up with a beauty for me, saying, 'You've never won the Dally M player of the year. I reckon it might be your turn this year. Dally M points often go to the team's playmaker, and that's you. Give it a go. Make it a goal.' He set me a target, and I thought I was up to it. He could see how fit and content and motivated I was, like never before at that stage of a season.

I had won the Provan-Summons Medal, the equivalent of the Rothmans Medal in the year Super League and the ARL were divided. But I'd always thought that the result was a bit too cosy. Laurie Daley got the Super League award as their best. I think it was more of a political decision to give it to me than a true representation of the season. I thought that player of the year was a fair goal to aim at. I'd given myself a good chance of winning the Dally M a couple of years earlier but I'd missed out when Trent Barrett won it.

Records were never right at the forefront of my thinking. For instance, there's no reason why I couldn't have gone on playing games for Australia and New South Wales and most probably knocked off all the records for most caps, and for most caps as captain. It just wasn't like me to worry about things like that. I'd had enough, and just hanging around for records and awards ... well, that seemed selfish to me. Plus I wasn't up to it.

But the Dally M was a good target. It was achievable. I'd had a good year just gone, and we had a tiptop side. So why not? I reckoned it was going to be my best year in the premiership. And it started off according to plan: the Roosters towelled Parramatta 32–14 and I laid on three tries. Even luck went my way with one or two fortunate bounces. I distinctly recall walking out of Aussie Stadium at the end of that first round match thinking to myself that, having played with such tremendous intensity, it was going to be another big year for the Roosters and for me. We trained with intensity and played that way too.

Then we outlasted Newcastle in a really gritty win. Next we came up against my old club, Penrith, the following week at Aussie Stadium, chasing the club's twelfth straight win. I was having a blinder. My head was focused. I had two tries on the board. But there's no doubt that Penrith is the Roosters' hoodoo team — they love to beat us. And I think the fact that I was there just made them all that more determined. In a newspaper column, Ricky Stuart said the Panthers had it over us. Our assistant coach, John Cartwright, himself a former Penrith hero, reckoned they just loved to 'come down from the mountains and rumble with us'. I think it was the new version of the old 'fibro v. silvertail' battles of the 1980s between Wests and Manly. Anyway, that was the end of our winning trot. They nailed us by a point.

I was happy when we struck wet conditions at Aussie Stadium for the Round 6 game against the Broncos, and everyone slowed down to my pace. I put on a couple of tries, and scored two myself, and Ricky Stuart made me feel 10 feet tall that day by telling the media, 'Brad's the best leader I've ever been associated with'. That from a bloke who played under Meninga and Daley at Canberra. Ricky's compliments were a reward, I think, for the hard work I was putting in at training. It was his way of publicly thanking me.

This game stands out in my mind. From the first set of six tackles I took on the line, put a kick through and 'Finchy' scored under the posts. I scored another myself later on and had a hand in a couple of others. So there I was, still getting the plaudits. I figured I was on track for that goal as Dally M player of the year.

After that win, the team had a day at the races at Randwick. Everybody who was anybody was there. I felt really proud to be a Rooster; the club had come so far. I'd really come to love it over the years. Still do now, even with my playing days behind me. What I'd like to think I've given in return is yeoman service and a sense of self-belief. They had the ability before I and others joined the club, but they didn't believe they could win. When we came together as this tight and talented and dedicated group in the late nineties, we gained not just in club playing strength but in strength of attitude. You don't reach that many Grand Finals in the space of a few seasons unless you believe in yourself, trust your team-mates and respect them, and that's been taken to a whole new level in the Roosters.

I want to make this point, too: it must not be an attitude at player and coaching level alone — it has to permeate down all the way from the president, the club board and the chief executive. The players and coach can't achieve great things without input from the boss and his board. They have to be helpful, passionate, compassionate and considerate. When I first started at Penrith that's the way it was in the Panthers, and it brought success on the playing field. In the latter years there the board became divided and uninterested, and the team suffered. The one thing I can definitely say about the Roosters is that if you wanted help from the board, you got it, no questions asked. It's not just comforting for the players and the coaching staff; it's absolutely essential if you want to win. A football club is one big team — at least, it should be. The team is not just the mob who runs out onto the paddock every weekend. The bloke in the suit at the board meeting is no less a part of the picture than the bloke scoring points. Everyone — and I mean every single person associated with the club — has to be committed, content and caring.

By Round 17 the Roosters were running fourth and I was about to hit a big milestone, playing my 300th first grade game against the Rabbitohs at Aussie Stadium. It was a memorable game for me: I scored a try, had a hand in three others and even kicked a goal. And for good measure I got into a rare fight, with Souths forward Justin Smith. I guess it was just a game in which I wanted to tick all the boxes, and I can happily say I succeeded. It was hugely satisfying. But I knew in the back of my mind that this might not be the giant year I'd hoped for a few months earlier.

I should say, though, just how much that 300th first grade game meant to me. It's one thing to get the big money and the adulation, but for me, there's nothing more satisfying than giving service in return. I didn't want a big deal made of it, though. In my 250th game we came up against Manly, and there was this whole week of 'Let's win for Freddy', and we got blitzed. The same thing happened when I played what I thought was to be my last ever State of Origin game in 2001. You know, 'Let's do it for Freddy'. And we were trounced then. So I was over all that by the time my 300th game came around. Twice bitten.

Despite that, it was comforting to be so warmly praised by some of the biggest names in the game's history. It meant a lot to me in the week leading up to the 300th game. Bob Fulton said I was 'the greatest of my generation'. Johnny Raper said, 'I've always loved his attitude to the game. If you ask him to do a job, he's always willing and never complains.' Graeme

Langlands added, 'He's always been an honest and fair player. There's no dirt in his play.' Well, when you read that stuff in the newspapers, you can't help but swell with pride. And I had to laugh at Wally Lewis, a dyed-in-the-wool Queenslander if ever there was one, when he said, 'He's a pain in the arse. You get so sick of talking about him. You can't help it.'

I organised a couple of private boxes in the stands at Aussie Stadium for Marie, and sponsors and friends. I made sure there were Roosters beanies and scarves on every chair. I was more worried about them having a good time than any fanfare for me. The club put on a terrific spread later, and some nice words were said about me. I deliberately played it all down, but the whole day is a cherished experience, I can tell you; it goes to the very heart of my career as a footballer. I might not have been the best ever. I might not have lived up to mine or others' expectations at times. But in those 300 games I'd given value for a long time, and every time. If I stood out from other players, it's for that fact alone. Whether it's down to attitude or resilience or the way I was made, or simply good luck, I was able to stick around for a long time at the highest level, and return dividends to those who'd paid me a lot of money. No one can take that from me, and I can hold my head high for my durability and service, if nothing else.

I won't bore you by describing the remainder of that season, game by game. Except to say that by about Round 17, even though the Roosters were back in fourth place on the ladder, I felt I was playing the best footy of my life. I was in control. The team that would beat us eventually in the Grand Final, Penrith, played host to the Roosters in Round 20, and it's another game that sticks in my memory. Penrith were on a huge unbeaten run to the finals, and it was a ground record crowd. I've never aimed up against my old club. I'm not sure why. It's something people like Gus Gould have often asked me to explain, and I can't come up with a satisfactory answer. Whatever the reason, I dearly wanted to turn it around on that day, to put the Panthers bogey behind me once and for all. Our lead-up was terrific, even going to the trouble of staging a mini training camp in the west for a couple of days beforehand. And the result was a first half of football that was absolutely dazzling. By half-time the Roosters led 26–0 and Penrith were lucky to get to nil. I scored a try, played a part in others and felt I'd played pretty much as well as I could ever hope to play.

Coming out for the second half, we won a scrum and the ball came to me. As I ran past Penrith's Luke Priddis I copped a slap in the face, but I kept going as Scott Sattler and then Tony Puletua stepped into my path. I jigged and turned back towards Priddis, but somehow Puletua picked me up and dumped me on my left shoulder. The sound of bone crunching on hard ground was sickening. I thought at that instant that I'd broken my shoulder, and it's extraordinary the thoughts that go through your head at such a time. In a split second I'd pretty much canvassed the whole season and my playing future. In the moment before the pain hit me, coursing through my brain was the thought that I was at the peak of my form one minute and carrying a shattered shoulder the next.

I couldn't work out what had happened in the tackle. All I knew was how much it hurt. And how loud the crack was. I'd never really had serious shoulder problems in the past. I just thought, *Well, this it — it's all over for Brad.* I went off, of course, and the doctor told me I'd dislocated the shoulder, and then he popped it back in. I was screaming in pain. 'What should I do now?' I asked, and surprisingly the answer was, 'You can keep playing if you want', so I went onto the reserves bench. The Panthers had fought back to within eight points, so I went onto the field again. Craig Wing made a break then put me through for a try, and I ran across to put the ball down — just like the day I went on as a schoolboy all those years ago. I ran past the same hill and placed the ball in almost exactly the same spot. If I'd looked up and seen all my schoolmates there on the grass, and it was 1989 again, I would not have been surprised. Talk about a flashback! It was a lovely déjà vu moment for me.

The shoulder injury was to continue plaguing me after that match. It hurt like hell when someone came at me on my left shoulder and I tried to tackle him. It also sent sharp pains coursing through my upper torso whenever I was tackled. I should've taken time off but didn't. Deep down I knew I needed a rest, but the team came first. In hindsight, I managed that injury very badly.

We beat Canberra and Cronulla and then came up against Souths in Round 23 at Aussie Stadium. Anthony Minichiello's brother, Mark, ran straight at me and I went in to effect the tackle — third defender in — and came away with my left arm hanging loose. That was it for me — straight off. Running up the race and into the dressing rooms, the team doctor and physiotherapist looked at me the way a vet looks at an ageing dog when it's time to put him down. It was a 'this is going to hurt me more than it hurts you' kind of look. I don't know how much pain *they* were actually in, but I was hurting like all get-out. As they manhandled my shoulder back into place, I was in bloody agony.

I missed the next game against Manly, came back for a loss to the Warriors, and then it was off to Canberra for a cracker of a game in the final round, which we won 23–16. I wasn't selected to play, but I travelled with the team. The day before the game my old mate and our trainer, Ron Palmer, pulled me aside and gave me a spiel about how the team needed me. I knew it was coming. For the record, Ron, I was always going to play, but I loved the ego-boosting speech.

By season's end the Roosters had worked into second behind Penrith on the ladder, and we would meet them in the Grand Final. Before that, though, we had to overcome the Bulldogs in the first preliminary final. Our clashes with the Bulldogs are invariably tough and physical — they sapped our energy. It's not the sort of epic arm-wrestle you want leading into a Grand Final, but nonetheless, I was confident we would win. I thought we were ready.

I have nothing but the utmost praise for our forward pack in that 2003 Grand Final. They were awesome. We smashed into

Penrith; Penrith smashed into us. And no one took a backward step. You can't imagine how soul-destroying it is to work hard all season, get that close and then lose a Grand Final as we did that day, 18–6. If nothing else it was a memorable match, mostly, I suppose, for Scott Sattler's covering tackle on a flying Todd Byrne.

Penrith were the best side all year, and I don't begrudge them the premiership. I still have a very warm spot for them. I wasn't at my best. It wasn't my greatest game ever. I had to laugh at Ricky Stuart, who said he was going to say something to me in the dressing room before the game. Says Ricky, 'I was going to ask him how he felt, but I could just imagine those eyes looking up at me as if to say, "I've played 400 of them. How do you think I feel?"' I suppose, if anything, I was feeling the pain of a long season. I'm not a bloke who plays at his best when I'm hurting. Some are, and I admire them. Luke Ricketson is one who comes to mind. He's got a fabulous constitution and will. If you need him, he'll provide, whatever the circumstances.

Anyway, the Panthers did us over again. Our bogey side, as Ricky Stuart had quite rightly stated in his newspaper column earlier in the year. They were better than us in the Grand Final, but I do think our guys were heroic. I wish I could've been more help.

The ironic thing about that season was that my goal of winning the Dally M player of the year had had the rug pulled from under it: the awards were cancelled. Every year since 1968 there had been an award to the season's best and fairest. The one year I had a great chance, it was called off. The Rugby League Professionals Association — the players' union — had been in dispute with the NRL over pay issues. When the association decided to boycott the Dally Ms, the League was left without any option but to call the whole thing off. Later it was revealed, in the *Sunday Telegraph* I think, that coming into the last round, Penrith half Craig Gower was one point ahead of Clinton Schifcofske and me. Craig was the best player all year, I'm sure. Without that late shoulder injury, though, I would've given him a run for his money. But he plays half his games injured, so my whinge means nothing.

So I missed out all round. No premiership and no Dally M. But it didn't matter, because I was about to land the greatest prize of my life.

father freddy

Marie's pregnancy in 2003 brought a strange calmness to my life. I found it fascinating to follow the baby's growth on the various scans, and to observe the physical and emotional changes in Marie. I know it must be a strain and a source of serious discomfort for the woman, but can there be a more amazing experience than to have a child growing inside you? I hear women say that men have all the pleasure in producing a baby and women all the pain. I don't go along with that. The fact that a woman can achieve that — to grow a human being and deliver it — is a mind-blowing achievement and a blessing, not a curse.

It's a cliché, I know, but it's true: nothing in your life can ever beat the arrival of your first child. Nothing compares with it. It was certainly that way for me with our beautiful daughter, Demi. Except that I almost killed her a day before she arrived. Since the woman does most of the work in all of this, I'll let Marie take over at this point:

> Demi was born on 23 December 2003. Why Demi? Well, I've always liked the actor Demi Moore. So has Brad. As soon as I fell pregnant, we settled on Demi for a girl. Brad chose her second name, Centaine, from a character in books by his favourite author, Wilbur Smith. Centaine

was the courageous and tragic heroine of the novels *The Burning Shore* and *The Power of the Sword*. But we couldn't work out a boy's name. If it'd been a boy, he would probably have gone through life without a name. We just couldn't think of a good one. So I guess it was a girl or nothing. I was all set for the birth at Prince of Wales Hospital, Randwick. Except Brad nearly killed me the day before.

We went for a drive in the car. It was a stinking hot summer's day. We stopped at Clovelly because Brad needed to go to the hardware store. We'd had the air conditioning on, so when he stopped the windows were closed. He was only going to be a minute, and jumped out of the car without opening the windows. His old team-mate Bryan Fletcher happened to be in the hardware store, and he and Brad got to talking about football, and Brad forgot all about Little Miss Pregnant left back in the car. I couldn't unlock the doors and I didn't have a key to switch on the ignition and open the windows.

After ten or fifteen minutes, I was dying. I had no phone. I couldn't call for help. There was no one passing by, and even if there had been, the windows were tinted and no one could have seen inside anyway. After twenty minutes I'd ripped all my clothes off. It had to be 50 degrees or more in that car. And I was one day away from being a mother. I was in sheer panic. Honestly, I expected to die. I could see the headlines in the paper the next day: 'League Hero Tragedy', and pictured Brad being led away in handcuffs, charged with manslaughter one-and-half times. I don't know what I would've done if Brad hadn't shown up after about twenty minutes. I'll never forget the look of horror on his face when he came back. He practically clawed at the door handle to get it open. He carried me to a shady spot, ran over to get a drink of water and some ice, and I stayed there until I cooled down. Brad was speechless, but it didn't matter, because I was doing enough talking for us both, and it was all insulting!

Things were much more relaxed when it came to the birth. Brad was there, holding my hand. He brought some lovely food and expensive champagne for all the visitors, and there were so many flowers that they were streaming out into the hallway. I went through ten hours of labour. Brad was well into his photography by then, and he'd brought in his video camera, tripod and digital still camera. You should've seen him. The doctors had put up a sheet and Brad kept pulling it down so he could get his cameras focused for the birth. The doctors were going off their heads. It was a sterile area, and here was this crazy expectant father putting his head and his camera into the middle of their delivery activities. All I could see was Brad's head and a camera popping up over the sheet every few seconds.

I mean, that's Brad. To a tee. Same as what happened at the hardware store the previous day. Once he gets focused on a project, whether it's on the field or off it, he can't be swayed or turned away. He was just caught up in the moment, clicking away, oblivious to everything. The doctors were telling him, 'Get away, Brad. It's a sterile area.'

When Demi appeared, Brad started crying. He was trying to say something sensible, but all that came out was 'She's beautiful … thank you … oh thank you … thank you … I love you, babe … thank you.' I'm having a little cry now, thinking about it.

I'll never forget that wild, panicky look on Marie's face when I accidentally locked her in the car a day before the birth. I just thought, *My God, what have I done?* But we were laughing about it an hour later. Well, I was laughing at least. Maybe not Marie.

When they induced Marie in the hospital room, there was a cast of thousands. My mum was there, Marie's mum and sister, too, and my nana. Marie's best friend, Angela, who works for a pediatrician, and her husband, John, were a massive help. It was like a Broadway show or something. I could've sold tickets. I had the tripod set up with the still camera at the end of the bed, looking lengthways from Marie's feet to her head. And I was walking around with the video camera like a Hollywood director. Everyone knows how stressful and painful it is at childbirth. I'm sure I wasn't making it any easier. I was thinking I should be giving Marie a Grand Final–type motivational speech or something. But it wouldn't have gone down very well. Honestly, I was the one who needed the propping up. Just looking on was painful enough for a wimp like me. I don't like the sight of needles or the smell of hospitals, really. I'm not good with that sort of stuff. I'm a wuss and a wimp, if the truth be known. Don't tell anyone. And I couldn't believe how weary I was getting. Lord only knows what it was like for Marie.

Marie wanted a natural birth, but in the end a caesarean was best. So she was taken down the corridor into the theatre, and I followed with a 2-metre tripod and video camera under one arm and my still camera under the other. As I walked in the nurse said, 'Look out, it's Steven Spielberg!' Before they could attend to Marie I had to sign an autograph for the nurse. Marie just looked at me in disgust, as if to say, 'There's a time and a place for everything and this is not the time to be signing autographs for the nurse'.

So I set everything up — cameras, tripod, the lot. Mostly all I got were shots of the doctor's shoulder, so Spielberg's job is safe. I don't know how to describe what I felt when Demi's little head appeared. Suddenly I went calm. Marie was in no pain. It was all very quiet, and a miracle was happening before my eyes. I was incredibly relaxed and contented, holding Marie's hand and watching events unfold. When Demi was fully out and beginning to wail, Marie said, 'It's a girl, isn't it?' The doctor told us: 'Yes, and a beautiful girl she is too.' But I was looking down at a part of the cord still there, and wasn't so sure. 'Are you certain, doc?' I asked. Bloody stupid Freddy! Then they got me to cut the cord. Well, it was already cut, and I was getting a completely unnecessary shot at it for ceremonial purposes, I suppose. I wanted to cut the real one, but it was too late. I went ahead anyway. At least it looked good for the cameras.

I did get one special moment on video. The baby was screaming and crying, but the second they put her on Marie's chest for the first time, she stopped. It was like there was an instant bond, like Demi knew that this was Mum and everything was going to be all right after all out here in this strange new world.

When I was younger, playing up, playing footy, I never thought about having children. I never wanted any. Now I can't imagine life without Demi. I can't understand why couples choose not to have children when they are able. Each to his own, I guess. I'm not lecturing. It's just my two bob's worth on the subject.

I have to say, I didn't play a huge role in the first few months of Demi's life. It was never a conscious decision of Marie's and mine that it would be her who got up in the middle of the night to attend to Demi's needs. We had monitoring systems, the works. And I learned to sleep through all of them, not because I was lazy or uncaring or unwilling to do it, it was just that football always came first in my life and it was hard to change that. In order for me to stay successful at football, I needed the rest. I know it sounds selfish, but I'm not about to apologise for that. Marie was sensational in taking care of Demi, and she saved my footy career in that last season. And I will say this: I'm more than making up for it in retirement, and the devotion I had to football is now diverted completely to Demi and Marie.

Whatever rewards I reaped in my final year of playing are equally down to Marie, no doubt about that. As the team leader, I couldn't afford an off day. I had to be up and positive, always. I saw other players who had to look after young children while their partner worked, and they'd come to training flagged out. I have the utmost respect for motherhood. From what I've seen, it's no less demanding or stressful than a high-powered corporate or sporting role. Hats off to the mums and the Mr Mums out there. You've got my undying regard and respect!

So I didn't have a lot of interaction with Demi early on, which I found difficult, because I have this need to be liked. You feel a bit uncomfortable when your daughter avoids you and goes straight to Mum. That's certainly not the case since I quit footy, though — I can't imagine ever being away from her side for very long. And as the 2004 Grand Final drew near, I'd crave coming home to see Demi crawling as fast as she could across the floor to get to me, smiling and gah-gahing all the way. Money can't buy the glow and the warm feeling that gives you. It's the baby's face early in the morning that gets to me the most. When adults wake up, they look like absolute crap. When Demi wakes up, even if she's crying at the time, she's positively angelic. Pick her up and suddenly the tears turn to a laugh, and there's a contented coo-cooing sound like a pigeon feeding, and you can't help but feel 10 feet tall. Not that we lost too many games that last year, but if we had, it wouldn't have felt so distressing, knowing I could come home to *that* smile.

There are some things I'm pretty clumsy at, like dressing Demi. You know how guys can't wrap presents without making a mess of it? I'm a bit like that when it comes to putting her little oufits on. I've given up. Nappy changing I never minded, though. Like all fathers I've been shat on, spewed on and peed on, the whole box and dice. One time I was attempting some really arty photos of Demi and I in the nude, and I'd set the camera and adopted the pose with Demi cradled in my arms, and she dropped a smelly load right in my hand. The camera went *click* and, well, the photos won't be appearing in this book. Suffice it to say Demi has a most contented look on her little face, and I haven't on mine.

From the moment Demi arrived, we were never frightened to introduce her to the world. I have photos — yep, that intrusive camera of mine again — of Marie breastfeeding under the sails of the Opera House. Demi's a terrific kid, really, always with a smile on her face. If I go to the local coffee shop with Demi on my shoulders, I'll often come back alone. They love looking after her for a while. So do our neighbours at Highgate — they take her for an hour or so. Never once has she come back stressed or unhappy. I suppose all parents beam with pride and say the same, but she truly is just an adorable kid.

As for the pictures, they contain some treasured memories. Maybe I'm not yet a Hollywood director or a famous photographer, but I'm hooked on it. I never was until we moved out to the beach house, and on this really stormy day, with huge seas running, I looked out the window and there were two fishermen in wet-weather gear, complete with bright yellow hats and full-length yellow coats. The wind was whipping up salt spray over the waves behind them, which towered over the two men and their beach rods. And overhead there were these purple and grey storm clouds, with just a splinter of sunlight knifing through. I couldn't wait to get on the beach and start taking photos. The only thing I'm sorry about was that all I had was an old camera I'd been given as a present. You could search for a scene like that for the rest of your life and not capture it again — a bit like the perfect kick or the perfect pass, or the perfect tackle or intercept, the ones you dream about.

The truth is that now I never go far without a camera. I was smitten from the time I saw those fishermen. I spend a fair bit of my money and time on the hobby. I've never had lessons or anything, but I read about it a lot in magazines and books and I'm convinced that, just like footy, the best teacher of all is experience. Go out there, do it, make mistakes and learn from them. Experts can show you what aperture and speed are all about, but mostly you have to go out and become familiar with lighting and background. I print my own pictures, too.

Sometimes I feel like a bit of a wanker walking around the city and snapping off pictures every so often, because I do get recognised. People wonder what's going on. I don't mind any more, except that the first question is always, 'What are you doing, Freddy?' and it's pretty damn obvious what I'm doing when I'm holding a camera to your face and looking through the lens. I'm not having a haircut.

From out on the balcony of the apartment at Highgate, facing west, I've taken the biggest collection of sunset pictures in the world, I reckon. But none of them matches those first pictures of the one who has become the sunshine of my life, my gorgeous little Demi. So I'll continue to stick with photography in my retirement from football.

I can tell you one hobby I tried and failed at, and won't be wasting much time on again: cooking. They still tell the story at The Rocks fire brigade about the time I tried to cook some special chicken dish in my apartment across the road from their station. It was meant to be a welcome home dinner for Marie and Demi. I got distracted and the oil caught on fire. I put out the flames, but there was smoke everywhere. Now, I imagined the sprinklers in the ceiling would come on if there was a call-out to the fire brigade. When they didn't, I thought that everything was fine and I'd caused no problem to anyone but me. Stupid me didn't realise the smoke alarm was outside in the corridor. So when I opened the door to let the smoke out, the alarm went off. The next thing I know there's half a dozen burly fireys in full uniform and helmets running up the corridor with axes drawn. I'm standing there with a grin on my face and a charred piece of what used to be poultry in my hand. One of them looked at me, looked at the charred remains in my hand, and said, 'Seems like you just won the ashes, Freddy.'

nobody's perfect

What do they say? Into each life, some rain must fall. But they didn't tell me it would all tumble down at once. Because in April 1999 I had a mother of a storm dump bucket-loads of rain on me. They reckon it's calm at the centre of a storm. Well, I was right in the middle of a beauty and I can guarantee it was anything but calm. I've already mentioned that on countless occasions I acted like I was here for a good time not a long time. But I've always strenuously avoided doing the wrong thing publicly, even more so since I'd been handed the captaincies of New South Wales and Australia. I wore those titles with enormous pride and there's nothing I would ever have done to disrespect them. I admit, though, that that's not how it looked when news broke that I was found falling-down drunk outside Glebe police station in Sydney's inner west.

There have been various versions written and broadcast about how I got there and what happened afterwards, but for the first time, here is the real story.

I'd split up with my longtime girlfriend, Stephanie Ford, weeks earlier, and had spent a harrowing day at home at Collaroy with her, separating what was hers from what was mine. There were no major arguments, but we'd been together a number of years, and as anyone who's been in that situation knows, it can mess with your mind. I wasn't sleeping well.

The Roosters played a club game at the weekend against North Sydney and I chose to stay close to the city that night, in the Holiday Inn at Coogee. I hadn't been drinking. In fact, we were on a three-week booze ban. I hardly slept a wink that night in the hotel. I put my head down at about 1.30 a.m. Maybe I dozed off at 4 a.m. Things were spinning around in my head about the broken relationship and club football and the Anzac Day Test match which was coming up in just over a week's time. I think most players would vouch for the fact that you don't sleep too well after a game. And this night was particularly bad. I was exhausted by early morning, and then I had to go to training with the Roosters at 7.30 a.m. In addition, I'd had Channel Nine television cameras following me for days for a segment on *The Footy Show* called 'A Day in the Life of Freddy'. I'd been on my very best behaviour for weeks.

After training I went home to Collaroy, then drove back to attend a sponsor's function in the city, and next a prearranged drink with the Roosters players at around 2 p.m. at the Orient Hotel in The Rocks. We gathered out in the rear section, where the TAB and the poker machines are, and the players wandered over in dribs and drabs. We had a few drinks there ... quite a few, I'll admit. As the evening drew near we were figuring out what to do next. On a previous occasion I'd been out on a boat for a night called Wild Boys Afloat. Essentially it's a girls' night out with male strippers. You have a few beers, hang out the back and watch the girls having fun watching the blokes. So I thought I'd call my mate who managed Wild Boys Afloat and see if some of the players and I could join them that night. The answer was 'please do'. So a dozen of us hopped on the boat for a cruise around Sydney Harbour with about sixty girls and a few male strippers. And more beers. And still more beers.

Afterwards there were varying reports in the newspapers about my behaviour on the boat and when we docked. The *Sydney Morning Herald* broke the story more than a week after the event. And then its rival, the *Daily Telegraph*, kicked in for their lot. They quoted a passenger saying the players were 'rude and obnoxious', pushed past paying customers to get free drinks, and made the cruise an 'atrocious nightmare'. Someone called Catherine was quoted as saying she 'had the pleasure of watching Brad Fittler urinate off the wharf when there was a toilet 200 metres away'. I'm not saying it didn't happen, but I just don't remember it. I was drunk. Very drunk. I'll go along with the function manager Corey Sen's version. He told the newspaper, 'The players behaved very well. They stayed upstairs and had a few beers on the stern deck. They left together and were very friendly.' That version will do me. Personally, my memories of the night are lost in a haze of alcohol and fatigue.

After the boat returned we went to a Chinese restaurant in Darling Harbour, then to an all-night bar for still more drinks. The last thing I remember is walking across the old Pyrmont Bridge toward the cab rank on the eastern side of Darling Harbour. I waved goodbye to Ivan Cleary — I remember that much. And I got into a taxi; I remember that, too. I won't deny I was as drunk as a skunk, but I was tired more than anything. What happened in the next half-hour after that is anyone's guess. I blacked out. I can't tell you how I got from the taxi rank to Glebe police station. I can only imagine I fell asleep in the taxi, or the driver's English was poor and he didn't hear the directions I was giving him in a drunken slur that must've sounded like Swahili, or I simply fell immediately asleep in the back of the cab. However I got there, I was dumped outside Glebe police station. But I do have a distinct recollection of getting out of the cab. I sat down on the footpath, curled up and went to sleep. I didn't abuse anyone or cause any trouble or make a noise. I just crashed out, right there on the grass. I know I wasn't rude or loud or messy. I was wearing these light-coloured jeans, and there was scarcely a mark on them.

Anyway, the next thing I remember is a tap on the shoulder. I looked up and there's a passerby who'd alerted the police, and a policewoman nodding and smiling and trying to get me up. They were really nice about it. They took me inside the station and let me go back to sleep for three hours across a few chairs.

It was by then the morning of 18 April. I'm told pictures of me were taken sleeping like a baby inside the station, arms neatly folded. Regrettably, I couldn't hunt any of them down to show you. I was certainly cooperative, too exhausted to do anything else. No charges were laid. They very kindly put me in a cab when I woke up and wished me well. That was it, as far as I figured.

The following day I was named captain of the Australian team for the Anzac Day Test match. We went along to the Olympic Stadium and played New Zealand. All was smooth sailing. Until the newspaper hit the streets the day after the Test match, with the predictable headline 'Blind Freddy'. Very creative! The father of one of the policemen at Glebe — an avid Penrith supporter, as it turned out — had let the story slip to Roy Masters at the *Herald*.

The revelations came at the worst possible time for rugby league. Sacked Australian hooker Craig Gower and reserve forward Nik Kosef were being threatened with fines of $50 000, and deregistration. Gower had been dumped from the team. Kosef, along with Manly trio John Hopoate, Cliff Lyons and Neil Tierney, got caught up in a Kings Cross bar brawl. And Cronulla chief executive Peter Gow was stood down after a fight in a Chinese restaurant at the Sharks Leagues Club. Four North Sydney players had run amok in Wagga Wagga, and Souths' Julian O'Neill had disgraced himself in Dubbo. There were demands for tougher penalties for poor off-field behaviour, and even a special tribunal set up by the League and an alcohol summit to examine misdemeanours.

I'll admit it was probably poor timing to say so, but I made the point that a few years earlier such incidents would have been let slide or swept under the carpet. I thought then, and I think now, that Craig Gower was persecuted unfairly.

Well, that didn't endear me to officials, or to the media. And I'd already found myself in hot water before the Test, on a completely different issue, this time over a sponsor's function in a building near the Kokoda Trail Walk at Concord in western

Sydney. They were to announce that Wizard Home Loans was sponsoring the Anzac Test. Only the New Zealand captain Jarrod McCracken showed up. It was meant to be a photo opportunity with a couple of Kokoda Trail veterans and one of the Papuan fuzzy-wuzzy angels there for the pictures. I was supposed to be there, too, as the Australian captain. When I didn't turn up the New Zealand press got a hold of it and called it an 'Anzac snub'. According to the Kiwis I'd thumbed my nose at Anzac veterans and the Anzac spirit, and those who'd fought so bravely at Kokoda.

The news also hit the Sydney papers. It was a time when the whole Anzac legend was gaining new strength in this country, so it was an easy thing to make me look like a proper dickhead for snubbing the Anzac ideal. For that one I plead not guilty. I was all ready to go; I'd taken my dress-up gear to Australian team training, where I was told there'd be a car to take me to Concord. No car turned up. I went back to the Holiday Inn, where we were staying, and still no car. I told the Australian team management, and they said, 'Don't worry. It's too late to go now.' What was I to do? I didn't even know where the function was taking place. I've mentioned my love of Papua New Guinea and its people. The last thing in the world I'd want to do is offend them, and I wouldn't deliberately offend a digger if my life depended on it.

So it was in this climate that, a day after the Test, it was revealed that I'd been found drunk outside the Glebe police station eight days previously. People were clamouring for my head. The question being asked very publicly was this: is Brad Fittler a fit and proper person to lead his country, or even play for it? The League asked both me and my club to show cause why I should not be heavily fined. A number of players came out strongly in support of me, and for that I'm for ever grateful. Laurie Daley was one; so was my old friend from inter-district matches at school, Terry Hill. And I could always rely on Phil Gould to back me up. He told the newspaper, 'Freddy asked for permission for one night on the drink because we'd been on the road, playing away from home for three weeks, in Auckland and North Queensland. He hasn't hurt anyone. He hasn't interfered with the public. He's gone where we tell all our kids to go when they've got a problem — to their nearest friendly police station. He showed good sense to get help.'

I was being threatened with a fine of $5000. With all the evidence I've presented above laid out to the NRL, there was no fine or penalty imposed in the end. My manager, Wayne Beavis, fronted up with support from the Roosters, and the NRL backed off. The NRL issued a statement that said, 'In the light of the comprehensive submissions, and of Brad's expressed regret at the incident, the NRL will not pursue a fine proposed in a recent breach notice given to him. Independent police reports refute details of media accounts of the Fittler matter.'

Do I think the Glebe saga was wrong? Of course I do. I was irresponsible. And whatever criticism came my way, I thoroughly deserved. But after all of that, I was off scot-free. Well, financially at least. But it took an enormous personal toll on me. I went into what I now know was a severely depressed state. I found myself curled up in the corner on occasions, barely able to move, let alone face anyone in public. That went on for weeks. I was wrong. Very wrong. No question about that. It damaged my reputation, and my health and wellbeing, for a long while. Physically and mentally, I was a wreck. Maybe they should've taken the Australian captaincy from me. I think if I'd done the same thing now, given the new focus on player behaviour and alcohol abuse, that's what would've happened, no questions asked. So maybe they should've relieved me of the top job. What a blow that would've been!

As I said, I was right in the centre of the storm swirling around me. I copped an absolute hammering for a month. And there was already a dark secret in my recent past, a skeleton in the closet that's never been reported. I figured that the story would get out, and that that would be the end of me. Surprisingly, it never did. I'm going to 'fess up now. It represents one of the lowest points in my life. I debated with myself whether or not to tell this story, but the book's about my life, and it happened, so I'm going to. I'll tell it straight. So here goes.

Just before I started my last season with Penrith in 1995, I went down to Sussex Inlet on the NSW south coast for a holiday, and to visit my family members who lived there. I stayed in a hotel. On the first night we all went out to dinner at the local RSL. My uncle was there. My aunty, too. And a friend, Carl Macnamara, plus a number of other family and friends. There was a woman who seemed to have positioned herself so that she was at the table next to us the whole evening. So it came time for the RSL to close, and I was about to leave when I started talking to this woman. I'll call her Dianne, but it's not her real name. I asked her to accompany me back to the hotel. And in the morning she went on her way. It's not the first one-night stand ever, even in a relatively small town like Sussex Inlet, I'm sure.

Fast forward more than a year, and I'm settling in to the good life on the twenty-second floor of the Highgate apartments near The Rocks. I was on top of the world. I'd just started my first season with the Roosters. Then I came home from training one evening and my girlfriend at the time couldn't wait to tell me what had happened. She seemed to be in a pretty distressed state. I asked her what was wrong. She said a woman had arrived at the front entrance of Highgate, buzzed my apartment number and said she wanted to see Brad Fittler because she was downstairs with his baby. She got through the security and knocked on the door. 'I want to see Brad Fittler. This is his child,' she said, thrusting a baby towards my girlfriend. My girl told her, 'Brad's at training. You can't see him.'

I was stunned at this revelation. Absolutely knocked off my feet. I didn't have a clue who it might have been. I'd long since forgotten about the one-night stand at Sussex Inlet, that's for sure.

A few days passed and I thought no more of it. When you're in the public eye you have strange people coming up to you with fantasy stories all the time; I figured this was just another one of those. So I was home and there was a knock on the door. It's a security building, and I thought the only person it could be is the concierge, so I opened it without bothering to look through the peephole. It was a lady I didn't recognise at all, with a baby in her arms. I said, 'Hello, can I help you?' and she said, 'Yes, you can hold your child. It's a boy.' Now at this point I still had not a clue who she was. No idea at all. I said, 'Look, I'm sorry, I don't know you from Adam.' Then she mentioned the one-night stand and it suddenly dawned on me that I might be in trouble here. Straightaway I called my lawyer and my manager, and arranged a DNA test to see whether I was indeed the father.

I was still awaiting the results of the test when I was getting ready for that massive opening of the Planet Hollywood restaurant in George Street in the city in May 1996. I was invited to walk the red carpet, and it was going to be a huge night. Sly Stallone would be there; Charlie Sheen too. I was all set to take some mates along, including Shorty, my closest friend, who was sharing the Highgate apartment with me, plus Sean Garlick and David Gyngell.

I needed a new suit, so earlier that day I took the BMW out of the garage below Highgate and planned to head for Marcs in Oxford Street in Sydney's Paddington with a couple of girls I knew to help me shop. We drove up King Street, across the intersection with George Street and then Pitt Street, and then across Castlereagh Street. I went through an amber light as I turned right at the intersection with Elizabeth Street, and thought the car behind me was awfully close. Suddenly, *bang*! The car behind me slammed into the back of my BMW.

My first instinct was to stop and pull over, because we'd had an accident. As I did that, the car slammed into the back of me again. I didn't know what the heck was going on. Then I looked in the rear-view mirror and saw that the driver was Dianne. She had her foot firmly fixed on the accelerator and I had my foot just as firmly planted on the brake. Smoke was pouring out the back of my car and the front of hers. I couldn't control the BMW — she was locked onto the back of it and pushing me into oncoming traffic. She was trying to harm me and my passengers, no doubt about it. As I struggled for control I took another look in the mirror — she was seriously angry and determined to put me away.

She pushed my car for 100 metres. Traffic was looming on the left, rushing down from Macquarie Street and that half-moon St James Road that borders the northern end of Hyde Park, and from the right coming out of Elizabeth Street. We're not talking about 3 a.m. here — this was the middle of the day and the heart of the city. I was headed for a very serious broadside from one of those cars when she finally slid off and careered into two parked cars, knocking them onto the footpath and narrowly missing pedestrians.

I just gassed it and took off. A few hundred metres down the road I caught sight of a policeman and blasted the horn to get his attention. I was too petrified to get out of the car, and so were my two passengers. All I could think about was that this woman was out to harm me. I told the police what had happened and guided them back to the car wrecks. The woman was still sitting in her car, which was badly damaged, and when she saw me she got out and came toward me. I called out to the police to grab her, and that's what they did.

The matter went to court and she lost her licence. I could have lost my life. The penalty on one of the charges was a three-year loss of licence, $750 fine and court costs.

And it didn't end there. The DNA test came back positive, and this indeed was my baby son ... *is* my baby son.

Later that year, I was in hospital getting an operation on my groin — I mentioned it earlier. And I had a call to the hospital from security at Highgate to say this woman was standing outside the building with the child and holding a big placard that read, 'Will someone please feed Brad Fittler's child!' They moved her down the road a bit, I was told. And when my flatmate, Shorty, came home he grabbed the placard from her and pushed her even further down the road. An hour later the police arrived at Highgate to charge Shorty with assault. It was a hell of a mess.

Anyway, the upshot is this: the boy is nine years old. I don't see him or his mother. I've had no contact since 1996. And I continue to pay child support for his upkeep, as I've done all along, backdated to his birth date. I'll continue to pay that amount as long as the court compels me to do so. I don't wish to mention the boy's name because I don't want to identify him. Maybe his mother hasn't told him about his real father. I don't know. I certainly don't want him reading about it here for the first time. That would not be fair on him.

There are two ways of looking at the dilemma: the first is that I was wrong to have sex with a stranger and not use a condom; the other is that I should be totally responsible for my actions and bring up the boy in style. I agree with the former, but not the latter. I was given no say in whether or not the pregnancy went ahead. The mother came to see me and informed me about it only after the child was several months old. It wasn't as if she couldn't have found me if she'd wanted to. No, I firmly believe a financial contribution is quite sufficient. I understand it could be hard on the boy, but the mother has to shoulder much of the blame for the way she went about things. I know what many people's first reaction will be: Freddy's father ran away when his mum was pregnant, and now Freddy's running away from his own son. None of that sways my opinion on this at all. The fact that my father ran away before I was born, and I didn't meet him until I was eighteen, played no part in formulating my opinion. It's a matter of right and wrong, unrelated to past history.

I don't know how the future will play out. All I will ever be with the boy is honest. Whatever happens happens. I can't say how it will go. I have my own family now. Who's to say what might change? I'm a football player, so I'll tackle it when it comes at me. I can only hope that he grows up in a stable environment. I do think about him. Whether he thinks of me

— what he thinks of me — whether he even knows I'm his father ... I haven't a clue.

Looking back now at Dianne's behaviour — and having gone through the experience of living with a newborn baby — I can understand how she was probably going through some stress at the time. Especially if you add postnatal depression to the mix. I have the greatest respect for all mums, because it's one of the toughest jobs in the world.

state of origin – the comeback

Once I'd finished with State of Origin in 2001, it was a closed chapter in my life. There was never a scrap of a thought in my head that I ever wanted to try it again. Ever. I've heard people say it was always planned that I'd be back as a reward for my long service. Not true: State of Origin was dead and buried for me in 2001.

I do think, though, and I've said so before in these pages, that I played my best football in 2002 and 2003. No two ways about it. I had no doubts I was up to representative standard, but absolutely no inkling that I would ever be back, and no desire to ask the question. Whenever media talk got around to the football I was playing in those two seasons, it was invariably said that without the extra burden of representative games I was playing more relaxed and fitter and healthier, and the decision to quit Tests and State of Origin was paying dividends. And that sort of comment was absolutely spot on.

So around came State of Origin 1, 2004, at Telstra Stadium, and I didn't go. Nothing stands in the way of my Wednesday evening boys' night out. Every Wednesday we gather at a mate's place or my house at Collaroy. It's not like the old days, though, at South Penrith. It's quiet, mostly alcohol-free and very innocent. We sit around playing video games, mostly the Tiger Woods golf game, and take the mickey out of each other. There's usually half a dozen of us and an overweight wonderdog named Buster. One of the regulars is Ryan Girdler, a State of Origin hero in his own right. 'Girds' and I have been close mates for a dozen years. The other guys aren't footy heads. There's a carpenter, a musician, an osteopath and usually three footballers — Chris Hicks, Girds and me. They're all terrific and funny guys who take your mind off football for the evening. I find it helps so much to ease the tension, particularly as finals time draws around.

Anyway, this particular boys' night out corresponded with Origin 1. We got our Tiger Woods golf game and takeaway food out of the way early and sat down to watch the game on television. That seemed a much better option for both me and Girds — sitting there with the log fire burning, waves lapping at the beach a few metres away, and a bunch of our closest mates with us — than braving the crowds at Telstra Stadium. During the pre-match commentary, the cameras panned across the NSW dressing room. I could almost feel the nervous tension among the players. Some were pacing up and down ... others sitting down, almost in fear of what might happen ... still others were listening to music. I said to Girds, 'Thank God we're not doing that!' His reply was, 'You're dead right there, Freddy boy. Have another bit of pizza.' I was perfectly relaxed and comfortable; I knew the players would be anything but.

It was an interesting contest without reaching any great heights. The killer blow — Shaun Timmins's field goal that won the match for New South Wales 9–8 — was magic enough, I guess. But when it was over, my mates and I weren't especially thrilled with the standard of football. We were far more interested in the standard of play in the Tiger Woods video golf, which resumed very quickly after Timmins's goal. Looking on as an outsider, one of the intriguing things about the night was the pride I had in watching fellow Rooster Craig Fitzgibbon. I told my mates to watch how much work he got through, and right on cue he was in absolutely everything. You had a blinder, Fitz.

Since my retirement from rep footy I watch team-mates play those games the way a mother hen looks over her brood. It never ceases to make me swell with pride, the way they represent themselves, their families and the club at the very highest level.

As the days passed, and the NSW injury toll grew, I had a sneaking suspicion Gus would ask me to play. Let's face it, there weren't many other options at five-eighth, with Timmins, Barrett and Scott Hill all unavailable. So it wasn't a total surprise to get the call. I knew the way I'd gone out of Origin in 2001 played more heavily on his mind than on mine. It had gnawed away at Gus for all that time, I know that for a fact. He's a perfectionist. He hates loose ends. And to him, my going out of the Origin business with a whimper instead of a bang was a loose end. An itch that needed to be scratched, for him much more than for me.

The way the call came through has been talked about a fair bit. Marie and I were staying at the Collaroy house for the weekend and I was out on my surf ski on a perfect winter Sunday. Marie took the call. Gus asked if I still had my Origin socks in the drawer, and mentioned something about 'This is the knock at the door — it's time'. Marie didn't pick up on that last bit, but I did straightaway. When I came in from the surf Marie told me Gus had rung and I didn't need to know why. I just said to her right away, 'What do you reckon? Should I play?' She answered without a second thought: 'Of course you should, Brad.' I thought I was up to it. No ... I *knew* I was up to it. Especially the way the Roosters had been playing.

And, in a way, I was ready for a new challenge. I think at that moment, too, I overcame one of the things that has held me back in life: I've always worried about what other people thought about me and what they had to say about me and my life and my game. I've always found it hard to rise above that. So I figured it was time to jump in and relish the opportunity, not sit back and wonder if people would say 'He's too old', or 'He's getting favoured treatment from his mate, the coach', or if I failed to play well, the inevitable, 'I told you so — why did they pull him out of the old folks' home?'

One of the hardest things in life is to cop the bad and the jealous and the ill-informed things people say about you, and stay strong to the belief in yourself. But I was ready to step up. It was time to move out of my comfort zone. In the final season at the Roosters, I was virtually playing second fiddle to Brett Finch, our halfback. I'd dropped back a bit and let Brett take charge of the team, and he was doing a grand job. My role had become more organisational. Now a real test had been handed to me, and there was no way I was going to say no to it. But I didn't ring Gus back right away; I thought I'd have some fun at his expense. I let him stew a bit. You know what they say: you have to get older, but you don't have to get more mature.

After a couple of hours I called Gus and told him 'OK', and he said I had to be at the team get-together at 2 p.m. the next day at the Crowne Plaza, Coogee. In the morning I had what I thought was a mere video session with the Roosters — it was supposed to be just a matter of reviewing the previous game on the screen. But Ricky Stuart told us to put our gear on and get out onto the field. He wasn't happy with the way the Bulldogs had dealt with us in the match just gone. So he proceeded to flog us in one of the hardest training sessions I can ever remember. I don't think we'd trained that hard since Sticky came to the Roosters. So by the time I arrived at the Origin rollcall that afternoon, I was totally buggered.

I shuffled in feeling a little uncomfortable. I didn't know many of the players. All the focus had been on my return. Some might've been jealous or sceptical; some might've liked me, others not. I didn't know. I made a point of going around and shaking hands with everybody. I just wanted to be one of the troops, but that was difficult with the front and back pages of the newspapers full of my comeback, and all the TV cameras aimed at me and not them. It was amazing when I arrived —

there must've been eight television cameras, and press photographers clicking away like I was a rock star or something. I was quite excited by all the attention and found it extremely flattering, even after all those years.

I had to keep my feet on the ground, though. I made a special point of not reading any of the articles or watching the television reports. Most sportspeople will tell you they don't read anything that's written about them, and then their girlfriends or their mums bring out the scrapbooks the person has diligently kept his whole life and they spill the beans by saying he can recite every word in every article. I'm not going to say I don't read the stuff — I do. But it can influence your thinking, and I deliberately wanted to go into this training camp with a clear head.

I'd worked out what I was going to say at the news conference — how I was only coming back because of the injuries, and that I was very thankful to be given the chance, and generally that I wanted it kept as low-key as possible, and this was just for one game and one game only. I'd said that morning to Ricky Stuart that I thought I only had one Origin game left in me. That's the way I felt at the time. I avoided any discussion of the controversy that preceded the first game — the dropping of Anthony Minichiello and Mark Gasnier, the grog and the SMS messages. The truth is that I didn't want to have a beer all week anyway and I was glad of the new, stricter regime.

I have to say that I was crook all the week, and unsure whether I was up to it. I never really recovered from the flogging Ricky had given us on the Monday morning. Training session was heaped on training session, and a few days later, when Gus eventually said it was OK to go out and have a beer, I was way too fatigued. I'd picked up a cold and I was weak. I went home to Highgate and slept for two days, starting to have second thoughts about whether I'd have the energy reserves to get through it. What had kept me going all week was chatting to the young blokes like Luke Lewis and Luke Rooney. I remembered when I'd first played Origin, in that second game in 1990, with blokes like Ricky Stuart and

Des Hasler and Brad Clyde, and I'd watched every move they'd made. It was like that for me in that week in 2004, and I found myself relishing the task of chatting with the young guys, offering suggestions at training if a move didn't quite work out the way it was supposed to. The respect they showed me, and the warm welcome I got, was really touching.

What's also interesting, coming in as an outsider, is pegging the leaders, the pranksters, the dedicated trainers, the footy heads and the air heads. Big Willie Mason pretty much took control. I had a wrap on him from the first time we met.

We went up to Brisbane as a team on the Sunday. I had a room on my own, and that was good. It was another mark of respect, I suppose, for my advancing years. The thing I've always noticed about State of Origin is how quickly the whole shebang comes and goes. The days before a game seem to last only minutes, and the game itself only seconds. As we got on the bus going out to Suncorp I said to Matt Gidley, 'Don't blink mate, you'll miss it.'

The route to Suncorp was lined with people in their maroon jerseys, a few blue ones among them, but not very many. There was good-natured cheering and jeering and finger pointing. Some flicked us the bird, and others just waved or gave us the thumbs down. I'm an emotional person, and that trip was about as emotional as I've ever been on the way to a game. I just thought to myself how lucky I was to be part of it again. I cried, openly, unashamedly, right there on the team bus. Ask me what was going through my mind that made me teary-eyed and I can't tell you for certain. Everything, really. Where I'd come from. The last time I'd played Origin in Brisbane. My family. The baby. Being blessed with the ability to play a game that had so many people so completely passionate about it. Everything. I remembered my first Origin experience. My uncle Matthew Wozsatka took me to the SCG to watch an Origin match when I was eight years old. We stood on the old Hill in the pouring rain and watched Greg Dowling scoop up a drop goal attempt from Wally Lewis, and score under the post. It was a moment I'll never forget.

I was completely overtaken by this Origin moment too. I was choked up and sobbing. It was night-time, of course. The bus was darkened. I was sitting on my own. I don't think any other player or official caught me. In a bus full of people, with hundreds more lining the roadway, it was an intensely personal and private time.

Once at the ground, I was totally focused on the game. The game plan was to shut down Darren Lockyer, who had missed Origin 1: we wanted to tire him, to see if we could put him off his kicking game. I had my defence to worry about too. I had a job to do, and that was all I was concerned with. That consumed me in the dressing room. There were no thoughts in my head about the old bloke making a comeback. All that was paper talk now, something for the TV commentators to rabbit on about. I had a footy game to play, and suddenly that was all that mattered to me. We were beaten of course, 22–18, but I thought New South Wales played well and I did nothing wrong. Perhaps I should've taken charge a little more towards the end, but overall I was delighted with the way I went. When you analyse it, Queensland scored a couple of tries from kicks — there's always an element of luck in that — and I reckon the referee, Sean Hampstead, gave us the rough end of the pineapple. There were at least a dozen decisions he got wrong. So I thought there was a good chance New South Wales would win the series in Sydney, even at that stage.

In the dressing room later we were discussing what had happened, and what we could've done better. Willie Mason came up to me and asked if I'd be playing the final game. I put my hands in the air and told I him I was unsure. Then Danny Buderus, the captain — and a bloke for whom I have massive respect — came up and said, 'You're playing the last game. That's all there is to it.' The next day, back in Sydney, I rang Ricky Stuart and told him, 'I know I said before that I didn't want to play any more games than one, but I'm going to play the decider.' I didn't say anything to Gus, but I did show Roosters boss Nick Politis the courtesy of telling him. He was noncommittal: 'Do it if you want' was all he said. I can understand why the Roosters were concerned. In the papers the next day, Sticky was quoted as saying he didn't think I should play, but there were politics going on behind the scenes at the Roosters in which I wasn't involved. I guess they thought my duty was to them, not New South Wales. Anyway, the point is this: my mind was made up from the moment Danny Buderus spoke.

Of course every day I'd hear the question, whether it was from a reporter or just someone I passed in the street: was I going to play in the final game? I stuck with the line that I didn't know whether I would or not; I thought that was the best way to turn down the spotlight. The last thing I wanted was the attention to be on me for a few weeks, perhaps adversely affecting my role at the Roosters. And as I've said, on most occasions when the focus is on me, it's turned out disastrously. It wasn't until a couple of weeks later, on the day they picked the team, that I rang Gus and told him I'd play if he wanted me.

By the time the team was chosen for the decider, and we were in the training camp, I felt 100 per cent better than I had the previous time. I even went out for a drink with the boys at the Clovelly Hotel. It had been ages since I'd been out for a drink, even with the Roosters, and I thoroughly enjoyed it. Later that week we all went down the south coast to Ulladulla to shoot *The Footy Show*, and I got to know my team-mates even better. I was in the perfect head space — I could not have been more contented than I was in the lead-up to Origin 3. Gus was his usual self, playing motivational mind games. He gathered us together on the Sunday and asked us as a group whether we thought they'd picked the right players. Then, over the next few days, he'd see each player on his own and casually ask, 'Did we do the right thing in selecting you?' The answer was always 'Yes', naturally. My first Origin coach back in 1990, Jack Gibson, used to do something similar. What it does is reinforce resolve and commitment and self-belief.

I felt we had the right team to win. Some big match players were back, people like Ben Kennedy and Trent Barrett. My brief history playing alongside Trent was fabulous, and I knew our combination would be first class. We've been good mates for years. For some reason we hooked up as kids and got on famously, and we've stayed good mates. We're both sponsored by adidas and managed by Wayne Beavis, so we meet up at functions regularly, even though we're in rival NRL teams. Gus asked me before the team was announced who I'd prefer at halfback; I said Finch or Barrett. I thought Brett Finch had a top game in Brisbane. The original plan, so I was told, was to bring Barrett off the reserves bench, but that's no place for a bloke as good as him when he's in the mood to explode. I would've been happy with either. It wasn't my choice in the end anyway.

Once Trent was in the side, and training camp started, we spoke often. He's like me in a lot of ways — a footy nut. He lives and breathes it. We spoke about who'd kick and when, who'd go for the charge-down, where the kicks would be aimed, how we'd work the defence. And we talked about those things over lunch, at dinner, later in the evening, all the time.

Every player in that team was superfit and in form. On the bus trip out to Telstra Stadium, the first hint of self-doubt came into my head. For some reason I was worried about my defence. It had been fine in Brisbane and I was fitter and stronger now, but sometimes you just can't stop those negative thoughts from sneaking into your brain. I started to wonder whether I was too old. Stupid, I know. But the harder you try to rid your brain of those thoughts, the more ingrained they become.

Gus had a plan for that last game based on a book about teams and individuals called *Good to Great*. He highlighted one team in particular, a group of high school cross-country runners in the United States who finetuned their attitude as much as their speed to go from average performers to national champions two years in a row. Their motto was:

We run best at the end.
We run best at the end of practice.
We run best at the end of the race.
We run best at the end of the season when it counts
    the most.

Later, in his column in the *Sun-Herald* newspaper, Gus wrote about how he adapted it to this game: to be best at the end of the run; best at the end of the tackle; best at the end of the set of six; best at the end of the half; best at the end of the game; best at the end of the series. It really struck a chord with me. I was driving everyone mad at training, yelling 'Let's be best' at this and that. And I did the same in the game, right up until the final whistle. I didn't let up for a second. Even at the end, when we were 20 points up, I was yelling, 'Let's be the best at the end.' Someone, I don't know who, yelled back, 'It's all right, Freddy. You can shut the f--- up now.' But I knew what Queensland were capable of. I wasn't going to let them have even a tiny sniff.

Really, the match was never in doubt. It was the perfect side playing the perfect game. The score was 18–8 at half-time, with the match in the bag. One of the most interesting aspects occurred just before the kick-off, when I bent down to adjust my boots. I was lost in some strange head space and almost forgot the game was about to start. I had to run across to get in position. The TV cameras focused on the adidas brand as I tightened the boots, and being a sponsor of mine, as adidas was then and still is today, some bright spark in the media figured I did it deliberately to publicise the product. Sometimes I wonder whether people like that even bother to think before they turn on the word processor. It's the final seconds before a monster game, and you think to yourself, 'I know … I'll give a plug to my sponsor.' As bloody if! It's an insult to me and the corporate executives to suggest that we'd collude in some way to do that. I think the world of that brand as a sponsor; they've been terrific to me. As it turned out, and I stress *later* turned out, adidas used that shot in advertising posters under the heading 'impossible is nothing'.

Just before half-time, on the last tackle, Craig Wing went into dummy half a couple of metres from the Queensland line, wide out to the right. The obvious thing was to get the ball out to the open side on the left, where all our players were spread. This is where experience is such a good teacher. I noticed out of the corner of my eye that the Queensland defenders were heading that way, too. I knew Wingy would give me the ball if I called for it. I'm his captain at the Roosters — he's not going to say no. There was a very narrow blindside, maybe 2 metres wide, and only Queensland's Petero Civoniceva and Rhys Wesser between Mark Gasnier and me and the try line. I knew I could get to Petero's outside and draw Rhys's attention long enough to leave 'Gaz' in the clear. To explain it logically like that is difficult, because it all happens in two or three seconds. It's funny how sometimes you read all that and see it all so clearly unfolding, and you know what's going to happen before it does. All in a split second.

Our override call at the Roosters is 'Henry'. There might be a set play in place, and someone calls 'Henry' and that overrides the set play, and the ball goes instantly to whoever made that call. So I called out 'Henry' as loud as I could, given there were 80 000 screaming fans in the stands, and Wingy instinctively popped me the ball. Just as I suspected, Petero was left inside, Rhys was coaxed into coming at me, and it was a case of money for old rope as Gaz put the ball over the line untouched. Most probably Gaz had to do most of the work, but I'm claiming the try — sorry, Gaz. You hear the term 'football brain' and I guess that's what they mean. It might be a brutal, body contact sport most of the time, but there's ample room for thought and the art of gentle persuasion as well.

I suppose the most memorable take-out from the game is my charge-down try five minutes from the end. What was going through my head was Gus's 'be best at the end'. I didn't want to stop. I wasn't going to leave a scrap of me out there. Part of the team's preparation was watching the video of Origin 2 and particularly the nonstop running of young Luke Lewis, which was also coursing through my skull. 'Keep going, mate — be best', I just kept saying to myself over and over. I saw Darren Lockyer trying for the chip over the wing, and the thought did strike me that I was a rough chance of charging it down. I ran as hard and fast as I could, and threw my hands up high to knock the ball down. When it hit me and went up in the air, time stood still, I swear. I could see that ball spinning over and over in slow motion, and I could clearly read the brand name of Steeden as it spun at what seemed to me a deathly slow speed of about one revolution every minute.

In truth, it probably turned over twenty times in the second or so it took me to grab it. I didn't have to change speed or direction. It bounced perfectly for me. Landed right in the breadbasket. There it was, the fairytale all over again. Right place, right time, just like it's been my whole life. Here was one of the great moments of my life, a few metres to run, no one near me, and only to plant the ball down for my eighth Origin try, the most amazing one of them all. I was on my own, ball tucked firmly under the right arm and my left arm pointing skywards with the index finger raised. In the photos I look like I was yelling, and I was. Nothing that made any sense, mind you. Just 'Yeah! Woo-hoo!', mindless stuff like that, overcome by the moment. I've spoken before about the half-dozen times in my life where I've been part of what I can only describe as an out-of-body experience. That was one of them. There was my body running toward the line, hootin' and hollerin' with joy and excitement. I was looking down on it all with a wonderful sense of relief and fulfilment.

I couldn't wait to put the ball down and find a team-mate to embrace. I kept running, both arms in the air, until I found somebody in a blue jersey. We'd created something magical together, all of us, and I wanted to share it with them. At the end we held a 36–14 lead, one of the most emphatic Origin wins. But within a few minutes I was over the hump of that emotional high. I was suddenly too tired to stand. I was gone. Players were embracing and hugging each other. I didn't have the energy. I saw Gus and he was very emotional. I made my way over to him, and we embraced. The win, and my part in it, was the perfect way to repay his kindness in giving me the opportunity. It was an extremely warm and fulfilling experience and a way for me to say 'Thanks, Gus' in the best way I knew how. But the fact is, I'd hit my emotional high the second I put that ball down for the try.

There was the traditional lap of honour, but I could hardly complete it. I knew where Mum was sitting, near the players' tunnel leading onto the ground. I went over to her and she was bawling her eyes out. We hugged for a long while. I get so wrapped up in the game that I often forget the effect it has on people close to me. To see Mum like that, so deliriously happy, was a moment I'll never forget. That's a great feeling. They even dragged her into the dressing room after the game, along with her boyfriend, John, and a couple of my very favourite people, Uncle Russell and Aunty Kim. That's probably the first and only time a player's mother and aunty have been in the dressing rooms immediately after a big game. I doubt that's going to happen again for a long while.

Gus got up and thanked all the players. Danny Buderus did too, and made special mention of how glad he was it finished on a high note for me. I got up and thanked everyone for the opportunity. I've said it often enough in these pages, how emotional I get. I feel things like that to the very core of my soul. That I was given the chance, and everyone helped me achieve it, meant so much that I wasn't able to express it in words. Just a little thing, but Luke Lewis — who is going to be a champion player — asked me to sign his jersey. He was just a kid in his first Origin season. The fact that my presence had made an impact on him to the point where he wanted my signature on his jersey was something money couldn't buy. I signed it 'Mates for ever'. I see a lot of myself many years ago in him. He's had it pretty tough growing up, and supporting him is a very caring and compassionate mother, Sharon. There are a number of similarities in our backgrounds.

Much was made of Gus's attack on the press in the news conference later. He was well wound up. 'I don't deserve the shit youse f---in' give me, not one word of it,' he said. In reference to criticism of those shots of him walking up the tunnel before the end of Origin 2, he told them, 'You people said I left Game 2 too early. There's two ways to look at that. Either I was leaving Game 2 early, or I was getting a head start on Game 3. You tell me what happened tonight. The shit youse dished up to me after that, I'll remember. You go hard. Go as hard as you like. I'll remember.' The packed conference in the bowels of the stadium was stunned. So were Danny Buderus and I, seated alongside him. I didn't think any of it took the shine off the game, not one little bit. I thought it was excellent. But it was going to get ugly if someone didn't put a subtle stop to it pretty quickly. I casually rose to my feet, took Danny Buderus with one hand and Gus with the other, thanked the assembled media and concluded it, hoping to God they ended the conference there. Never a dull moment when Gus is around.

I went back to the Crowne Plaza at Coogee for a short while only and had a couple of beers. That was all. I chatted to Gus and NRL CEO David Gallop and a few of the players. Roy Masters came up to me and said something about a fairytale for a kid from Ashcroft. I said, 'I've had a fairytale my whole life.' I spoke about coming down from the emotional high of scoring that try. That's why I think highs of such magnitude have to be dealt with carefully. You get so high, you have to come down with a crash eventually. Same as the Grand Final win with the Roosters in 2002. I was like that, crashing back to earth. I was at the point where I was spiralling into an overwhelming tiredness, so I excused myself and went home to Highgate.

I find it very hard to sleep the night of a big game. Even the second night after one. It's at times like that I get my solace, my peace, my rest, on the balcony of our apartment at Highgate. When I got home it was probably three in the morning. The place was dark. Demi was fast asleep. It was an unbelievably warm and calming feeling to look down on my sleeping six-months-old baby and think how innocent and how beautiful she looked, and know that she'd played a role in exorcising my State of Origin demons simply by coming into my life. Marie and I chatted for a while. I love getting to hear about a game from her perspective, how the crowd reacted, and what she was going through at each point of it; how she'd bought six beers for our mates, and people nearby in the crowd thought out loud that someone had better marry her quickly. 'Mate,' someone apparently called out, 'she goes to the footy, and shouts beers as well. Marry her!' 'Nah,' said one of my close mates, 'I can't. It's Freddy's missus.' I laughed my head off. Any remaining tension was lifted off my shoulders in one hilarious moment.

Later I stood out on the balcony on my own until the sun came up and reflected on where I've lived, what I've lived through, where I've come from, what I've done with my life to this point. It's a wonderful view, as I've mentioned, over Darling Harbour and out to the west of Sydney. I can see Ashcroft in the distance and right out to Penrith, and I can't help but remember where I came from. It's the one place where all thought of football drains from my head. I know what you're thinking: I'm a head case. And I am.

Ever since I was kid, I've thought about footy seven days a week, 24 hours a day. When I'm in the car I'm thinking about who we're playing this week and who's my opposite number, what can I do to get over the top of him. That's just how I am. If I'm watching a game on TV, I'm not on the lounge but out there in the middle with them. Marie tells me I throw my arms about, put my shoulder into tackles, shape to kick a football. And all this happens on the couch at home. She's given up asking if I want a drink or something to eat. I just don't hear. I'm fully, totally, completely focused on the footy, even if it's the two lowest teams in the competition. So now, maybe, you understand why a 3 by 5 metre stretch of apartment balcony fifteen floors up is so important to me for winding down. No need to repeat it, but I will: I'm a head case. And proud of it. It partly explains why I've given thirty years of my life to the game.

One bit of football has been cast out of my head for ever as a result of that night — the decider in State of Origin 2001. It's been replaced by the wonderful memories of 2004. I've got my mate Gus Gould to thank for that. For that, and for very much more.

gus and me

I suppose Gus and I forged our tight bond for the first time at the end of that troubled year, 1992, at the Panthers. I'd lost Ben Alexander, and the team was on the downslide. Our club was in a fair bit of upheaval; some players had gone off the rails. I think Gus was concerned that I might get caught up in all of that at the expense of my own career. I was already a fixture in the national team, a veteran of a premiership win, two Grand Finals and a Kangaroo tour, and there was a chance, at least in his mind, that I could've sat back, let it all wash over me and maybe never be seen again at the top level.

He called me up at the end of the season and asked if I'd go around to his house at Leonay, which is a very stylish suburb just the other side of Penrith, in the foothills of the Blue Mountains. We sat out on his back veranda, overlooking the golf course. He asked me how I wanted to end my career, and where I wanted to be in ten years' time. I was twenty-one — such thoughts had not even entered my head. Best I let Gus tell the story of what happened next:

I said to Brad, 'I'll tell you where I think you can go. I think you can be one of the all-time greats.' I mentioned names like Wayne Pearce and Bob Fulton. I went on: 'You can be remembered as one of the best ever. But you're not going to achieve that the way you're living your life at the moment. I understand the stress and pressure you're under. But you need to make some changes. Some very serious and drastic changes. If you're prepared to, I'll help you. But you need to redirect your goals and attitudes.' Brad looked at me and I didn't know if he was going to say 'Get nicked' and walk off. Instead he said, 'What have I got to do?' I suggested he come and live with me for a few months. Brad said, straightaway, 'I'll do it.' And the next day he came and took possession of one of the rooms downstairs. It's not as though we were hanging out together, but it was a comfort zone for him. He'd have breakfast there, and dinner. I didn't have much by way of cooking utensils — a vertical griller and a microwave — and I taught him how to use both.

We'd have a chat after dinner, and more often than not he'd be on the phone to a friend and off he'd go, usually grabbing the keys to my car as he left, and bringing them back at a late hour. That went on throughout the off season 1992 to '93. Before that he was a special young player and I was a coach, and there wasn't much more between us. We had a firm bond from that point. And I'm certain it stopped him going off the rails. He could've gone either way at that time. That would've been very sad. He was wayward, no doubt about that. But he was never a bad kid. He'd always own up if he did something wrong. And you couldn't stay angry at him very long. It was a career and a life well worth saving.

My strongest image of that period is not the father–son chats over breakfast but coming home late at night and finding Gus invariably moulded into the couch, dressed only in his underpants, feasting on Twisties and Coca-Cola. Not a pretty sight, I can tell you.

That association strengthened through the years Gus coached State of Origin — 1992 to 1996 — and in those initial years at the Roosters. I suppose I gave a fair bit back, not just on the field but as a magnet to attract new players to the Roosters. When Craig Fitzgibbon came to the club, for instance, I called him to recommend the place and outline our plans for him. We had an England captain in Phil Clarke, the Papua New Guinea captain in Adrian Lam, and suddenly the club that had dwelled at cellar level for so long grew in stature. It helped give the Roosters a platform to recruit some good kids, and to buy players like David Barnhill and Richie Barnett and Scott Gourley and, later, Brett Finch.

The peak of the bond between Gus and me was obviously the State of Origin comeback in 2004. I know he felt really sorry for me, and sorry for the team, when I'd gone out with a whimper three years earlier. At the end of that match he came up to interview me for Channel Nine. It was supposed to be a happy farewell interview. It was miserable for both of us.

In truth, I might never even have played that series. I was going to give the representative stuff away after the 2000 World Cup. Gus came over to the World Cup for Nine and covered the final at Old Trafford, when we beat New Zealand. He came down to the dressing room afterwards, expecting an announcement that I'd be quitting rep football. But they'd announced that there was a Kangaroo tour coming up at the end of 2001, and I was going to stick around for that. So I was exposed to that lamentable finish of the 2001 State of Origin series when really, when all was said and done, I didn't want to be there. It made me feel twice as bad at the end.

Anyway, roll on another year, and Gus comes back to coach the Blues and I'm retired from rep footy. And there's absolutely no doubt I would have stayed retired for ever if anyone but Gus had been coaching the side. I remember as the series drew near, a worker at a building site I visited asked why I wasn't playing State of Origin any more. I said I couldn't be bothered. It was absolutely the wrong thing to say, to belittle something that was so important to him and had played such a role in my life. I've never spoken lightly of the series since, and never will again.

People live and breathe the game, and there I was, acting like a jerk. As if Origin didn't mean anything. Of course it did. I'll be eternally sorry for what I said to that worker. I'm not a fan of cynical people, and there I was being a cynical dickhead myself.

New South Wales went into the 2002 series as underdogs, and on the day of Game 1, Shaun Timmins pulled out with the flu. Matt Gidley was the replacement management wanted, but he couldn't be found. Chances were he was out fishing, or in a pub somewhere getting ready to watch State of Origin on the TV with his mates. Unbeknownst to me, Gus Gould was ready to call me as the fill-in. He was about to pick up the phone to ring me when Matt Gidley was found. So I was literally only a split second away from making a State of Origin comeback in 2002. The Blues won the first game pretty handsomely and Gus called me up and told me how close I'd come to putting on the blue jersey again. He said he was worried about Game 2, and if I wanted to play I could. I said, 'No, thanks.' The Blues lost Game 2 narrowly up there, and then drew the last.

In 2003 they played on the reopened Lang Park for the first game and the Blues won after Gus put plenty of heat on Andrew Johns, which occupied much of the media's time in the lead-up. I was curious about their supposed rift and just wanted to wish them luck, so I telephoned Gus the day before the game. They happened to be on the team bus. I said, 'Put Joey on the phone.' I spoke to him about Gus and wished him all the best. I told Gus, 'Joey's fine. You'll win tomorrow, and Joey's Knights will probably win the premiership now.' That game was the best thing that happened to Joey.

I knew Gus felt it was important to wrap up the 2003 series in Sydney because he didn't want to be heading back to Lang Park for the decider. He rang me up again before Game 2 saying, 'No pressure, mate, but I've sort of earmarked you for this match. I think we can win. It's a good chance for you if you feel like having one more.' My reply: 'Then what will I do? Will I have to play Game 3?' It just didn't seem fair to the rest of the players for me to enjoy the fruits of a series win then drop out for a match that didn't count. Gus was insistent. 'This is how I planned the series,' he told me, 'to win Game 1, then for you to come back and help me win Game 2.' I decided against it because I felt guilty. 'Maybe next year, mate.' Anyway, the Blues won Game 2, 27–4, and the series, and got spanked in the last game. So — and this has never been revealed publicly before — I came within a hair's breadth of returning to State of Origin in both 2002 and 2003. I thought about it, and declined, but in the back of my mind hoped it really would happen one day.

The catalyst for my Origin comeback in 2004 was publicly announcing my retirement from football after Easts played Canberra on 2 May. If ever I was to play State of Origin again, it had to be in the last few months of the 2004 season. I'm sure Gus knew that, and formulated a plan to get me on board. After the injuries leading into Game 2, it almost became a necessity that I played. I was excited at first, then apprehensive. Here's Gus's version of events:

Coming into camp for Game 2, Freddy was very worried. I didn't get the feeling leading into that game that he was going to get out there and blow the opposition away. It was more or less like 'I hope I get by without doing anything wrong'. After the game, even though we lost, he was much happier. He knew he was up to it. Later that week, at Roosters training, he was jumping out of his skin. On the Friday night, the Roosters belted Newcastle and Freddy scored the first try. The confidence he gained from State of Origin had done him the world of good.

I spoke to him on the Saturday, and he said he really wanted to play Game 3. I said, 'I really want you to play, too.' He wanted to be assured he'd be picked. 'No trouble,' I said. 'You'll be picked. You're in. Get yourself ready to play Origin Game 3.' None of that was made public. We both played it down. It suited him, and it suited me as the Blues coach. No point letting Queensland know our true plans.

He was totally different in camp this time. He was like a kid again. He took the team out drinking and dancing, something he hadn't done himself for years. At training, he was on fire. On match day, he was primed. I didn't make a big deal of winning it for Freddy, certainly not in his presence anyway. On the Sunday, when he left early to attend Demi's christening, I gathered the rest of the blokes together at Wentworth Park after training and told them how much it meant to Brad, and how much it would mean to them to be part of a series win alongside him. And how much it meant to me as well.

I spoke of his courageous decision to return to the fold. And how he'd be guaranteed to put everything on the line. I said to the blokes, 'If you could just find some little bit extra for him, I'd really appreciate it.' I actually tried to say all that before Game 2, with Brad present, and got too emotional and broke down. I couldn't get the words out about how much he meant to my life, and how much I'd like to see him go out of State of Origin on a winning note. I could only get the words out when he wasn't there. Stupid, isn't it, for a grown man. But there it was.

In the dressing room just before Origin 3, there was a really awkward moment. I was sitting on the bench, getting a rub, and Gus came up to me, hand outstretched. I thought that this was the moment where he'd give me the big speech about what it all meant, and then shake my hand. I put my right hand out to shake his. But he didn't want to give me a talking-to at all. He was just trying to go over one of our plays. 'I don't want to shake your f---in' hand,' he said. 'I'm just telling you about one of the plays.' That's why he had his hand out, indicating the direction we'd go on that particular play. We both fell about laughing. It was so embarrassing. But it was a perfect, if impromptu, tension-breaker. Anyway, the game was won and then came my charge-down, and the try. If it was an emotional moment for me, I can only imagine what it meant to Gus. I asked him to put it into words if he could, and this is what he told me:

> I thought about all we'd been through together, right back to the early days at Penrith, and how this was the ideal theatre for you to go out the way you deserved. There were 80 000 people out there in the stadium where they held the Olympics. We were winning so convincingly, and you were playing so well. I craved for a moment in that game that would be yours alone. When you charged the ball down, I screamed out from the bench, 'Sit up, sit up.' Here was that grown man again, talking to a football, demanding it bounce perfectly for you, Freddy, which it did. That was the greatest moment I've seen in football. I was so happy for you. It was special for you, and just as special for me, too.

At my tribute dinner at the Shrangri-La Hotel, with a few matches still to play, Gus summed up my career this way:

> When Brad finished against the Warriors last weekend, he'd played 444 first-class matches. That is, top grade premiership, representative and Test matches — 444 of them. It's extraordinary and will never be matched again. That's 444 over sixteen years at around twenty-seven matches a year. He only played a few in the first year, so if you take that off, in fifteen seasons of professional rugby league, he's averaged twenty-nine games a year, every year, for fifteen years. In 99 per cent of those he played the full 80 minutes, in times of limited and unlimited interchange. You can't play that many games unless a lot are played with injury, under pressure, or under stress.
>
> I just find it absolutely unbelievable that one man can contribute that much in that period of time. I've seen him

too injured to train, but he trained nonetheless. Too injured to play, but he played anyway. Too injured to stay out there, but did. And when he was like that, hobbled by pain and stress, he could still turn games with his passion and courage and toughness and desire. These are the things that define him and define his career.

He wasn't always so complimentary, though. I'll never forget the time he was coaching the Roosters and I thought we were all a bit flat. I said to the head trainer, Ron Palmer, 'Maybe Gus is training us too hard.' Ron dished me straight up to Gus on a platter. That night the phone rang, and it was Gus's voice saying, 'Freddy?' I responded, 'Hey, Gussy, how ya going?' In response I got this avalanche of bile and four-letter words: 'Who the f--- do you think you are? You want to be coach, go be a f---in' coach. Somewhere else. At the moment, you're a player and that's all. Be a player, and shut the f--- up!' I never got a word in before he slammed the phone down in my already bruised ear. He takes a couple of days to get over those things, deliberately, I think, so the message doesn't lose its impact. You learn to stay out of his way. Then it's as if nothing happened.

Gus has seen them come and go in the blue jersey. He says, 'Laurie Daley is the best Origin player I've coached, and Greg Alexander the most gifted, by a long way. But when you combine everything together, with Freddy's leadership, impact, longevity, durability, toughness and courage, there's never been such a complete package in the history of the game.'

It's hard to say how different my life might have been if Gus had never entered it. Could I have steadied the ship on my own? Most probably not. What can I say? Just this: thanks, mate. For everything.

going about your business

It's only in recent years that I've taken an interest in my financial affairs. I was reckless with money in my teens and early twenties. I never really had a head for business. Let me give you an example ...

For some reason, when I was nineteen I decided I was going to buy a business. I went out and bought a truck, and a lawnmower and all the equipment to start a lawnmowing operation. I figured I needed a job. Then I thought to myself, *Why own the business* and *do all the work? Why have a dog and do your own barking?* So I hired a couple of young guys to cut the lawns, using my truck and my equipment. I gave them the keys to the truck. Of course this was Penrith, not the north shore of Sydney. I never saw the truck, the equipment or the employees again.

I suppose that with maturity and responsibility you start to understand that a career in football doesn't go on for ever, and you'll have to plan for what happens afterwards. Can I make this point, though: there is insufficient financial management training for all young people in school, and particularly for people in my sort of position, young sportspeople who make good money at an early stage in their lives. Way too many young lives are getting off to a seriously bad start with mobile phone and credit card debts that can never be repaid.

I would like to see the Department of Education and Training institute a financial counselling scheme in all schools. How many young people are ruining their lives by getting heavily into debt, their credit rating shot to pieces and still not out of their teens? It's one thing to concentrate on the obesity problem, but what about the financial recklessness problem? I was just fortunate that my career continued and the money came naturally, and that a lottery win called Super League came around when I was at my peak. And that I had someone as astute and scrupulously honest as Wayne Beavis to manage the money.

I dare say if I'd been injured in my first or second season at Penrith, and my career had been cut short, I could be back now in a pokey western suburbs flat, where I started. Anyway, that's not the case, and I'll devote a chapter to explaining the business of being Freddy. It's not just about being paid to play footy, and to endorse a certain product. It goes beyond that when you become a public figure. I've always known that people enjoy being associated with a good sportsperson, particularly in Australia. I think that imposes a responsibility on you to act with patience and kindness in return where possible, whether it's a fan buying you a pie or a major sponsor offering money. With the former, it's just a few seconds out of your day to say 'Thanks', and to provide an autograph if they want one. It can be invasive and tiring and can shove whoever you're with at the time into the shadows, but I see responding with courtesy as a duty, and it's one that makes me feel good, too. People from all walks of life have been incredibly generous to me over the years. Why, I don't know. Because I could play football, I guess, and some folks like the reflected glory, but I think it goes beyond that. I'm a firm believer in the basic goodness and generosity of spirit in people. I can only speak from experience, and that's certainly how it's been for me.

In the early days, you can imagine how superprotective my mum was in any contract negotiations or major financial decisions. It was clear by the time I was a regular first-grader at Penrith that I needed more than just Mum and a local solicitor looking after me in business. I needed a specialist manager. Enter Wayne Beavis.

In the stands at Penrith Park one afternoon, while I was getting ready to play, Wayne sat himself down next to Mum, seeking to sign me up. The way Mum tells it, Wayne asked if she'd heard about him and Mum replied, 'Yes — so you're starting from a long way behind.' Straight to the point, my mum! Wayne himself tells the story with great relish: 'She had the guard up when it came to her precious boy, Freddy,' he recalls. 'She told me she was looking after him, and I'd need to do some hard talking to convince her someone else could do it better.' The two met again a short while later. Not long after that, convinced that the best way to look after my own financial affairs as well as provide for the rest of the family was to sign with Wayne's management company, that's what we did. And more than a dozen years later, he and I are very firm friends. I'll let Wayne tell what he found when he first investigated my dealings with money:

> It was disastrous. It was like he thought there was no settling, that you spend on and spend up for ever, and there will never be a day of reckoning. If it wasn't yours yet, borrow the money from the club and buy it. That's how he thought. There was no need to worry about money, it was always there from some avenue. It was a bottomless pit. Or so Brad figured. Reckless and disastrous. There are no other words for it.

I had the house at South Penrith at the time. Soon afterwards I went into the new estate at Glenmore Park. I still have no idea where the money came from to buy the first place. Wayne tried often to talk to me about income protection and building assets and quarantining money for the future. It all sounded fine, but the truth is I didn't want to know about it at the time. I just wanted to play football and enjoy myself.

As for contract negotiations, they weren't all that hard in the late eighties and the early nineties. There wasn't the scope for discussion that exists today. Players were paid according to a set schedule: a Kangaroo earned X, a State of Origin player Y, a regular first-grader Z. You'd sign the contract and that was that.

Wayne organised my contracts with Don Feltis, the Penrith chief executive. 'The discussions were always pleasurable,' Wayne recalls. 'Don loved you like a son.' Other clubs were interested, but I never intended to leave the area. I had money from the club on tap, they provided me with fast cars — what else did I need? As long as I had the swimming pool and the good stereo and TV at home to go with it, I was content. On the occasions where I got into trouble with local authorities — and I outlined those earlier — I didn't need management to sort things out. In Penrith it was a case of 'out of sight, out of mind'. There was no scrutiny on everything I did like there would be today.

Wayne also organised my last contract at Penrith. I was one of the highest-paid players in the game and at the peak of my form. But I continued to improve in subsequent seasons and perhaps, even at $150 000 a season plus extras, I was giving value in return. The best part about it was that Wayne organised for Penrith to attend to my expenses out of that money. The house payments came out of it, and all the other bills were met *before* I got my hands on the lump sum, not after. I was given enough spending money to keep me occupied — not unlike a kid getting pocket money from his parents. But it's the best thing that could've happened if I was ever to build assets.

The real change in both my financial status and my attitude to it came with the arrival of Super League. I had no sponsors when I left Penrith. I was still, as Wayne Beavis likes to put it, 'wild and woolly'. I was in no position to be responsible to a serious sponsor. Then I became captain of the Roosters, captain of New South Wales and captain of Australia, and I was in a position to attract sponsors. I bought the block of land at Collaroy, and Mum's house at Sussex Inlet, and I was on the springboard to financial comfort.

When I got my Super League cheque in 1995, I came to the realisation that there *would* be a day of reckoning, and it wasn't all that far down the track. I'd be playing for another seven or eight years, and I needed to put my foot down as far as asset-building was concerned and start preparing for retirement from the game. I must have surprised Wayne. At about the age of twenty-seven or twenty-eight, I'd call him regularly and want to sit down and discuss where the business of being Freddy Fittler was actually heading. At the age of seventeen or eighteen, I couldn't have given a stuff. I'll admit, the change was dramatic.

Property was always going to be the smart way to go. I might have paid too much at the time for the Collaroy and Sussex Inlet properties, but it certainly doesn't look that way now. I also bought a unit in Bronte Road, Waverley, in a small block of twelve, renovated it and sold it a few years later. I went into a commercial property in Hurstville with a group of business partners, and made good money. And I bought the apartment in Highgate in Kent Street. More recently I purchased a semi at auction in Clovelly, in Sydney's eastern suburbs; it's a 1919 home I'm trying to renovate.

I've sat and listened to the financial experts — people like Mark Bouris from Wizard, Jack Elsegood wearing his property developer hat, Wayne Beavis, and Manly sponsor and part-owner Max Delmege — and soaked up their knowledge. Every time they passed on a financial axiom, like Mark's favourite — 'Borrow to buy property and pay cash for shares' — or Wayne's 'Take something for yourself, but always leave something for the next bloke', it would go into my brain and stay there. The difference between me then and now is that these days I know how you make money, and what you need to do to make money, and how you recognise opportunity. Problem is, of course, there are a lot of people out there chasing the same opportunity.

Jack Elsegood — racing car driver, footballer, dapper man-about-town — is a remarkably astute and interesting bloke. At first glance you wouldn't think that a tycoon's brain lies within, but it does. The two of us were involved in buying some land at Bayview in Sydney's north. I had no idea about DA approvals and whatever else we needed at great cost and legwork; it was a foreign language to me. But I enjoyed the learning experience just as much as the profits. By then Jack was an old hand at property development and council approvals.

When I was involved in commercial property at Hurstville I came to learn about yields and the importance of interest rates and good tenants and the availability of car parking. Now *there's* a funny story: the Bank of Cyprus was a tenant in that building, and I only found out later that Roosters boss Nick Politis was on the board. I'd ring him up each month and cheekily demand the rent.

Sponsors came into my life in a serious and permanent way from that first year at the Roosters. As always, I needed a fast car; I asked Wayne to go get me one. Little did I know that it would result in a long and still ongoing relationship with BMW through Trivett Classic Cars at Parramatta. I get a new BMW every few months and in return attend corporate functions and help them out in other ways. Wayne made the initial approach. He went to see them on a Wednesday and called me the next day while I was on the golf course. He said, 'I've got you a new car.' I said, 'What kind?' 'It's a BMW.' Well, that made my day. It ruined my golf, mind you. I went up to the showroom and saw the car they were giving me. It was amazing. I drove it very carefully ... until I got around the corner. Every car since has been just as amazing, and the relationship gets stronger and stronger. The dealer principal, Greg Duncan, his wife, Glenda, and their children, Matthew and Kirsty, have become dear friends.

Adidas also came on board. Marketing manager Jim Tanzey wanted to sign an individual rugby league player, and I was first in their sights. That, too, is a happy and lasting relationship that has continued after my retirement.

I also have an arrangement with the Nine Network, but that's fairly small-scale because I've never been totally comfortable in front of the camera.

My other major backer is Wizard Home Loans, for whom I attend functions and fulfil other roles they require in publicity and promotion. That relationship started in 1996, and it's been terrific for helping me to understand the power of money and how to grow a portfolio of assets. I was very conscious, though, that my core business was playing football, and I was getting well paid for it: that's where my major duty lay.

I could have had many more sponsors, but I simply didn't have the time and energy to devote to more than those I've described here.

The outrageous dollars of Super League had dried up by the time it came to negotiating a second contract with the Roosters. I took a two-year deal and then, in my final year, a twelve-month contract. I took a significant pay cut to stay at the Roosters in my last season. It's not easy for clubs to stay within the salary cap, and the Roosters had been very good to me for a long time, so I felt I had to repay that kindness by accepting less money. I could have gone elsewhere for more, but it made sense to me to stay where I was. In fact, it never seriously entered my head to do otherwise.

The only thing I've been a little sorry about in my career is that I haven't been able to accommodate all the requests for my time. I couldn't tell you how many bag-loads of letters arrive, asking me to attend a birthday party as a surprise for someone or other. Charities, companies, fans — they all want a little of your time or money or league souvenirs. I've always done my best, but I can't get to them all.

So as I approached the end of my playing career, what could I look forward to in the years ahead? Undecided at this stage. But something at the Roosters, I'm sure, in development, or coaching or administration. I'm looking at a number of options in that regard. There'll be an ongoing association with Nine. And I want to do some work raising awareness of the problems in Papua New Guinea. What I needed first off, though, was rest and relaxation for a few months.

the end is nigh

During my last couple of seasons with the Roosters, I felt entirely on top of my game. I was infinitely fitter and stronger, no longer with a youthful body but, instead, with an understanding of how to preserve the one I'd grown into. When I was younger, too, my head was somewhere else, always wondering about the next night out or the next date. What I had for those last couple of seasons was strength of body and peace of mind to match. I knew exactly how long my energy reserves would last each match, and the work ethic required to maximise those reserves. For eleven or twelve years of my football career I had made it hard for myself with late nights and rushing around, which take a huge toll on your body. I got smacked around enough on the field without doing it to myself off it. But you can't put an old head on young shoulders, and no one can tell you to grow up and wake up. It took me a long time to mature, as a player and as a person. And with that maturity came an understanding of how long I could stay in the game, and how I'd cope when the final curtain was drawn.

So for the last two years I looked forward to coming home to Marie and Demi and just kicking back and relaxing. I'm a much more rounded person now, I think. The little things make me happiest, like holding Demi in my arms as she nods off to sleep, taking a walk around the harbour foreshore, seeing friends, snapping off pictures, or whipping Marie at a card game. Well, to be honest, she beats me fairly often, but I refuse to quit the game until I win. I can't help it — I'm competitive. That's all there is to it. It drives her mad, but I simply won't let her leave until I've won. Maybe that will change now I'm no longer playing football.

I'd been fixed on retirement almost from the start of the 2004 season. Along with my manager, Wayne, I always tried to plan twelve months ahead. Wayne and I first spoke about retirement around New Year's. I needed to make up my mind whether, if I was to play on, it would be here in Australia or in Britain or France. The salary cap has made a huge difference to players like me in the twilight of our careers. I'm talking about players who are accustomed to earning large fees but who may no longer form part of long-range plans for a club. They become dispensable, and almost impossible to squeeze in under the salary cap restrictions. I'm not saying that's such a bad thing, as it provides a springboard for young players in what's becoming increasingly a young person's game. The problem is that it's hard for established, long-term players to see themselves being, in some cases, suddenly undervalued. That's why England or France become an option. You get used to the luxuries of life, and the possibility of ending your playing days making your family comfortable and well provided for in the north of England, no matter how harsh the climate, becomes rather attractive. I had several offers to play the 2004–05 season in England, and the money was double what I got in my last season at the Roosters. That's to say nothing of a luxurious lifestyle to match. It was quite tempting. For the first half of my life I had nothing, but I enjoy having money now — it gives you options — so it's hard to say no when much more of it is on offer. I was seriously thinking about it. I don't mind it over there. I could've played with Leeds or Wigan or the London Broncos.

So the decision had to be made about the 2004 season and beyond. Why did I knock back all that money in England and France? Basically, at heart, I'm a loyal person. The Roosters had been good to me; I felt I should be good to them. That's why I signed on for one more year in the red, white and blue. But even before the season began I was convinced that it would be my last, even though the official announcement would not come until six months later. I ended up taking a pay cut, but those heady days of Super League free spending were long gone anyway. From my first contract at the Roosters to my last, there was a pay drop of about 10 per cent. I'm not whingeing — it's not 'poor Brad' or anything. To be paid a very decent sum of money to do what you love is like winning the lottery. Honestly, the money wasn't such a massive issue. I was set up in family life and in business, and I wanted to be with friends in a great team that had a good chance of winning another premiership.

I had other concerns at the start of 2004. My left shoulder was operated on, and I wasn't sure how it would stand up to one more year. I had keyhole surgery to remove scar tissue and cartilage, and I wanted to get photos of it all just as I did for Demi's birth. Strangely enough, though, the doctor wouldn't let me click away while he was doing the operation. So we compromised: I got a mate, Gregg Porteous, to take the video footage and photos for me. Because it was keyhole surgery and they didn't slice me up, the pictures aren't too graphic. Pity, really — I wanted shots that would make the front page of *The Lancet*. Don't laugh — I was almost as interested in the photographs as what the doctor was doing to my shoulder. I want to star in some fly-on-the-wall hospital documentary like *RPA*. I could handle it. I'm up to it. I mean, that's real-life drama. I don't care if I'm the subject or the cameraman. Anyway, I digress. The football field beckoned again, not a field hospital.

I thought I'd make it through the season with a quiet start. My intention was to glide through early training and the pre-season matches without extending myself. At least, that was the theory. In practice, it was nothing like that. I can't ever remember a more strenuous or demanding couple of months of preparation for a season. There were no easy days. I'd come home like a cripple, and I spent the first three weeks of the year bent over, unable to straighten up from the rigours and hardships of pre-season training. My shoulder was weak and I couldn't do much weight training, so I wasn't building muscle, just breaking it down each session. Pre-season training hurt me like it had never hurt before. My body was wracked with pain, day in, day out. I had to stand up to eat Christmas dinner. No kidding. It hurt to sit up straight at the table.

In hindsight, I wouldn't have had it any other way. Without the background work I'd never have made it through two State of Origin matches and another season. But it was at that moment, while on my feet to eat Christmas dinner 2003, that I made up my mind that the next season would be my last. I decided there was no way in the world I could put myself through that regime again. I'll take you through one week of it, the week that sticks sharply in my mind now, and you can see how you'd go.

This particular week was in December 2003. Monday was a heavy conditioning session with long runs then short sprints in the heat of a summer's day. We'd run several kilometres, have a short rest, then do a series of 150-metre and 300-metre sprints with practically no recovery time in between. If you grabbed a moment, it would only be to throw up. It lasted several hours and it was torture. Put your hands on your hips or behind your head — look like you're done in — for a second and you'd have to do an extra load. Squat on your haunches or sit down and you'd be there running until dusk.

Tuesday was the first serious weights session of the new season. And anyone who's tried weights after a long lay-off knows what you're like the next day: you can't move from the muscle strain. You're like a mechanical man. A stick-man. Then it was Wednesday and those dreaded steps at the southern end of Coogee Beach in Sydney's eastern suburbs. The circuit included a steep flight of steps then a kilometre road run with an Everest-like gradient, back down and start all over again. It's tough. Finish one then start another. No rest for the wicked. Try doing that circuit a few times and see whether the money league players get is worth it. It was on the second circuit, I think, that I saw one of our players sprawled out on the footpath, throwing his heart up. I just wanted to be there with him. I felt exactly the same way.

Then to Thursday, and it was off to Kurnell, in the south of Sydney, for sand-hill drill. It's a throwback to the fifties and early sixties, when the legendary old track coach Percy Cerutty pioneered running up sand hills to prepare his famous charges like Herb Elliott. I can tell you that it hasn't become any easier in the intervening years. The hills out by the oil refineries stretch up steeply about 100 metres. You form a line, holding hands to ensure no one drops off, and up you go at full pelt. Then straight back down and up again, piggybacking a team-mate. You love having big blokes in your team on the football field — but not at a time like that. When you have to carry someone on your back up a steep sand hill at full throttle, you want him to be an apprentice jockey, not a front-row forward.

You pretty much find out right there who's mentally tough and who's not. Some people are naturally faster; some are naturally stronger. But it's your tenacity, will and character that's tested in drills like that, not your natural talent. Those new to it might wonder why the coaching staff is putting you through such torment. The fact is that the coach is guided by what he sees at that time as to who'll stand up for him on the field months later, when the same blowtorch is put to your character in a vastly different arena.

In a training session like that, being hunched over, dogging it, giving out faltering body language, complaining, arguing with each other or the coach — they're all bad signs. The way you train, that's the way you play. See an opponent on the field with his hand on his hips, hunched over, and you know he's gone. You know his reserves of energy and will are sapped. It gives you heart and strength. It lifts you. Body language is so important. Even when you're gone to Gowings, you mustn't show it to your rivals. And the best time to get all that right is in training. I remember that day at Kurnell clearly. I've written previously of attacking a young player for showing signs of weakness on the sand hills at the start of the 2002 season. This time one of our young blokes had his hands on his knees, throwing up in the sand. It wasn't him being sick that annoyed me — it was the hands on the knees. I screamed at him, 'Get your f---in' hands off your knees!' He continued throwing up, but with his hands raised over his head like a soldier surrendering. It's funny now when I tell the story. But I'll guarantee you it wasn't funny to either of us at that point.

So then it was Friday, and it just got worse. We went to Wentworth Park for sprint training. Now I've never been a speed machine; I'm not all that light in the loafers. So when I was made to do fifty sprints of 100 metres each, with only a short recovery between them, you can bet I was a wobbling bowl of jelly by the end of it. You don't do the run-throughs at your leisure, either. You have to complete each sprint inside a certain time limit. If you don't, you do it again. That sort of stuff hammers me. My back goes first, then my hamstrings. So there's Monday to Friday. And no rest at weekends.

The next day we had a 'beep' test. We had to make it from one marker to another, 20 metres apart, before the beep sounded, and then back again. The time between beeps got shorter and shorter, and we ended up doing about 150 of these breakneck sprints trying to beat the beep. As soon as it finished, they made us do another. That was unheard of in my time. Then followed our penalty. For every point you were behind, it meant doing a 50-metre sprint. We ended up doing fifty of them. The last one I did in my swimming costume — clothes were too heavy.

There's a typical week, then. And that went on for more than four weeks. It's torture — there's no other word for it. I'm sure it's banned under the Geneva Convention for the treatment of prisoners of war, and if it's not it should be. After that madness had finished at the end of January, they took us on a trip to Coffs Harbour. That seemed like a nice break, a reward for all the hard work of previous weeks. But it was no holiday camp. One evening they got us up at midnight, took us to the steepest hill on the north coast and said, 'Run, come back and run again, and do it till you drop.' We crawled back to the hotel at daybreak.

I'd come home during those first weeks and Marie would just say, 'Oh, you poor old crippled thing', and burst out laughing. She gave me no sympathy at all. I'd lie in a bath full of Epsom salts for hours and moan with the pain. When I woke up each morning I'd go in to the bathroom and sit on the toilet and sort of defrost. I'd move one hand, then get the arm working, then the shoulder, move my head a little, and start on the other side. I'd try to stretch out my legs, one at a time. I'd sit there for half an hour before all four limbs worked. That's how sore everything was. Then I'd try to stand and walk. My brain would be sending messages to the extremities, but the lines were down. It was a very telling time in my life. A crossroads. There were times when I wondered if I was up to even that last season. Many times, in fact.

Anyway, it's rock-and-a-hard-place stuff. I didn't want to ever face that again, and I didn't want to play again without enduring it. At that point, there was only one option: quit. I've heard others give the standard response about impending retirement: 'I'll go on playing as long as I'm enjoying it.' In a sport as physically demanding as rugby league, that's arrant nonsense. You go on playing as long as you're physically able. When your body's giving out, you give it up. Simple as that. And my body was giving up. I went to training sessions knowing I was going to get flogged, and wondering whether I was up to it. In the end, I went and did the best I could. But it was very, very tough, physically and mentally. And if it became too tough, I had to stop. For ever. I couldn't take the money and give nothing in return, no matter how much I needed it. Some players do, and I don't blame them for it. You have to fend for your family. I'm just saying that I couldn't do it.

In April 2004 I was starting to get sick of the questions about whether that year would be the end, so I called Wayne Beavis and told him this would be it. I was ready to call it quits. I'd known that since Christmas, and so had Marie and my family and a few close mates. Ricky Stuart, the coach, had known for a while. The Roosters were looking towards 2005. I asked Wayne to call the club and let them know. He spoke to the president, Nick Politis, and that was the right thing to do, informing the club that had been so good to me that it might need to make other arrangements for the next season because I was not going to be there. Overtures were made to me to reconsider my position, but I stayed firm.

There were two approaches from rugby union clubs in France by fax and email and phone calls, all of which which I knocked on the head, and then a more direct one from a French-based agent. I did not treat the approaches lightly and made a number of inquiries to establish how tough it would be and what sort of lifestyle I could expect. The response I got was that tremendous pressure would be placed on my head if I failed to perform. I really do love the country, and France is a place where I'd like to spend some time in the future. I've enjoyed my trips there. In this case, the deals would have meant a house and a car and more than half a million dollars per season. But after a fair bit of soul-searching, I said no — or *non*, I guess — to the French. The commitment they needed was more than I had to offer.

As far as the retirement announcement was concerned, Wayne told me that the best thing to do was hold a sponsors' function and make it all official. Nick Politis wanted it that way so that the Roosters' major backers found out first. My response was, 'No thanks. Leave me out of that.' It didn't sit well with me. I just didn't want to make a big fuss of it. The whole thing was playing on my mind for weeks; it was a real burr in my backside. I wanted it out of the way, quickly and with no major fanfare. I devised a plan where I'd wait for a game, preferably at Aussie Stadium, where we had a win and I played all right, and

I'd just come right out and announce it out of the blue. Such an opportunity came after we beat Canberra 28–8 at Aussie Stadium on 2 May 2004.

It was my 318th first grade game, and one of the most momentous, as it turned out. It was on my mind that if we did win that game, I'd make the announcement. And by half-time, leading 22–0, I knew that this was the day. So we won, and I scored a try, and we were in the dressing room later, getting ready for the usual post-match news conference. I said to Sticky, 'I'm going to say it now. I'm quitting. I can't be bothered dealing with it any more.' And, twenty minutes later, it was all over. Clean as a whistle. I said some honest and earnest things about the club, and made the point that I'd love to go out on a winning note in my last season, the way other great players like Mal Meninga, Glenn Lazarus, Royce Simmons and Terry Lamb had done, winning a premiership in their final seasons. So it was done in the best way for everyone — except poor Wayne Beavis. He'd walked from home in Woollahra to the game and left early because we were a long way ahead. He'd walked back home again and just got inside his front door when I rang him. Here's how Wayne recalls it:

Bloody Freddy — timing's never been his long suit. I'd literally just turned the key in the front door after walking home and the mobile phone rings. He says to me, 'Where are ya?' I said, 'I'm home, mate, where are you?' As if I didn't know, because the full-time hooter would barely have sounded. He says, 'I'm about to make it known at the news conference that I'm retiring. You'd better come back.' Walking to the game and walking back home had just about exhausted me. Now I had to turn around and do it again. I made it there just as he did his thing. Just like that. Out of the blue. For me, the worst possible timing. For him, perfect timing. The time felt right for him and he made his decision then and there. No spotlight. No fuss. No trumpets or drum rolls. Right place, right time. That's Freddy to a tee.

If I thought that way my whole life, it would be selfish, I know. But it was best for me to get it over and done with. There are occasions when you have to think of others and be aware of their needs. That was a moment in my life where the only one I had to please was Brad Fittler.

gringo freddy goes to jail

One of the joys of playing football is the fabled end-of-season trip. Mostly you can't tell stories of what happened because you and your team-mates occasionally get up to mischief you don't want others to know about. But I'll tell a few stories now, one particularly at my own expense — when I finished up in a Mexican jail robbed blind and fearing for my life.

I'll start in Hawaii. I'd had a few drinks one evening on an end-of-season trip. We were watching these fit young guys run halfway up palm trees and then do backflips, and land, upright, with a perfect ten. I announced to everyone that 'I could do that'. Someone suggested I drown a tequila first and then take a shot at it. Full of drink and blind faith I ran at the palm tree, got a little way up, attempted the backflip and actually made it. I wouldn't say it was a perfect ten ... more like a wobbly six of a landing, but still I made it, and all the players and the locals carried me off like a conquering hero straight to the bar, where it was free drinks for all. By the end of the night, standing up had become hard enough, without gymnastic tricks as well.

Drinking games and me were never a good combination. Once I was travelling through Egypt, and got caught up in this stupid game of snorting salt, sculling tequila and then pouring lemon in my eye. Where's the sense in that, I hear you ask? Well, there's none. I had a migraine for days afterwards. I was on a cruise on the Nile and screaming out in pain. An Egyptian doctor stuck some sort of needle in my bum and fixed it, so I carried on. I was fascinated by Egypt and the pyramids, and then made it down to the plains of the Serengeti, and from a hot-air balloon watched the annual migration of a million wildebeest and zebra in search of new grass between the Serengeti and Masai Mara. I went whitewater rafting and bungy-jumping on the Zambesi, too, all the thrill-seeker stuff.

That was all pretty frightening, but nothing like the time I flew in a fighter jet as part of a *Footy Show* stunt. I couldn't believe it but the pilot gave me the controls at one point, and I started doing Top Gun stuff, tumbleturns and belly-rolls. Just as incredibly, we came through it and landed safely.

You'll understand why I'm starting off this chapter with adventure and travel success stories when I tell you about this next one: the nightmare in the beach resort of Cancun, Mexico. The Roosters' end-of-season trip coincided with the World Series baseball in the US, so each night we'd go to a bar — the same bar each night — watch the game for a while, have a chat and a few drinks. At the end of one session, Andrew Walker and I decided we'd kick on to a local nightclub. I have to say, though, that we were both pretty well behaved on this particular evening. We didn't get up to much, just having a few more drinks and checking out the locals. We caused no trouble whatsoever. The fun really started when it came time to leave the place. I got separated from Andrew and then found myself surrounded by half a dozen strong-armed bouncers pushing and jostling me. I think the bar staff might have tipped off the bouncers whenever a gringo came in with money and jewellery and a bit too much booze on board. I had US$700 in my pocket and a flash Tag Heuer watch I'd bought in England a couple of years earlier. It was my first piece of decent jewellery.

So there I am caught up in all this, wearing a shirt and shorts and thongs, and with the cash and an expensive watch, and I figured I'd better make a break for it. I thought, *C'mon, Freddy, you're an athlete, you can outpace a few muscle-bound Mexicans*. Problem was, I was half-tanked and below my best. I kicked off my thongs and took off across the car park, ran 100 metres or so and leaped over a grass hedge. I was puffed out, but I figured they would be too, and wouldn't be continuing the chase. I poked my head up over the hedge and four monster blokes as big as Blocker Roach were staring down at me. I was too exhausted to run any more. I just put my hands up and surrendered.

They took me to the police station, which was something out of a bad western movie: just four chipped cement walls. The police had jeans and T-shirts on. It was very dodgy, and quite frightening. They took my watch off, emptied my pockets of the money and dragged me down to this cell which was already occupied by someone with a face straight off a Most Wanted poster. My cellmate couldn't speak a word of English, and in any case I didn't care to carry on a conversation with some Mexican psycho with whom I was sharing a very tiny space. For all I knew he might have wiped out his entire family with a poisoned taco. He certainly wasn't in there for a white-collar crime. Unless he'd murdered a priest.

I was absolutely bloody terrified. I've been in moderate trouble with the police, but never to that extent. I'd never been locked up. Until then. And as far as I was aware, no one else knew I was in there. I could have been made to disappear, and they'd still be trying to clear up the mystery to this day. Brad Fittler and Harold Holt — where did they go? I suppose it was a couple of hours later when they came in, grabbed me and threw me out of the cell. I was terrified, I can tell you. I did ask what happened to my watch and money. The answer was predictable: 'You come with nothing, gringo — you leave with nothing.' I just took off for the lick of my life. Watch or no watch, money or no money, I didn't care.

There was one funny aftermath. Andrew Walker was waiting outside the police station for me. I didn't stop to chat to him.

I kept running straight past him, and then they grabbed him. I couldn't have cared less. Bit cowardly, I know, but I'd had enough by then. I didn't look back until I reached the team hotel. David Barnhill was in the foyer. 'Where you been, Freddy?' he asked. I couldn't get the words out I was so puffed and still scared: 'I ... uh ... jail ... uh ... robbed ... Mexican bastards.' That was about all I could say before I fell down. Nothing about Andrew. I'd forgotten about him. Apparently they threw him in the cell too, and got what they could before they let him go.

Now that I think of it, there's another funny postscript. I rang the insurance company from the hotel and they said I needed a letter from the local police to confirm that the watch and money had been stolen. So I went to the Cancun police headquarters the next day, and it was exactly the same blokes who'd thrown me in the cell and stolen the stuff the night before. I just threw my hands in the air and said, 'Oh, don't worry, forget it. I'll cop it sweet.' Another gringo ripped off.

End-of-season trips weren't always spent in dingy bars and the odd police cell. There were times when we mixed in some pretty lofty company. Nick Politis spent plenty of time in Los Angeles. I'd go there from time to time with people like Luke Ricketson, Jack Elsegood, Mark Bouris from Wizard and David Gyngell, the boss of the Nine Network. We'd stay in a luxury hotel in LA, travel everywhere by stretch limousine, dine at legendary establishments like the Ivy, and all the starspotters would wonder which famous rock group we belonged to. Little did they know that we were a bunch of perfectly ordinary blokes from Sydney who'd done OK for themselves and were carrying on like Lord Muck because we could! We spent one night in a club where the DJ recognised our accents and played Men at Work's classic 'Land Down Under' song. We danced our asses off, then looked over and spotted Prince with his bodyguard.

It never ceases to amaze me what great knockabout company hugely successful and high-powered business achievers like Nick, Mark and David can be when they are away from the stress of the office. I count them as good mates. You know my background as a kid from the western suburbs. I always figured people like that would be stuck-up and out of reach. It's not that way at all. They're not different, and they're not to be pilloried. They're to be admired for what they achieve. A boofheaded footballer like me gets all the accolades, but here are people who create great enterprises through their skill and commitment and dedication, employ hundreds and sometimes thousands of people, and contribute endlessly to the country, and for that, people where I come from see them as spoiled, snotty-nosed rich bastards. It's short-sighted, unfair and untrue. There's no difference between what a successful businessman or -woman achieves, and what a sports star achieves. Both need training, energy and skill, and the mental toughness. Their exploits are hidden away in a few lines in the *Financial Review*, and we're on the front and back pages of the daily newspaper. It doesn't make much sense to me. Again, just like footballers, there are good ones and bad ones. The reporting's no different. The bad ones get all the publicity.

My favourite place of all — outside Sydney, of course — isn't all that far from the ranch. It's a place called La Jolla, just north of San Diego. Beautiful houses, amazing coastline, clean and pristine, lovely walks, seals sunning themselves on the rocks below. Football has taken me to a lot of places around the world. But there's only a few I could live in: Sydney, La Jolla and maybe France.

the people you meet

I've mentioned some of the important and successful people I've met, whose company I treasure, through my association with the Roosters, and Wizard Home Loans, Nine and BMW in particular. I've also been lucky enough to meet some of our sporting greats. But there's one encounter that will stick with me for ever: I'm talking about meeting Superman himself, the actor Christopher Reeve.

Christopher was in Sydney early in 2003 to speak out in support of stem cell research. As you'd know, he was wheelchair-bound and paralysed from the neck down as a result of a riding accident. The sister of one of our Roosters players, Peter Cusack, had a connection with Chris's family from her days as a babysitter and nanny for the Reeves in the States. And through that affiliation, Christopher Reeve and his wife, Dana, and children came down to a Roosters training session at Sydney Athletic Field. I suppose I spent about thirty minutes with him, along with Ricky Stuart and Peter. I've met inspirational people in the past who have overcome massive hurdles in their lives. Former Penrith player John Maclean is one — he's now a paraplegic, and the only wheelchair athlete ever to swim the English Channel, and the first to finish the

Hawaii Ironman triathlon. Meeting him, and listening to him speak, was an uplifting experience. But nothing matches that time I spent with Christopher Reeve.

We spoke about football, and about the miraculous things that doctors can do these days, and about the prospect of stem cell research one day curing paraplegia and quadriplegia. It's a Holy Grail of medicine, isn't it, up there with curing cancer.

I'll tell you why that incident will never leave me and why it's so firmly fixed in my head. You get all this adulation as a footballer. You're called a hero. But a hero is someone like Christopher, who used his own tragic accident to help the future of mankind. And a hero is someone like his wife, who cared for him dutifully without a hint of complaint or pity.

At one point — a little thing — his hat fell off, and his wife picked it up and put it back on his head at just the right rakish angle, and smiled lovingly as she did it. He smiled back, and the love and the loyalty between the two of them radiated around them and enveloped us. It was a very tangible thing; it made us positively glow in its reflection.

The heroes, too, are these incredibly skilled and devoted doctors and researchers Christopher told us about. What I did on the footy field, people paid money to see, and they cheered me until they were hoarse. But I was no hero. I wasn't saving lives or working for the betterment of humankind. To be in the presence of someone like Christopher Reeve — a true hero — made me feel very humble, and quite moved. I was in awe of the bloke. I walked away from our meeting a different person — I'd been touched quite deeply. And I knew — God forbid — that if anything bad happened to me in the next tackle, I'd be able to cope because I'd look on him as the perfect role model.

When news of his passing came through, I was really upset. I'd been at the dentist earlier in the day to have a tooth pulled. I was feeling in pain and uncomfortable, and cursing the world. But I can only imagine the pain and discomfort that man endured stoically and with tremendous dignity for the last nine years of his life. The day Christopher Reeve died the NSW

Premier, Bob Carr, who was instrumental in bringing Superman to Sydney, issued this statement: 'Christopher Reeve was simply the most impressive human being I've ever met.' Mr Premier, they're my sentiments exactly.

And let me tell you about meeting a very different type of Superman: Kerry Packer. He was a prominent figure in the Super League–ARL fight, backing the traditional game against Rupert Murdoch's raiders. Not long after I'd signed with the Roosters I was summoned to meet Mr Packer in his office at Australian Consolidated Press in Park Street, Sydney. On my way to that meeting it was hard not to recall earlier contract discussions many years before, and meeting club backers and sponsors from Penrith and in the local juniors. I'd go with my mum. There'd be cheese and biscuits, and debate over a few thousand dollars. Now it was hundreds of thousands — nigh on a million a year — and the man I was meeting was Australia's richest tycoon. Talk about a world of difference in less than a decade. Thongs to Gucci loafers!

Anyway, I walked into his office with Gus Gould, Wayne Beavis and Nick Politis. Kerry had his feet up on the mahogany desk, leaning back, hands behind his head It was just the way you'd imagine it should look when you walk into Kerry Packer's office. He was the king of all he surveyed, no doubt about it. Just like Nick, Kerry was dead keen for the Roosters to win a premiership again. He said to me, 'What will it take to win a premiership?' I thought about it for a moment, cast my mind back to the Penrith Grand Final win, and answered, 'You have to build up your junior base, get some good young kids coming through the ranks, and develop a real feeling of club spirit and tradition.' I rambled on for a minute or so about how it would take a few years to build up a group of bright juniors and mould them into a premiership-winning side. To his credit, Kerry listened patiently. When I eventually finished, he took his feet off the desk and leaned forward until his face was a few centimetres from mine. 'Waste of time, son,' he said. 'I'll buy one.' When we did finally win a premiership in 2002, ten of our players had come up through the junior ranks. I think we were both right, Mr Packer!

Later I had the opportunity to visit Kerry Packer's stud, homestead and golf course in Scone in the NSW Hunter Valley. What a showplace! There I was with Gus, sitting around, chewing the fat with Australia's richest man. He just wanted to talk about horses and cricket and football. It's funny how being a good sportsman in this country is so valued that it gains you entrée into the very best of company.

I met Prime Minister John Howard after a State of Origin series win. I understand it's just a photo opportunity, and political figures don't have time to spend hanging around with mug football players who've just won a game and are more intent on tossing beer around the room. But I was so excited when he came into the dressing room that I just threw an arm around him, the way you might do when you excitedly greet an old mate. I'd never met him before, obviously. When I look back on it I'm not that proud of what I did. It was pretty disrespectful. But I had a chance to apologise later. Marie and I were invited around to Kirribilli House for Christmas drinks with the PM. Can you imagine it? From rags to riches, Penrith to Parliament. I stood there, the only guest not wearing a tie (well, I wasn't going to be uncomfortable), quite unable to believe I was in this position. Freddy having private drinks with the PM, indeed! Marie was done up like the Queen of England and looked like a goddess. There's that fairytale of my life, again.

I believe that in a democracy like ours, no matter who the prime minister is, you should show great respect. As it turns out, I support his policies and I think he's been a terrific prime minister for this country. I was like a pig in mud that whole evening. I loved it, and enjoyed the PM's company immensely. He had a couple of beers. There were no cameramen, no news reporters. The cricket was on the TV. I think, towards the end of the night, the security people were trying to move us on and leave the Howards in peace. I said to the PM, 'John, let's give the others the brush, and you and I will sit here all night, have a few beers and watch the cricket.' I think he'd have been in it, too, being a well-known cricket tragic. But Jeanette Howard put a stop to that: 'Off you go, Brad,' she said, and I knew it was time to pull the pin.

Not everyone I meet because I'm a sports personality makes for a pleasurable experience. I meet all types. Let me tell you about my male stalker. Every player has his fans, and most are a joy to have around. For instance, every weekend at Aussie Stadium in that final season a boy named James and his sister and little mate would meet me at the car when I arrived and walk with me to into the ground. And when the game was over they'd wait outside the dressing room and walk me back to my car. I always found it quite uplifting to have them there. I'd always look around and hope they were there when I turned up. Lucky charms, in a way, and it made me feel good. They were great kids. But this stalker, Andrew, was something else. Very weird, very spooky, and alarming.

He was a few years younger than me, and I used to see him quite regularly at the footy and at training over a couple of years. I think he lived in Brisbane, but he would often turn up to games in Sydney. He'd always want to chat, get some photos and some more autographs. I'm always as nice as I can be. But with this bloke I always felt there was something not quite right. One Origin series, staying in the ParkRoyal in Brisbane, a call came through to my room the day before the match. It was this fellow, who said he had to see me right away and could I come downstairs so he could show me something. It was match day and just before lunch. So it wasn't convenient, and I didn't want much to do with him, but I said OK and down to the foyer I went. I thought he had something for me to sign.

Instead he showed me a three-page letter and said, 'Please read this'. The first sentence was, 'I know I'm a bit mixed up but, Brad, I'm very much in love with you.' Well, I didn't know what to think. I don't care if anyone's gay or straight or whatever; it's their life, and good on them for it. Stand up proudly for what you are. If someone gets enjoyment out of looking at pictures of me, so be it. Guy or girl, it's up to them. But I don't want to be told about it. I don't want to know about it. I said to him, 'Look, mate, you feel how you want to feel, but I don't want you coming near me again.'

After that he continued to turn up at Roosters training in Sydney. Whenever I arrived at training, or when I was on the way out, he'd call over to me: 'Brad, I have to see you, please.' I just brushed him off. I was quite restrained. In the old days blokes would've just smacked him in the head and moved on.

I was told he had dozens of photos of me, taken through the windows of the beach house at Collaroy. There was no fence around it at that time. I reported the matter to the local police. After that, he pretty much dropped off, thank God. Like I said, it was spooky and very disturbing.

It's a most difficult and fine line to walk among the fans. Sport gives people hope and joy they might not otherwise have in their lives. Of course, there are highly successful and motivated people who are equally consumed by the love of their chosen sport. The Roosters boss, Nick Politis, is one — he lives and breathes it. But when support becomes obsession in the ordinary fan, as a high-profile player you have to take a step back. The sportspeople I admire most are those who retain their humility, and are equally at home among princes and paupers. That's a very difficult thing to do: you are paid vast sums of money, lauded as heroes in the newspapers and on television, people jostle with each other to get your name signed on a bit of paper, and in all of that it's easy to lose your sense of reality.

Australians love their champions to be approachable, perfectly ordinary and a little bit vulnerable — leave a beer half-consumed on the bar, go out and beat up on the world, then come back to the bar to finish off your beer and shout one for everybody else. Australians also like their champions to be flawed, I've found. It makes them seem more human. Supporters can relate a little more if their champion is not a robot.

Take Greg Norman, for example. He's one of the guys in sport I admire most. Whenever he was in contention for a major, I never missed a moment, whether it was 1 a.m. our time for the British Open or later in the morning for the US tournaments. But we know him best for the golf tournaments he might have won and didn't. Those dozens of young Australians making their way on the professional golf circuit around the world owe a great debt of gratitude to Norman for blazing a trail with class and distinction. He took on the world pretty much on his own. To lose as gracefully as you win — well, that's the mark of a gentleman as far as I'm concerned.

I got to play a round with Greg as a guest at an opening for the course he designed, Pelican Waters on the Sunshine Coast. Ryan Girdler and I stood on the first tee, crowds gathered around and cameras clicking away, and I was shaking like a bloody leaf. By some miracle my ball found its way onto the fairway, but I can't imagine how a professional golfer stands up to that pressure eighteen times every working day.

The great West Indian batsman Viv Richards was there too, and Girds and I hooked up with him afterwards. Now, I figure Girds is a very good-looking bloke, and the girls like him, but when it was a choice between him and Viv Richards, there was no betting. Viv has a voice like honey pouring from a jar, smiling eyes that would melt an iceberg, and skin like Old Gold chocolate. The girls kept edging closer and closer to our little group, and we knew they didn't have their sights on us. I started to feel feminine elbows nudging Girds and me out of the way.

One of my favourite sports stories is about Viv. An Australian fast bowler whipped one past his helmetless head, and on the way through told him, 'Didn't you see the ball, Viv? It's round and red.' Richards smacked the next ball over the fence, and told the quickie, 'You know what it looks like. Now go find it!'

I've mentioned my friendship with Nine boss David Gyngell. He introduced me to John Cornell, formerly Paul Hogan's loopy, lifesaver cap-wearing offsider, Strop. For that I'm eternally grateful, because John is one of the most inspiring and interesting people I've met. As a businessman he proved to be extremely astute in backing the *Crocodile Dundee* movies, driving the World Series cricket revolution on behalf of Kerry Packer's PBL, managing several of Australia's outstanding cricketers and recognising the investment potential of the Byron Bay area of far northern New South Wales. These are just a few of his success stories. When I'm asked if I could be anyone else in the world other than Brad Fittler, my public response is always, 'I'm happy being me.' Privately, if I could be anyone else I'll tell you now it would be John Cornell. He and his wife, Delvene Delaney, are a delightful couple. Delvene could pass for a young woman of twenty. Like John, she's bright and forthright and intelligent.

Some of the most riveting snippets of conversation I've had in my life are with John as he recounted his role in World Series cricket, travelling the world on behalf of Kerry Packer to sign up players. The parallels with Super League brought it all a lot closer to home for me.

At the other end of the scale, you get to meet weird and wonderful people and go to unusual places as a prominent sportsperson. As an Australia Day ambassador I travelled to Cobar in the far west of New South Wales, and I was meant to be met by the mayor. I didn't expect a state reception or anything on arrival, but I figured there'd be a bloke in a suit at least. Instead there was a fellow in stubbies, thongs and a singlet. I said, 'Can you take me to the mayor, please?' He said, 'I *am* the mayor!' We had a terrific time, competing in goat races and downing beers at the local RSL. It was just about as Australian a day as you could possibly get.

I regard the former Australian cricket captain Steve Waugh highly for the length of time he spent at the top, and his gritty determination. There's been no more positive sports champion in my time. He always believed he could win, and instilled that feeling in his team when he led them onto the field. These are attributes I tried to emulate. And I suppose Pat Rafter is the quintessential Aussie sports favourite. When he wins, he smiles and shakes his opponent's hand. When he loses, he smiles and shakes his opponent's hand. No difference. He's natural and humble, the way Australians love their sports stars. I love them that way, too, particularly when it comes to Rafter. He also came from humble beginnings, and had a devoted family to back him with love and inspiration.

I'll mention one other whom I've met a few times, and whose company I thoroughly enjoy. That's the basketballer Andrew Gaze, the Australian flag-bearer at the Sydney Olympic Games. Another humble, low-key champion. A big achiever without being a big-noter. I'd like to think I can go out leaving that sort of lasting impression myself.

backing up and staying up

Looking back over my career, the pillars that mark the way are the premierships, the Test series wins while I was captain of Australia, State of Origin triumphs as captain, and the Origin comeback. But if you ask me what I'm most proud of, it's none of those. All were moments of magic, but I'll sum up what makes me most beam with pride in one word: value. I gave value to those who had faith in me. In fifteen and a bit seasons, I never missed more than three games on the trot. I never missed a match because I was sick. In a game as damaging to your health as rugby league, that's no small feat. I'd like it to be the way I'm remembered. It helps me sleep to say, truthfully, that I gave value to the club and to the game. To back up year in, year out — and to stay up, game in and game out — takes extraordinary self-discipline. You have to learn how to play injured. Sometimes I wish I hadn't, like when I carried rib cartilage and then shoulder problems. I always looked at it this way: you can lie to your coach, you can lie to the club doctor, you can lie to your team-mates. But you can't lie to yourself. If you can play, you play. That's it.

I had a test for the way I applied myself to playing and training, preparing for a season, and caring for my health and body during the year. It's pretty simple: it's called Man in the Mirror. You stare at yourself in the mirror, and know that you can't lie to yourself. If you've been slack, the Man in the Mirror will let you know. And there's no harsher critic.

What you eat and drink is a big part of that, of course, so I'll start with that angle first. Growing up in the seventies and eighties, there was no great concentration on the nutritional value of the food you ate, and not the variety there is today. No stir-fries or sushi, for instance. It was meat and two or three veg on a good day. Fish and chips on a Friday. Occasionally a roast on Sunday. Take it or leave it. Spaghetti bolognese now and then was about as exotic as it got. I ate pretty much whatever Mum put in front of me, except brussels sprouts and chokos. No way, that stuff. When they were on the plate I made a quick trip mid-meal to the bathroom to spit them out. 'Beautiful, Mum,' I'd say when I returned to the table. 'Any more of those chokos?' Having already made sure there were none left, of course.

There was one kind of milk, the full-cream type, and there was actually a layer of cream on top, and if anyone in Sydney knew what soy or tofu were, it hadn't yet reached the wilds of Ashcroft. To me a balanced meal was keeping my peas on the fork. Every day of my life — every single day of my life from the earliest I can remember until I left school at seventeen — I had Vegemite sandwiches. Still do, for that matter. You know how kids like to swap their sandwiches at lunch — you probably did it yourself: 'What've you got today, mate? Wow, that looks good. Swap ya half a corned beef for half of yours. Whaddya say?' Well, it didn't happen in my case. They always knew what I had: Vegemite and more Vegemite.

Was there anything better, though, than the day your mum worked in the canteen? You were allowed in the back to snaffle a drink or a pie or an ice cream or a Sunnyboy, and you were king for a day. You'd sit there, jealously guarding the treasure while your mates clamoured around for a bite. It was a wise investment, I found, to let one or two mates share the spoils. That way, when their mums were in the canteen, I got some as well.

I tried not to let a day go past without a vanilla Paddle Pop. Or I'd get a 600 ml glass bottle of milk and have the bloke at the corner store squirt some chocolate flavouring into it. I never had much money to spend at the canteen, but never saw any sense in it anyway. There was always a line-up of about twenty kids, and you'd spend half your lunchtime in a queue. With a couple of Vegemite sandwiches packed away there was ample time for running and jumping before classes resumed. I see grown men and women now in the city or down at The Rocks, wasting most of their lunch hour lining up to buy a sandwich. Surely it would be smarter to bring your own — Vegemite or otherwise — and spend more time relaxing and enjoying the views.

Maybe those snacks weren't always good for us, and it's quite a bone of contention these days as the focus falls on obesity in children. But here's the thing: back then, we never stopped running from the moment we walked out of class until it got dark, and I'm sure all that junk food was burned off before it took hold. So it's not just the junk food that's the problem: it's the lack of exercise. It's a point I made right at the start of the book when I spoke about the ghost town that is Ashcroft. You don't see kids playing in the parks and streets like they did back then. I understand that parents have concerns about safety. But I say let 'em run. Set the kids free. It's natural for children to run and play. They have so many reserves of energy and, blessed with the climate we have in Australia, it's a sin not to let them use up those reserves.

Computer games, I hear you say — how do you deal with kids' fascination with computer games these days? Well, we had computer games, too. Rudimentary, for sure, but I clearly remember a mate of mine, Scott, getting an Atari game. It was the big thing. You'd play it for a while, but after an hour or so you'd be desperate to get outside and kick a ball. My mates were not necessarily sports stars, but they could all swing a cricket bat or pass and catch. I'm not sure when all that stopped in our community. Certainly it's not the case now from what I can see. I know, too, that there's less open space these days than there was. But our favourite bike track was the street. We didn't need a velodrome. If we had some crates and a piece of board, we made a jump. Or we got a cricket game happening on a makeshift pitch between the laundry blocks of adjoining flats. Mass games of hide-and-seek or tip footy between kids from flats on our side of the road against kids from the other side of the road were legendary. The ends of the street were the boundaries. We were only allowed on the ground floor of the flats. And we went home when it got dark.

The science of what's best to eat was completely unknown to me as a budding sportsman, even through junior state and national representative teams. A healthy breakfast was a packet of Cheezels. I can't imagine a national squad in any sport without a nutritional counsellor now, but it wasn't like that then. We knew vaguely what was fatty and what wasn't, but the effects of a low or high carbohydrate diet were unknown to me as a young footballer.

I came back from the Kangaroo tour in 1990 a flabby mountain at 105 kg. Gus Gould put me in one-on-one training with a bloke called Dennis Bailey, doing stationary bike and rowing machine, and running until I dropped, and all that happened every single day for a month until the weight came back down below 100 kg. In England I'd been on the drink and I hadn't played often enough. It was a three-month tour, and it was cold, and we were having hot breakfasts and three large meals a day. It doesn't take long to lump on the lard if you're naturally predisposed to putting on weight. And without discipline my weight shot up until I looked like Marlon Brando's later-life stunt double. If I'd known about Man in the Mirror at that time, I don't think it would've helped — there wasn't a mirror big enough to see all of me in it.

It's amazing to think that this was not much more than a decade ago, considering the entourage that elite sports teams backing up and staying up

take with them these days — scientists, doctors, dieticians, nutritionists, hyperbaric chambers. It's a travelling circus. I think the first time I came across a nutritionist was in my final year at Penrith. She handed us all food diaries. That lasted a week. I think some of the people ate their diaries. It wouldn't have surprised me, not out there. It was simply unrealistic to put down in a book every single thing you ate for a week. You'd finish up filling it out all at once and never being truthful anyway.

The game itself was different then, too. Big was good. The average forward's weight on that first Kangaroo tour was about 115 kg. Mal Meninga, in the centres, was 118 kg; Marty Bella was 120 kg. You were expected to carry more fat. There were skin-fold fat tests, which I didn't do very well at. Compared with the greyhounds of today's game, we were old labradors.

We ate and did what we thought was right without any professional advice. Ryan Girdler and I would go down to Ron Oxley's gym and box for an hour and do 500 sit-ups every morning, then make our way down to a Sizzler restaurant for a large spaghetti bolognese and pumpkin soup. We understood that to be 'low fat'. It had to be, didn't it? Well, we now know it was pretty stupid if we were trying to keep the weight off. We thought battered stuff was fat and anything else was good. And we wondered why we weren't getting any trimmer.

When you're young, though, it doesn't seem to matter so much. You still bounce out of bed. You still get through games. You still have a skinful after every match. It was like an extension of the game back then, straight over to the club for beers as soon as the game was over. And the next day was the same: more beers. You didn't train until the Tuesday, and that was usually a conditioning run where you'd gallop around the field for a while and go home. It was tough conditioning work, mind you. But not the way it's all been revolutionised today. And I think Gus Gould is responsible for much of that, because he was young when he came to coach at Penrith, and he was brimming with bright new ideas. As a player, because youth was on your side, you mended — miraculously — and you backed up the next week.

I grew up in a culture of football where you played injured. There was more natural padding with the extra fat. A player's body these days is more athletic, and more vulnerable. And clubs are a little too protective, maybe. Anyway, I've never been much of a one for physiotherapists. I mostly found it tedious and not very helpful when I was young. I'd go to physio sessions on Tuesdays, but only to get out of the conditioning session.

As for injuries, well, they'd heal in time and maybe you played a little below par but there was never any thought of sitting it out. Within a couple of weeks there was a new injury and you'd forgotten about the old one. I found — and I don't suppose it's written in any medical journal or has a fancy Latin medical description — that if I hurt my knee, and I had a sore knee for a while, as soon as I hurt my shoulder my knee healed up. That happened to me my whole playing life.

I won't say I've disregarded medical and physiotherapy advice, but I've always found that common sense and the Man in the Mirror were enough to get me there each weekend. That and some back-up from Liz Steet, the physio at the Roosters. Until six years ago, I routinely played at 100 kg. For the last few seasons I played at 5 kilograms less. No one told me to lose that weight. I just came to the realisation that if my body was to carry me through for more of the same, I needed to take the strain off it by getting the weight down. I didn't need a doctor to give me that advice — common sense was enough.

Phil Gould had suggested many years earlier that I'd be best at 92 kg, but that was unrealistic. However, getting to and staying at 95 kg wasn't all that hard. Shedding those extra kilos made an absolutely massive difference to me. I would have been forced into retirement years earlier if I'd stayed at that old weight. With the pressure off injuries like the groin, in particular, I could carry on. That groin injury — I described the agony of it in an earlier chapter — could have ended my playing days there and then, halfway through. I had five operations, spent three weeks in hospital and three more weeks in a wheelchair. It took me a whole off season to make it back.

After that major operation in 1998, I'd lost weight naturally, and I made a conscious decision not to put it back on. Being in the city from the end of 1995, in an apartment block with its own gymnasium and sauna, made a huge difference on a number of fronts. First, I was removed from the temptation of a night out on the tiles with my mates out west several nights a week. And second, with facilities like that literally at my doorstep, I chose to use them. If I'd had to get in the car to go to a gym, or walk a long way, I might not have been so diligent about my condition. I'd train with the Roosters in the day, and at the apartment gym of an evening. But my eating habits weren't all that great, so I continued to stay at a high weight. It wasn't until I started to get sensible about eating, after the groin operation, that I reached, after all those years, an ideal playing weight.

I went four or five months without any bread or pasta, on one of those low carbohydrate diets. I'd eat potatoes and rice at dinner. But not eating bread for all that time when I was used to not much more than Vegemite sandwiches for half my life was a difficult thing to do. The funny thing about that diet — the only one I ever adhered to strictly in my life — was that it helped more with self-discipline than with weight loss. Once I was able to stop eating those things as I said I would, suddenly training became easier. Discipline in one area of my life led to discipline in another. *If I can do this, then why not that?* That's the way my brain was operating.

If I found I was putting on a kilo or two, I went and trained a bit harder. That's the way I kept the balance of my health and fitness after fifteen seasons. I weighed myself most days. And I had my bad weeks. And I've got another trick, not so much Man in the Mirror as Man on the Toilet. If the image is too much for you, then skip a line or two now. It's OK by me. But honestly, if I sit on the toilet and see a roll or two of fat, I know it's time to eat less and train harder. They don't tell you that at the Australian Institute of Sport, I'm sure.

Fruit is a huge part of my diet now. I never ate it much as a kid, but now I have between five and ten pieces a day, every day — apples, bananas, mandarins, oranges, pears, the lot. I discovered fruit in 1999, and I wonder now what I missed out on all those years. How can something that falls off a tree taste so good?

I make myself a smoothie with egg whites, banana and cashews, whipping it up so it tastes OK. I couldn't quite do the Rocky Balboa thing with the raw eggs in a glass, but more power to the people who can. Again, it's the discipline thing. And everyone's make-up is different. If it works for you, and you persevere, then good on you.

A typical day for me towards the end of my final year would've gone something like this: Weetbix and fruit for breakfast; fruit for after training; protein supplement; salad sandwich or a 'Freddy Special' for lunch when we trained at Wentworth Park (when I was on the no-bread diet, the shop across the road would make me a meal of schnitzel and salad, and it became known as a Freddy Special and now holds a permanent place on their menu); an afternoon snack of a muesli bar or yoghurt; and a good dinner of chicken or steak and steamed vegetables, washed down with juices and about 5 litres of water a day. No soft drink, no sugar in my tea, not much coffee any more. I think giving up sugar is one of the best things you can do in your life. Giving up salt is a bit harder, given Marie's Greek background, but we've been trying. And with all of that, I've found something remarkable: my body recovers better now than it did five years ago. There's something to be said for a settled and healthy lifestyle.

During the last three years of my career I was totally disciplined. It made me a better person. It did wonders for my confidence and self-esteem to know that, whatever the temptation, it wasn't strong enough to knock me off the right path. Discipline brings its own sense of satisfaction. And I'm not just talking about playing sport at the highest level. A little thing like taking a walk of a morning or evening, or walking to the shop instead of driving, or just putting the remote control aside for a month, and actually doing it all unfailingly for a set period of time, can give you a tremendous boost, and a sense of fulfilment. I recommend it to anybody.

Discipline's such a wonderful thing that I'm sorry I only discovered it so late in life. My advice to a young bloke looking at a career, as I was back in the late eighties, is this: enjoy the discipline, and never cheat on yourself. If the coach says don't have a beer on a Sunday and you sneak off and have one, well, it's probably not going to make a difference. But I'll tell you this: I've never seen anyone cheat on himself in that way and make it. Never.

Maybe I could have made a bigger impact in rugby league when I was younger. But I've adapted. And if I'd done things differently early in life, I might not have been around in the game so long. So I don't suppose I would change a thing about those fifteen years. But if there's a young person reading this and looking for one good tip, it's this: discipline yourself, and revel in it. I can't imagine ever deliberately dodging a training session. I never did when I was fourteen. And I never did when I was thirty-two. I loved the game and never wanted to be away from it.

And while I'm on my 'wise old Freddy' stool, here's another tip: there's always help available. There's a lot of good people who care. Never try to get through a crisis on your own. I had problems and issues as a kid, and because I could play football well there was always someone around to pull me into line or point me in the right direction. I'm a successful person because of that. Look for advice when you need it, and accept it. Work out who's got the best advice and follow it. Work out who gives bad advice, and let it go through one ear and out the other. Here endeth the lesson.

Stress played a big part in my life. Still does. I get terribly anxious about things. I think too deeply about aspects of football and life in general. Football occupied my head from the time I woke up until the time I went to bed, 24/7. Or at least it did until I retired. Discipline again: I had to train my mind to stop brooding.

Rest became a very big thing with me. In my entire last season in the game, leading into the finals, I had only two nights out with the team-mates — one in the off season, and one during the season. Apart from that I scarcely had any alcohol at all, and I didn't miss it. After a game I'd come home and put my feet up. I worked out that my team needed me on the weekend, not drinking after the game. It took me a long time to figure that out.

You can't do at thirty what you did at twenty: play a hard game, hit the grog, then back up the next day for training, and the next week for the another game. Modern training methods reflect that as well, with a big focus on rest and recovery rather than flattening you before a game. To give you an idea of a typical week at the Roosters: play Sunday; Monday, a swim; Tuesday, sprints and boxing in the morning and a heavy weights session in the afternoon; Wednesday, kicking and field drills; Thursday, weights and field drills: Friday, nothing; Saturday, field drills; and Sunday we played again.

We got our schedule for the following week after every game. No excuse for missing your share of the workload, that's for sure. The session on match eve was an interesting event that could differ markedly between coaches. Ricky Stuart at the Roosters preferred a sharp 45-minute field session without a dropped ball or missed drill. Chris Anderson, the Australian coach, figured there was no point leaving your best work on the training paddock the day before a game.

There's one aspect of backing up week after week that gives me some concern. I told you at the start of this chapter that I've never taken a sickie. That's true. But I've felt compelled to force-feed myself antibiotics at the first sign of a cold. Over a number of years I have taken antibiotics in huge doses. They tell you antibiotics don't cure a cold. Well, I've had a lot of them —

colds and flu — and never missed a game. I'm not sure, though, how my body's going to be able to fight off infection in later life; I hope I haven't become dependent on antibiotics. I know it's best to let the body build up its own defences, but that hasn't happened in my case. The problem is that footy's week to week, training's most days, and you have to front up. Without the antibiotics, that wouldn't happen. It's a penalty you pay. I don't like taking them, and as soon as I finished playing I gave them up. I guess that's an open invitation to the bugs to come on back.

Our health and condition were monitored regularly. The skin-fold tests, so dreaded in the early nineties, are now a competitive sport. There are groups within the Roosters who treat it as a competition to see who can improve most from the start of the pre-season until finals time. That's a great thing. And it just rams home how much the times and attitudes have changed in the game. There's a conditioner, a dietician, a doctor, a nutritionist, a physiotherapist, a sports psychologist and all the latest technology on hand with advice any time you want it. And sometimes when you don't. I've never been much of a one for sports psychologists. It's just me being old and stubborn, I guess.

I missed a game only once through illness. I couldn't really call it a sickie. It happened in a match against Cronulla during my time at Penrith. We stayed down in Cronulla the night before, and the only way I could sleep was on all fours, like a dog, because of this excruciating pain on the right side of my stomach. The pain was so intense and sharp, like a knife plunging in and out. It wasn't too bad the next morning, and I got on the bus to get to the ground with every intention of playing. I was half-changed in the dressing room when I went down like a bag of spuds, clutching the right side of my stomach. This is about forty minutes before the game, and there was no doctor. He was otherwise occupied.

I cried out, 'Look, I'm in a bit of strife here. I'm all cramped up. Can someone help me?' The answer was typically unsympathetic that close to game time: 'You'll be right, mate.' Finally the doctor appeared, felt around the painful area, told me my appendix was about to burst, and I was on my way to hospital before the kick-off. I'm surprised they didn't just give me a painkiller and send me on.

best of the best

I'm not going to rate players, coaches, captains and referees in order as the best I've played with or against or under in the past decade and a half. Nor am I going to tell you the meanest or the toughest I've ever seen. It doesn't do justice to me or to them to put them in order, nominating one over the other. Every match is different; it requires knowing your own, your team-mates' and the opposition's strengths and weaknesses, and how to use them or exploit them to your advantage. And every player, every coach, every referee has strengths and weaknesses.

But I do want to look at some of the pillars and characters of the game I've lined up with, or come up against, or just met over the years. My criteria are basically these: people who have changed the game for the better, or changed me, for better or worse, or simply made footy fun.

I'll start with coaches. Ron Willey was my first coach in the top grade, and I wrote a little about him earlier. He was an extremely likeable bloke, genuine, uncomplicated, straight down the line. Old Ron passed away a week before the 2004 Grand Final, and stories were lovingly swapped about his unique ways. I will never forget his warm-up sessions at training. He had this singsong way of controlling them that went something like this: 'One, two, touch-your-toes, three, four, jump-in-the-air, four, five, feelin' alive ...' Before every training session we all stood in a circle, held hands and pulled tightly against each other. At the point where the circle pulled apart Ron would run up to it, pointing at the players and saying, 'You're the weakest link', well before the TV quiz show of the same name made that call famous. It was comical then, and laughable now. But it worked. It was just a bit of light-hearted banter before the hard yakka started.

Ron's Thursday sessions were memorable. We'd train for an hour on the dot. Neil Baker would kick a field goal from 30 or 40 metres out and that signalled the end, like clockwork, week in and week out. Then it was up to a local pub called the Aussie Arms, funnily enough owned now by Ricky Stuart, for a beer-a-thon. It was a different era. But I'll always have fond memories of Ron Willey, because he was the first to show faith in me. I'd known the reserve grade coach, Len Stacker, having played against his son Peter, and he was always keen for me to play grade; I was apprehensive. But for both Len and Ron to pin their colours to me as a mere untried kid was pretty special. It got the whole train rolling to the point where it's only just reached the end of the line.

Gus Gould came into my life in 1990. I've devoted a chapter to his influence on me, but it's appropriate to include a little extra here. The real key to his talents was an understanding of how to massage personalities. He analysed an individual's character and personality traits, and worked on them to bring out the best in that player and in the player's contribution to the team as a whole. In a footy team you've got thirteen in the starting line-up, another four on the bench, and each one of them is different. The coach who brings in all the different ages and needs and personalities of each of them to form a cohesive, bonded unit will win every time. And that's where Gus's true talent lies.

When Gus came to Penrith, he put me straight back down to reserve grade. I think he was most probably marking the ground a bit, letting me know I'd come along a little too quickly. Oddly enough, I didn't play all that well in reserve grade, but when I came on for top grade I lifted a lot. It was easier for me, paradoxically, against better players. No idea why. It just was.

Gus was tough on me early on. He gave us all a huge rev-up about being late for training, and said he'd cut anyone who didn't get there on time. Well, I made sure I set my alarm for training coming up to an important game against Parramatta. Except ... I set it wrongly. Just an honest mistake. When I finally got to the ground Gus gave me an absolutely filthy look and said, 'You're in reserve grade.' I had a shocker. I tried hard, but played like a log. Geoff Gerard was the reserve grade coach and he was crook on me.

With Gus and me in those early days, it gets back to what I was saying about his unique ability to read character. He could see a young bloke learning about life and bound to make mistakes along the way. Some things I could get away with, and for others he'd pull me into line at exactly the right time. I was rough around the edges and impressionable. The train was moving, but a derailment was never too far down the track. Two major incidents prevented that, and Gus was instrumental in both.

Back from the Kangaroo tour and massively overweight, Gus hauled me over the coals and told me to wake up to myself. I've described that incident and its profound effect on me in a previous chapter. A year later, unable to dodge the pitfalls of a serious social life, I was convinced it'd better if I moved in with Gus. He offered me that opportunity, and I knew I wasn't playing good footy at the time, so I grabbed it.

I was still only new to the game when Gus took over as coach, but the thing that struck me most was his work ethic. He knew more about the game, more about us, more about the opposition through sheer weight of study and analysis, than anyone I'd known. He could tell you — and did — the hand in which every member of the opposing team preferred to carry the ball, and which foot that person preferred to sidestep off. Before each game we'd go through the whole opposing team, with Gus saying, 'He's a right hand carry, left foot step', or whatever. He'd know if a player missed tackles on his right side or his left. We'd go through all that in a video session a few days before the game, then get notes about it. It was like having a racing form guide on every runner up against us. I suppose that's where Gus got the format, racetrack punter that he is. And if we sucked in some of that information, we had to be better players. I swear he knew what each of them had for breakfast on match morning. I'm sure Gus had been doing that at Canterbury before he came to Penrith. But it was an eye-opener to us.

What it did, too, was inspire us as players to learn more about the game. We thought we knew it all until Gus came, and then we found out we really only *thought* we did. Having a player of Brandy's calibre allowed us to use this knowledge to advantage. We had set plays from every part of the field. For instance, if the ball landed in our back left corner from an opposition kick, we knew to move it across, then back one for Brandy's kick. Footy became easy, play-by-numbers almost, with Brandy leading us around. It was carefully choreographed, and then, when one of us made a break, we played footy, so the tries rarely looked programmed. But the year we won the premiership, there was never a game without a tightly controlled match plan. If things looked like going belly-up, we fell back on the match plan and it rarely let us down. No team ever won a Grand Final — certainly in my time — without a game plan to go to under pressure.

The set plays I'm talking about at Penrith were colour-coded. You had red plays and brown plays and yellow plays, and everyone knew them. It was like actors' scripts. I knew the lock's job, the prop's job, the second-rower's job, and could have filled any of those gaps at any time. Any of us could have. You knew their scripts as well as yours. Brandy was the director, and he called the plays, and you knew when the ball would be coming to you. Compared with what I'd known Before Gus, this was revolutionary.

Before games Gus would quietly go around to every player, reminding him of his task and the plan. We had some tough players who set out to intimidate and didn't need to be revved up by fire-and-brimstone speeches before games. But Gus could get emotional and fired up — make no mistake about that. There was a game against St George at Penrith where we led clearly at half-time and hung on desperately to win by just 2 points, 14–12. Gus was upset, to say the least. He was yelling and screaming at us. There was always a giant tub of beer, soft drink and ice in the dressing room after a game. At the height of his rage, Gus kicked the tub as hard as he could. Everyone winced, knowing it must have hurt. He said nothing for a few seconds, then cried out at the top of his voice, 'F--- that hurt!' Everyone broke up. So did his foot. He was limping for days. At least it saved us from another ten minutes of ranting and raving.

Bob Fulton was the next top coach I came in contact with, in the Kangaroo teams of 1990 and 1994. A lot of what he based his work on was the simple fact that Australia had the best team and the best players. He instilled confidence. He emphasised taking control and going forward. There was a game plan, but never so carefully constructed that it watered down natural skills. I remember going into every game under Bozo pretty much knowing we were going to win. In video sessions he only showed us the negative aspects of the opposition, always pointing out their weaknesses.

As a player, I'm told, Bozo was a fitness fanatic. I never saw him play, but he brought that fitness obsession to his coaching. We trained every day on those tours, rain, hail or snow. Worse than that, we even trained among the dog droppings at a ground in Manchester we called 'Dog-shit Park'. When you hit the tackling bag you had to watch where you fell. Splat! It didn't bother Bozo, though. You trained no matter what, and no matter where. I had the utmost respect for him.

The State of Origin coaches provided a terrific contrast. Jack Gibson was the first, and he was ... well, interesting. I was young then, and I found Jack very weird. It was the things he said more than the things he did. One of the first training sessions with him was at David Phillips Field in Kingsford, in Sydney's east, and the thing he emphasised most was this: 'Whatever you do, don't play tennis or squash.' Now, I couldn't work out what the heck that had to do with training for a State of Origin rugby league match. None at all, as far as I could see. Like I said, he was unusual.

Anyway, there was no Origin camp then — you trained and you went home, and by the time you came back tennis or squash were never mentioned again. In fact, I never even thought about that comment again until the year the Roosters won the premiership, a decade later. In the middle of that year I played tennis with a friend and twisted my knee. Jack had been right: it was a stupid thing to be doing. Not so weird after all.

Jack said something else which was gobbledegook at the time. 'Fred,' he said to me, 'you can never kick a ball high enough.' I had no idea what that meant. Until we played Canberra a dozen years later, trailing with a minute to go, desperate, and Jack's words came into my brain. I booted the ball as high as I could and Clinton Schifcofske, normally safe under pressure, dropped it. We won the scrum, and Brett Finch put someone over for a try. It was all down to a chance remark by Jack Gibson that had sounded like nonsense at the time.

Then there was Tommy Raudonikis, a breath of fresh air as Origin coach in 1997 and 1998. He'd make these outrageous and extremely crude comments. I enjoyed it; I thought he was hilarious. And it engendered a tremendous camaraderie and team spirit in the Blues. Detailed match plans weren't Tommy's go. He coached as he played — get ready for the contest, and rip in regardless. He'd consult the players first, rather than us getting advice from him. 'Whadda youse think?' he'd say. Tommy just made sure you were ready for the stink.

Contrast that with Wayne 'Junior' Pearce, the Blues coach for three years between 1999 and 2001. He had a massive passion for the game in general and for State of Origin in particular. He had a more serious approach, completely the opposite of Tommy. His style was was more stern and immediate. State of Origin was always renowned for team-mates getting together over a beer, and Junior didn't touch alcohol, so he came up with an unusual bonding session in his first year. Unusual — and disastrous, as it turned out.

Before the first match he took us up to Megalong Valley in the Blue Mountains west of Sydney, where the plan was to go horse riding as a group during the day, and engage in some self-expression and singing around a campfire at a mountain lodge in the evening. It seemed like a good idea at the time. And I loved it — it was cool by me. There were half a dozen of us confident about riding horses, and the rest were petrified. Brad Clyde and a few of the others were scared to get their horses out of a slow walk. Anyway, those of us brave enough and confident enough took off together at full gallop, playing Man from Snowy River, over hills and mountains. It was fantastic. We waited until we were out of view so as not to spook the rest of the horses.

Later on we caught up with the slow walkers, but it was too gentle. We moved to the side and broke into a canter, which immediately sent Brad Clyde and his lot into a full-scale gallop. They were out of control. Robbie Kearns fell off his horse onto rocks and broke his collarbone. He was knocked unconscious, and was dazed and bleeding. Clydey tumbled out of the saddle, too, and damaged his shoulder. Bryan Fletcher got his foot caught in some wire. The end result was that Kearns and Clyde missed the series. And abseiling the next day was cancelled. All our fault, I'm afraid. Mine, and the would-be Men from Snowy River!

To Junior's credit, he stayed strong under great pressure that first year when the Blues lost the opening game 9–8 when Mat Rogers scored all of Queensland's points, then levelled up 12–8 in the second, and drew the last game 10–all. We wiped the floor with a sub-standard Queensland team the following year, and then in 2001 ... well, I've put that out of my memory.

Chris Anderson as Kangaroo coach had a style I really liked. It was that flat-line attack, much favoured by the likes of Brett Kimmorley, who flourished under Anderson. That type of footy — very different, really — encouraged us to use the ball as much as possible. And it asked huge questions of the defence, with a side as strong and fit and fast as the Australians coming at it all the time. Chris is a bloke who handles pressure tremendously well, but he's obviously one who does it by showing a calm exterior and bottling it up inside — to the disadvantage of his own health. That showed up in 2001 when he was taken to hospital just before half-time in the third Test at Wigan, suffering chest pains, later diagnosed as a heart attack. At the interval the team manager told me, as the captain, and Joey Johns, and asked if we needed any assistance in the second half. I said, 'No, we're OK.' We were going all right, and just a couple of minutes into the second half we extended our lead even further. We were really concerned about Chris, but the best we could do to ease his pain was play as well as we could and win the Test, which we did by 20 points.

In situations where we were behind in games, or perhaps not playing as well as we should, Chris would never convey that to the players. The week after a win was the same as the week after a loss. I always found it quite incredible, how calm he was in tight situations. One area where he differed totally from other coaches was the last training session before a game. He never asked us to run at more than half pace. No point, he'd say, in leaving your best on the training paddock. The last session was always at half pace or slower. I found it kept us calm and fresh. And the bottom line is he made it a pleasant experience as well as an honour to play for Australia. He was liked and respected.

© NEWSPIX

LEFT The stand-out moment of my career: captaining the Roosters to win the NRL premiership in 2002.

© NEWSPIX

RIGHT Launching a Warrior missile. Richard Villasanti goes in head first in the 2002 Grand Final.

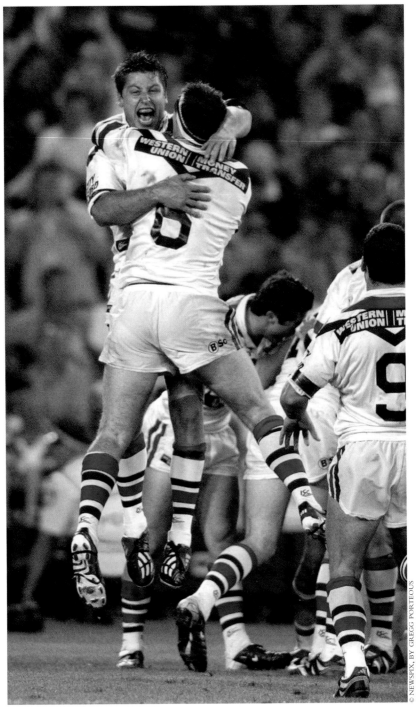

ABOVE Sharing the joy of a Grand Final win with my great mate and fellow Rooster, Luke Ricketson.

ABOVE LEFT Back for the Blues — State of Origin comeback in 2004.

ABOVE RIGHT The fairytale: a try in the decider and victory for the Blues in my 2004 return.

ABOVE With my mum, Christine, after the Origin comeback. She has always been my greatest fan and supporter.

RIGHT With another loyal supporter, Blues coach Phil Gould, at Telstra Stadium after the series triumph in 2004. A good mate repaid.

LEFT My last club game for the Roosters at Aussie Stadium. How overwhelming that people would stand in the lightning and hail just to say goodbye.

BELOW Boots 'n' all: talking tactics with Roosters coach and great friend Ricky Stuart in the dressing room.

ABOVE Leading out the Roosters for the 2004 Grand Final. You never forget a moment like this.

ABOVE In Sydney with Christopher Reeve, the most inspirational man I've ever met. Ricky Stuart and Peter Cusack look on.

BELOW With my favourite Aussie sportsman and boyhood hero, Greg Norman. Ryan Girdler and AFL player Robert Harvey look on.

ABOVE LEFT Marie and me on our way to the Dally M awards. No medal ever shone as brightly as Marie.

ABOVE RIGHT Demi at birth, so beautiful and vulnerable. A gift from the gods.

ABOVE My sister, Kate, and her husband, Jay, on their wedding day in January 2004. My brother, Nathan, and Mum stand next to the bride.

LEFT At my father's property: my brother Nathan (L), father Robert (centre) and me.

ABOVE Demi, and the miracle of birth.

ABOVE RIGHT 'So you're my mum!' Instant bonding between mother and child: Demi and Marie face to face for the first time.

ABOVE Mucking around with Demi, me and the camera, feet first.

BELOW A couple of kids at play: Demi and Dad.

ABOVE Doing the devil's work: mother and daughter looking 'horny', New Year's Eve 2004.

LEFT In photography, I've learned that the subject is everything. I just had to ask this couple in the Royal Botanic Gardens: 'Mind if I take your picture?'

BELOW I snapped this gentle shot of team-mate Peter Cusack strolling along an English country lane during the World Club Challenge in 2003.

ABOVE AND BELOW The ever-changing views of Sydney Harbour caught on camera from my apartment balcony.

In contrast, under Ricky Stuart our final sessions at the Roosters were invariably tough and fast, and we had tremendous success. So I guess the jury's out on that one. Early in Ricky's coaching career, Gus helped him out a little bit as far as being prepared and working hard. Ricky's passionate and has always done his homework. He works his butt off, and works the team devilishly hard, yet remains good mates with the players, and that's an extremely difficult thing to achieve. Ricky's very intense on game day. I hope I'm wrong, but he's in line for a heart attack, too, I think. He'll be one of the all-time great coaches.

I haven't been able to put my finger on exactly what makes a good coach. I know this much: you don't have to have been a good player to succeed as a coach. And just because you've been a good player doesn't necessarily mean you'll be a good coach. Some people just have a knack for it, an ability to transfer information to you in a way that's informative and understanding and passionate. You don't have to be particularly eloquent, either. Tommy Raudonikis is a perfect example of a bloke who had the knowledge, and a rare ability to drive a team to victory, without the grasp of vocabulary to deliver the stirring dressing-room speeches of a Gus Gould. His passion was enough — it painted a thousand words.

To captains now, and it's appropriate to start with the first and one of the most inspirational: Royce Simmons. I was fortunate enough to be able to spend some extra time with him as a young player, because in 1990 and 1991 we'd do extra training in the boxing gym once or twice a week. Just watching him working so hard, even in the twilight of his career, moved me to want to achieve as much as I could in the game. He was also the toughest bloke I've played with or against. Career-threatening injuries were nothing to him; he played right through them. That Penrith Grand Final win in 1991 is a stand-out example of his courage.

Brandy Alexander took over as captain for Penrith's premiership year in 1991, and he was an obvious choice because he so dominated everything we did on the field. More than any other captain, Brandy led by the power of his own skills. He knew where the ball was going minutes before it got there. He knew instinctively when to take on the defensive line and when not to. I followed him, and admired him. I have few better friends.

I was also lucky enough to play a few games under Mal Meninga in the Australian team. I'd held him in high regard for years. I found him to be a no-nonsense player, never given to foul play under any circumstances. I couldn't help but respect the man. I mentioned in an earlier chapter a game in Townsville against Papua New Guinea that stands out in my mind as one of the great displays of leadership by example, Mal taking charge on his own when the rest of us were turning in indifferent performances. In the last few seasons of my career as a captain, I tried to follow a lot of what Mal did. That is, pick my time to celebrate with the players, not lead the way to the bar, but be around when I felt I was needed. I understand now that Mal was looking after himself as well, but also doing the best for the team.

Then there was Laurie Daley as my State of Origin captain in 1992, '93 and '94, for a series win in all of those years. For those three matches a year, he did a fantastic job. I particularly admired his dedication when he was troubled by injury. He had an undeserved reputation as a party animal that tended to overshadow the extraordinary commitment he made to getting himself fit and ready for those matches. He was a great believer in paying you a compliment on the field and reinforcing the positive. If you were involved in a good tackle, he'd be the first there to slap you on the back and say, 'Good hit, mate'. And while on State of Origin captains, I do want to mention Danny Buderus in 2004. When you talk about strength and depth of character, you can't go past this bloke. He's salt of the earth. I'm a terrific wrap for him.

To players, and again I'm not ranking them in order, but I did admire Allan Langer so much. What he did for Queensland and for the Broncos can never be underestimated. He's the best club player I've seen, and by that I mean the bloke who, above all others, devoted himself to the team he represented. You always felt with Alfie that it was never about him, and always about the team. He's just a really likable character, and funny as hell. I'll never forget the sight of him sitting on the bonnet of a car in France on the 1990 Kangaroo tour, hanging onto the windscreen wipers for dear life as the car sped through the snow at about 60 km/h in one of his many pranks that went a little bit awry but ended safely.

Players who changed the game have a special place in my memory, too. Andrew Johns is one of those, as innovative a player as there's been in my time. When he and his brother, Matthew, introduced those angled, deceptive screw kicks that devastated opposition teams, it made us all re-examine our games. They pushed the boundaries. I'm sure the moves were well rehearsed — they pulled them off time after time in matches. And every time they did, another halfback or five-eighth or appointed kicker in the other team went back to the drawing board. Some of the most enjoyable challenges of my career were matches where I was playing against Joey, and before him, against Laurie Daley. I always tried to be perfectly prepared against those two. If I wasn't, it was curtains. Joey and I had some terrific and thoroughly enjoyable battles. For mine, he took footy to a new level.

I got the better of Joey once, in a semi-final in 2000, when I took an intercept from him and bolted away under the posts. It was the start of a second-half comeback and a win for the Roosters. The following year we played Newcastle in the semi-final, and they were all over us. It's funny in football, but when you've got the better of someone, and you know it, you just want to ram it home — make sure they know it as well. It's not a nasty thing, just good, healthy competition. And Joey knew he had the better of me and my team that day. I was in the defensive line, and he came at me. We locked gazes. He didn't bother about looking for a support player, or kicking around or over me. He could have done any of those things and most likely scored. Very deliberately, he chose to take me on because he knew he had the better of me that day. He stood me up cold, and scored.

And I'll throw in an underrated player that many won't even remember — he never made State of Origin, never made a Test team. He's the old Penrith lock Colin van der Voort. In our Grand Final win he opposed Canberra's Brad Clyde, who was acknowledged as the best lock in the world. Truth is, I wouldn't have swapped Vandy for anyone, Brad Clyde included.

Finally, to referees, and it's Bill Harrigan by a country mile. He was a leader in the field; a leader in fitness as well. I always found him to be a man of action and decision. That's what referees were lacking in my final seasons. I think that unless another Bill Harrigan bobs up soon among the ranks of premiership referees, the League is in huge trouble. Refereeing is in danger of falling apart at the seams. The problem is that referees won't make a decision. They are too reliant on others — the touch judge, the video referee, the judiciary panel. Taking responsibility away from the refs is only making them weaker. Bill Harrigan made mistakes, sure — we all do — but he made decisions and stuck by them, and I admired him for that.

Some thoughts, perhaps, on the game of rugby league as it is now, and how it can be in the future. Just as the future of the country lies in educating our children, so the future of this game depends on proper coaching of kids. I'd love to see other retired players come back to help out at the junior level. Some have, like my old friend David Riolo, and Marty Moore, and the League ought to encourage their participation and education as coaches. I know the League has excellent coaching programs in place already, and I think that's absolutely vital.

The standard of teenagers playing the game is exceptional. I watch players coming straight from school — Karmichael Hunt is the perfect example — and they carve up the senior ranks. It's getting to be a young man's game. You need speed and strength. It's extraordinary how robust and mature they are, so much more so than in my era. They're attacking weights in training far younger, and by the time they hit first grade, they're as big and as tough as tanks. I have no doubt that more teenagers will start to come into first grade, and my records as youngest State of Origin and Kangaroo player won't last long.

We've seen clubs struggle financially and that will continue. But I won't have it that players are overpaid. Millions of dollars change hands for TV and radio rights. Players deserve some of that. I hear it all the time: all you do is play footy, and you make barrels of money. Others earn their money pushing a pen, or operating a computer or driving a truck, and get paid their wage for forty hours' work. The pressure on a first-grade rugby league player never stops. It's constant from the first day of the week until game day. For me, every waking hour is devoted to the game. Or, at least, it was when I played. It isn't your run-of-the-mill job. No complaints, of course — I loved it, and lived for it. But most workers don't go to the office injured and concerned over what effects all this crash-bang-wallop week after week will have on their long-term health. I've spoken to leading players about their retirement — people like Paul Harragon. He's working about five jobs at the moment, he says, and still has twice as much free time as he ever had as a football player. It ain't easy, I'm telling you. It's not just eighty minutes a week and your name in the paper. It's all-consuming.

And not everyone's on $400 000 a season. Many first graders are on $50 to $60 000. They don't train any less. They still have to pay insurance and medical bills and tax. There's no time for another income.

I agree with a salary cap to curb the spending, but the salary ought to rise along with cost of living. It's been set at a low figure for too long. I would institute exemptions for players who have stayed loyal to the one club for all or most of their careers. You can always get a little more money by changing clubs, but the tribal nature of the game is best served if club teams stay more or less intact. It stands to reason that players who stick around at the same club are doing the club — and, more importantly, the game — a favour. They should be compensated.

But I don't advocate an age allowance. I don't want older players staying on too long for the sake of a few dollars when they might be blocking the path of young talent unable to make it onto the club roster. Certainly there needs to be more financial responsibility at club management level. One of Jack Gibson's favourite sayings was that a 'good front office makes a good front line'. The Roosters were always like that, soundly managed. So was Penrith early on. The fact that both teams won premierships was inextricably linked with good management as much as playing talent. You can't have the latter without the former.

To expanding the game, and I'm a big supporter of that. I can't understand why the League chose to postpone a decision on whether or not to add a team or teams from the NSW Central Coast, Queensland's Gold Coast and Wellington in New Zealand. There are huge fan bases in those places, money to back the teams, licensed clubs in a couple of instances, and good grounds and enough talent to go around. It's just ridiculous not to take the game to the people. With woolly thinking like that, there would never have been a North Queensland Cowboys to bring joy to so many fans in 2004, and so much concern to the Roosters in that preliminary final.

As for the final series, I'm backing a final eight against a final five. It gives an opportunity for emerging clubs like North Queensland to force their way in and gain experience of finals footy, as well as some extra funds.

Where I do compliment the League is in instituting counselling for players on the treatment of women and the abuse of alcohol. The image of the game has taken a battering over these issues. In many cases you're talking about young people with limited education coming straight into an arena where they are well paid and hero-worshipped by fans. That can be a lethal combination. But I think it's grossly unfair to single out footballers in general, and rugby league players in particular.

At a presentation in one of the country's best-regarded tertiary institutions, I observed — and participated in — larrikin behaviour no footballer I've ever seen would even dream about. If there's a problem with abuse of alcohol and women, it's a community problem, not just a football one. Social responsibility is one thing, but who wants to grow up too quickly? There's a difference between being irresponsible and being unlawful, and it's not a fine line. Being derogatory or intimidating to women is unacceptable. Drinking to the point where you don't know what you're doing, or are being an irresponsible hooligan, is equally unacceptable. But partying hard is not. You shouldn't forget that these are not worldly kids in a lot of cases. They're straight out of school, and often not from 'good' schools. You can't expect to hold them back on a short leash all the time. You have to let them live.

As for bonding sessions over a quiet drink, it's not just footballers who do that. Corporations do it. Business executives do it. Film cast and crew do it. And their camaraderie is enhanced by it. I played in teams all the time where your fate depended totally on the trust and faith you had in the bloke next to you on the field, and the faith he had in you. You have to know these people in depth, personally and privately. You have to know what makes them tick.

It's not like working in an office. If a workmate in your office has issues and you don't know him or her well enough to understand that, then maybe that might lead to a disagreement or a project being a little late. If it happens on the football field, you could lose the game or a limb, or both. When there's gossip, in an office at worst you hear it discussed around the water cooler the next day. Footballers do it and it's all over the front page for days, and some have their careers and their personal lives shattered. Where's the equity in that? OK, so we are high profile, and have a role model status. That's fine. But I repeat: many are just kids, fresh out of school. Rub them out if they're drunken hooligans and abusive or disrespectful towards women. I said earlier, and I repeat, that is simply unacceptable. But cut them just a little slack. I make that plea on behalf of the young players of the future, as I look to my own.

the final curtain

Despite a slump in form late in the 2004 season, the Roosters still managed to carry off the $100 000 prize for finishing at the top of the premiership ladder. A lot of the credit has to go to Ricky Stuart. He took much of the weight off my shoulders with a simple formula: 'I want the ball to go to Brad when he wants it, not when you want to give it to him', he told the team more than once. He maintained that when we were in trouble, players threw me the ball and banked on me to get us out of it. That became harder and harder as the years marched on. Ricky recognised that, and got much more out of players like Brett Finch by giving them additional responsibility.

Given the extra wear and tear of the Origin games on me, Ricky occasionally pulled me out of training early. I didn't like it because I didn't want to let anyone down, but it kept me going. 'If I pull you out,' Ricky would say, 'I'm doing it for a reason. The team knows your value on game day, not on training day. I like to see you having fun, being first here, kicking the ball round like you're fifteen again, not drained of energy at the end.'

Probably the last week of the premiership was the hardest for me because of the demands on my time, and that old problem with having the spotlight on me. I can play football in front of 100 000 people and not have a trace of anxiety. I'm in my shorts and boots and footy jumper, and it's natural. It's my comfort zone. It's a different story in a suit and tie, standing up to make a speech, or doing a TV interview, or appearing at a function. Over the years I've become better at it by following advice like taking deep, controlled breaths and slowing down for a moment when I get panicky, but I still have anxiety attacks. I can't tell you how much time I've spent in a function room or leagues club toilet, stripped of my suit, tie, shirt and pants, wiping down full-body sweats with toilet paper. That's happened on at least half a dozen occasions.

I used to get stressed about a month before a function. I'd have thoughts about where I'd be placed in the room, hopefully so I could make a quick exit, unnoticed. I'd start to get claustrophobic just thinking about it. These thoughts would swirl around my head every day and night for a month. I had many sleepless nights. And I'm sure the problem I've had since I was eighteen with the skin disease psoriasis stems from that stress and anxiety. One breeds off the other. I stress over whether a skin rash might break out on my face when I go to a function three weeks down the track, and then I stress even more over the function itself.

So it's in this light, with my problems with anxiety attacks, that I faced up to a tribute dinner for me on 31 August 2004 at the Shrangri-La Hotel in Sydney, then the last home game against the Parramatta Eels at Aussie Stadium, and all the interviews that accompanied my impending retirement. The focus on me was wearing, draining and time-consuming. Amazing, too, but difficult to handle. At training at Wentworth Park at the start of that week, Ricky Stuart pulled me aside.

'You've got to be greedy and selfish, mate,' he said. 'A lot of people are going to want a lot of your time. Remember how much it would mean to go out with another Grand Final win. Remember how much it would mean to the other players as well to run a victory lap with you in your last game. Doing just that with Mal Meninga was a highlight of my life. I want you to enjoy yourself. Take the phone off the hook, and don't worry about doing interviews outside the news conferences we organise. Much time and effort goes into making you happy at this club. I want you to be happy, OK?'

I was concerned about going to my tribute dinner, with 500 people and all the hoopla that went with it. I was flattered, of course, but apprehensive. That spotlight thing again. I even rang Greg Alexander on the way there and asked if he'd join me on stage and help me with the speech I was dreading. Years earlier we'd combined to deliver a speech at the University of New England in Armidale. Now, that was rarefied air for a couple of battlers from the bush. I was amazed at the way the teachers and students all got on the drink beforehand, and by the time we got on stage Brandy and I were flying high. We told stories and had the place in uproarious laughter. I stayed there for days afterwards and watched them getting up to all sorts of mischief like car surfing and generally acting the goat, making football players look tame by comparison. So I figured Brandy would help me out this time, too. Of course he said, 'No mate, sorry, you're on your own.'

I figured the best way to relax before the dinner was to meet up with my old schoolmates from St Mary's, and in the swankiest hotel room overlooking the harbour and the Bridge and the Opera House, I shared a drink with the boys I'd mucked around with in the playground at St Mary's High School at age twelve — Fitzy, Boppa, Shippo, Marcus, Reddo and me, back together again, dressed to the nines, raiding the minibar in a suite at the Shrangri-La instead of the tuckshop fridge at school.

Then we all went down to the ballroom in the lift and were confronted by half a dozen television and still cameras, and people everywhere. Reality hit home in a flash, literally. The boys were off. And I was right in the thick of it. Marie and I were shaking. The room was spectacular, and when I got to our table I picked up the menu and read the words of welcome from Greg Alexander, who'd written, 'I knew him as a fifteen-year-old mate of my younger brother, Ben. The only disappointment

Freddy will ever cause me is retiring. I wish he could play for ever. Thanks for the memories, my friend.' It was all I could do to stop crying. It set the tone for one of the most astonishing evenings of my life. It was truly overwhelming, all these powerful people saying such nice things about me. I never expected it, and I couldn't imagine how I'd deserved it.

I had a speech prepared in different forms, one written out fully in case I wasn't coping and another in dot points in the event I was feeling comfortable. In the end, I used neither. Following speakers like Nick Politis, Gus Gould and Alan Jones, it wasn't going to do me any good holding up a couple of flimsy bits of paper and waving them in the air. I guess because I spoke from the heart it all came out OK. How many people get to publicly thank those who have helped them along the way? That's a rare privilege. And it raised $150 000 for the Children's Hospital too. I told Wayne Beavis I'd only ever be part of a testimonial or tribute dinner if all the money raised went to charity. I should say this: you did an unbelievable job in making that evening happen, Beaver, and I'll never forget it. The night ended in the pub next door at around 4 a.m. with a happy, fun-loving group of mates swapping yarns and telling lies. Words can't describe the experience.

At the end of that week I had my last competition home game, against Parramatta at Aussie Stadium. As usual the team stayed in a hotel the night before the game, and as we were about to leave for the ground I caught a segment on the Sunday *Footy Show*, a tribute to my career. The tears welled up again. We always have a team meeting before we leave the hotel, and I turned up red-eyed.

It was an important game with a lot at stake, what with the minor premiership and the six-figure prizemoney that went with it. I knew the boys were primed. Just as we were about to take the field I called everybody together in a huddle and said, simply, 'It's been a pleasure.' I was about to start crying again, so to hell with the big speech, I just broke off and ran out onto the field. A try a couple of minutes in came as no surprise. I cut to the right in a classic scissors movement and handed it onto Craig Wing for a try in the corner. It was a procession from then on, and finished up 48–10. It all might have been a bit dull and boring save for a spectacular storm that sent down lightning and hailstones.

I find it hard to speak about doing that lap of honour at the end of the game. Several thousand people stayed out in those conditions just to wave goodbye to me. I don't like to dwell on how or why I've had such an impact on their lives; it could play around with my head, that stuff. My feeling as it was happening was that it couldn't be real. If I'd imagined it was real, it would have been impossible to keep my feet on the ground. All I can do now is thank them for making it another special day.

I didn't stay long at the club afterwards; as soon as the essentials were done I was off home to see Demi and Marie. It'd been two days, and that was two days too many. It was Fathers' Day, too. There was an unbelievable present waiting for me. I said to Marie, 'Is Demi awake? She can help me unpack my bags.' Well, not only was she awake — she crawled for the first time. How's that for an end to an amazing day?

The next morning's newspapers carried the page one headline, 'All Hail Freddy!', and a picture of me waving to the crowd as hailstones pelted down. Trouble is, you don't stay on top very long in this business. After the game I asked the Roosters management if I could have a rest from media engagements for a few days. I wasn't tired, or fatigued or anything. The truth is this: I was sick of seeing myself on TV and in the newspapers and hearing about myself on radio, and I figured so was everybody else. I was trying to do you all a favour, not get out of commitments. Under normal circumstances I would have attended a gathering of team captains involved in the finals series. It's a traditional photo opportunity on the Monday before the finals start, to publicise the series. With the approval of management I declined to attend, and they sent a very able substitute in the club's longest-serving player, Luke Ricketson. I've missed it before, and other captains have missed it before, too.

Well, the next day's newspapers gave me an absolute

hammering. I was caught on camera at our regular team pool session only a couple of hundred metres from where the captains had gathered. Nothing unusual about that — we always go to the pool the day after the game. Look, the bottom line is this: I was paid by the Roosters, and I was there for them. But let me say again, I was just sick of seeing my image in the damn paper, and I was certain everybody else was, too. Maybe I could've turned up and loafed through it, but I'm not there to please the NRL and jump when they say 'jump'. Anyway, they got an extra couple of days' publicity out of me by giving me a kicking. There was a week's worth of positive promotion for the game out of my tribute dinner and final match, then more by kicking the tripe out of me. The newspapers got a front page story one day out of my celebrations, and another the next day, out of my tribulations. That's why I just have to accept it, and not take it all personally, or even seriously.

The ironic thing is that no club in the game is more concerned about player discipline and public appearance and image than the Roosters. And it doesn't mean coaches and managers are on the lookout for breaches all the time. The players toe the line, unprompted. If a team-mate is seen being rude to a fan, or even slightly ignorant or ill-mannered, he'll be chipped by the closest player. If a player turns up late, his team-mates will give him a gentle reminder to be on time. If he does it again, the reminder won't be quite so gentle. But it comes from the team; we don't need to hear it from management.

A blot on one bloke is a blot on the whole team. That sort of attitude helps the young guys grow and mature, not just as players, but as men. And I watched them develop with immense pride in the last couple of years, players like Craig Fitzgibbon, Craig Wing, Chris Flannery and Brett Finch have all grown in stature and responsibility. They have fun, sure, but they know when to switch on, and I'd be the first one to chip them if they forgot.

Luke Ricketson is an interesting case study. He's got this playboy image, and certainly loves nothing better than a night out with the boys. I found in my later seasons that I couldn't go out at night and still be first to training the next day. 'Ricko' could. He'd have a night out but still be first to training, and train harder than anyone else. He was a shining example of combining fun with professionalism. There was never a hint of slackening off when it was time to work. Ricko is a fitness machine. And he'll make an outstanding captain, too.

There was a lot of talk of a so-called siege mentality at the Roosters, an us-and-them scenario similar to that which fired up the Broncos in the nineties. It's true that Ricky Stuart used that as a motivational tool; sometimes he went out of his way to create situations like that. He's a smart bloke and he knows what drives his players to new heights. When the papers give you a pasting, you can use that to your advantage. But reaction to criticism about being supported by the big end of town and the like was not in the manner of a club suffering from paranoia. I didn't feel like anyone was out to get us. It's just that the Roosters tried very hard to raise the game to a new level. And by doing so, we became a target. We pushed the barriers all the time. If we were disliked, it was jealousy because we created a culture of winning. The Roosters have to keep pushing the NRL, and that's good for the game. It keeps the game's minders on their toes. And it raises standards all round.

One problem it did create for the Roosters was always giving away the advantage of being the underdog. Everyone in this country loves an underdog. The underdog has nothing to lose; the favourite is a large and vulnerable and exposed target. When first markets came out for the premiership each year, we were always at the top. The tall poppy syndrome was alive and well. That's why supporting each other when everyone else wanted us to lose was so vital.

It was essential for the Roosters, more than any other club, to develop a close-knit unbreakable bond that others mistook for siege mentality. The Roosters came first, and anything else — including, at times, the needs of the NRL — came second. What was the result? The Roosters made four Grand Finals in my time at the club. They won one of those. On my last game day, all three grades were in Grand Finals. We won two of those. If developing this so-called siege mentality works for you, then go for it, I say. Maybe other clubs would do well to follow the Roosters' example, from management on down. It's a winning formula, simple as that.

Shaping a group of disparate men into a winning combination is a fascinating exercise. Young and old, quiet and rowdy, small and large, it takes all kinds. Some, like Chris Walker, always seeing their names and pictures in the paper. Others, like Adrian Morley, preferred being out of the limelight. You've got your playboys and your likable young lads and your stay-at-homes; your serious ones and your mad men. People who enjoy sipping a quiet beer, and others who become crazed animals on it. The Roosters were made up of all these personalities. The thinkers, the dreamers, the smart, the dumb, the space cadets and the lunatics. How do you successfully fuse them into a machine that conquers all? I think the answer lies in understanding, respect, care, forgiveness and compassion.

It's a brutal game. Tough men play it. But they won't survive in it without support from team-mates, with everyone drawing on each other. It's like a big family. There will always be bust-ups and black sheep, but you get nowhere with insults and admonishment and banishment. Father Chris Riley from Youth Off The Streets deals with particularly violent and abusive young lads and lasses, some of them the worst of the worst. He succeeds more often than not with what he calls 'tough love'. It's a term that applies to formulating a cohesive football team, too.

In my experience, the Roosters were a great big bunch of happy blokes. If there was ever an issue it was brought out, debated and resolved, not swept aside and allowed to simmer. An example: the Justin Hodges matter. He was a young bloke who came to the Roosters from Queensland, unsettled and unsure, and he disappeared back home. He didn't want to be in Sydney. When he returned to us, the first thing he did was come to the players and say, in front of all of us, 'I'm here to stay. I'm going to put the work in. I hope you'll have me back. I need your support.'

For Justin's good and the good of the team, there was resounding acceptance and care and understanding. People go through ups and downs, and personal crisis at times, whether you're a high-class football player or a housewife or you sell shoes in Myer. You make allowances for that. Like I said, the team only works through understanding, respect, care, forgiveness and compassion. They're not words you hear regularly in conversation about rugby league. But they are as important to winning a premiership as kick, tackle, pass and intimidate. Justin Hodges, in the centres, became a crucial part of our run to the Grand Final. He could've been lost to us. For weeks players sent him text messages of support and best wishes. The same thing happened when Anthony Minichiello ran into strife before State of Origin. It might've been text messages on a mobile phone that got him into trouble in the first place, but it was text messages of support from all his team-mates that propped up his spirits in those troubling times.

It often falls to the captain to help with form slumps that happen to every player from time to time. The coach can't do it all. You counsel the player, see if everything's right in his life outside the game. I had a valuable experience with one-on-one counselling regarding Brett Finch. He came to the Roosters from Canberra in 2003. We played the Raiders at Canberra Stadium late in 2002 and flogged them. It wasn't a usual occurrence down there. In fact, the Roosters broke an eleven-year drought in the national capital that day and it was my first ever win there. Finchy had a shocker for Canberra. We knew he was about to join our club. I shook his hand at the end and said, 'Very disappointed in you, mate. That was very ordinary.' Raiders captain Simon Woolford looked at Finchy and said, 'Did he just say what I think he said?' Brett replied, 'He did.' When Finchy came to us the next season, he told me he had been distressed for weeks over that. It was a lesson learned in being too brutally honest with young people in particular.

What you say as an experienced person sticks in their minds, and it haunts and hurts. Positive reinforcement works a whole lot better.

I just wish I had something positive to say about Grand Final day, 2004. Do I have to tell you about it? Guess so. But this ain't gonna be easy.

saving the worst
till last

And so to the finals series for the last time. Far from being nervous and apprehensive about the end, I was feeling particularly relaxed. For three or four years prior I'd tried very hard to lead by example at the Roosters. I'd deliberately tried to be first at everything: first to training, first to functions, first to the weights, first to drinks, if we were up for it. As the seasons wore on, age took its toll, and the arrival of Demi made further demands on my time, so that became increasingly difficult. Even with things like maintaining the right body language, not looking tired with head down or hands on hips. I was purposely trying to set an example for everyone else in everything I did, and I think that was the difference between me as a 'learner leader' in the nineties and a halfway decent one in the new millennium. But I can tell you that it's extremely taxing.

So as the end drew near, I got into the habit of noting in my head how many sprint sessions were left in my life, how many video sessions, how many weight sessions. Three of them to go ... two of those to go ... That sort of thing. I'd play it all out in my brain as the calendar wore down to what I hoped would be another Grand Final appearance. Perhaps even another premiership.

Canberra was the first finals stumbling block, and we were expected to win. It was tough for a short while. We knew they'd be aggressive. I always felt there was a similarity between that Canberra side and coming up against a side like New Zealand. I think the game plans were based on their opposition, and if that didn't work they had nothing to fall back on. They'd be pumped up in the rooms beforehand, thinking that if they bustled and belted early, they'd put you off your game. But they never did. I can't believe they didn't try something different. So Canberra came with that attitude again, smacking blokes high and ripping in early as if we might back off under pressure. Of course that was never going to happen. I suppose it's down to the coach to set the game plan, but I often think senior players take it on themselves to charge in without thinking about the consequences. And the consequence in that case was that we quite simply smashed them.

We had the week off after that, and we trained hard, especially on the day North Queensland beat the Broncos, a match I watched with a few other players in the Phoenix Hotel at Woollahra. I was always taken with the Cowboys. They were a real team unit. It didn't surprise me in the slightest when they knocked off Brisbane. I knew the Roosters were always going to be up against it facing North Queensland. I thought they were maybe just one player short of being a really top side, capable of winning the premiership.

As the Grand Final qualifier against them drew near, all the talk was that the Roosters only had to turn up to win. That would have been a recipe for disaster if we'd let ourselves believe it. The Cowboys had blokes who could score tries and a good game plan to set them up. And when a team's that high on confidence, they'll take chances that will more often than not pay dividends. It's a particularly difficult situation to prepare for. The obvious thing is to tell your team not to be overconfident. But that's like a prosecutor telling a jury that the bloke on trial did the crime once before, and the judge tells them to strike it from their minds. It's too late; the seed's already planted. It's the same planning for a game you're considered certain to win: the more you tell a team not to be complacent, the more the thought becomes pervasive. The last thing you want to do all week before the match is to say, 'Don't take these blokes easy', because they will. There's nothing surer.

I respected the Cowboys and I rated them highly. Coming into that game, our plan was to keep it pretty simple and run from dummy half as much as possible. Sounds boring, doesn't it? And it was. Maybe Ricky Stuart's plan was to get a tough, grinding win under our belt for the big one a week later. I'm not sure. There would also have been the thought in his mind that, being new and enthusiastic, the Cowboys would be quick off the mark to launch themselves into tackles. Gaps would be created close to the ruck. But — and there's no way to put this kindly — we played stupidly. No one extended themselves. During the game I wasn't all that worried — I always felt we had the class to win. Then they scored a try to level again with not too long remaining, and the thought crossed my mind that if they got into a position to do that one more time we might be in a little strife. Thankfully that wasn't to be, and we hung on to win 19–16 after the Cowboys had first levelled at 6–6, then 10–10 and later at 16–16.

I should talk about the incident in which Luke Ricketson felled their half, Nathan Fien, and therefore missed the Grand Final. As I made a tackle Fien came up and pushed me in the head. It was his first semi-final, and he was a cheeky little half, and I thought, *You're not going to get away with that*. I pushed him back, a little confrontation started, and then Ricko got up to see what he thought was his captain and mate in trouble. He just lashed out without thinking and collected Fien. In the end, I suppose, Fien's niggling worked: it got a player suspended. But I wasn't going to let him slap me in the head and think he'd got one up on me. No guilt from me. It was just a chain of events, something that happened in a second or two. Fighting the grading of the charge at the judiciary later in the week was pretty pointless. The more they showed it, the worse it looked. I did feel so sorry for Ricko. Here's what he told me about the matter:

> Funny, but I've only ever reacted a couple of times like that in my life, and both times it was in support of you, Freddy. It just gets under my skin when they push and shove you. It last happened five years earlier against the Dragons when you were cheap-shotted from behind. Remember that? After the Cowboys game you came up to me and said, 'Thanks, mate, for doing what you did', and that meant heaps to me. Didn't make up for missing the Grand Final, but it was some considerable compensation at least. Then when you rang me and asked if you could come into the judiciary hearing and speak on my behalf, well, I was touched again. It didn't help the cause, but that wasn't your fault.
>
> I'm sorry I wasn't there on the big day. You probably don't remember it, you were that focused, but just before you ran out to take on the Bulldogs I gave you a hug, looked you in the eye, shook your hand and said, 'Let's just get the cash.'

Ricko's right. The only times he's ever been in trouble are when he's come to my aid. It was just one of those unfortunate things.

And so to the Bulldogs in the Grand Final. They were hugely impressive against Penrith in their qualifier; Penrith simply ran out of numbers, ran out of troops. The reserves bench is always vital, but never more so than in a finals series. In the end, there was no one left on the Penrith bench to match up to the Bulldogs.

We knew the Bulldogs would be tough to beat. All week we spoke about hitting their edges — that is, moving their forwards around the field and striking at the line where the half and five-eighth would mostly be, about three or four defenders in from the sideline. The tactic in attack was to belt up the middle a couple of times, then have someone wider steaming onto the ball at the edge at full pace. Canterbury spread their troops and defend the whole field. This plan would open them up. The gaps would surely come. That's what it said in the game plan, anyway.

When you're given a plan like that you have to have faith in it, and believe in it, and implement it as best you can. And it was a fantastic plan. Then the weather turned a bit moist. But we stayed with the plan and paid the penalty, dropping the ball as it went to the edges and the men who were supposed to be creating havoc. We dropped the ball, and we dropped the ball, and we dropped the f---in' ball.

The start was fine, with that try after fifteen minutes from a left-foot screw kick of mine which landed in the lap of Chris Walker. They say you can't teach an old dog new tricks. Well, I'd been practising my left-foot kick for the last dozen weeks of the competition. I just figured it would come in handy one day. Chris Walker signalled to me the play before and it landed perfectly for him. I heard him yell, 'I'm inside ya', and then he called 'Mullo's', which was our call for a kick, named after our old player Brett Mullins, who was such a master at it. When it fell perfectly it was one of those nice, satisfying moments. It must've looked terrific on TV. But then I'm giving away the fact that I was too disappointed to watch a replay of the game. Truth is, I've never seen it, and don't wish to. Maybe one day. But it will be a long time in the future. It's all just too painful right now.

Those left-foot kicks almost paid off again later when I slotted one down the field and Luke Patten just beat me to the ball. I honestly thought for a split second that it was going to sit up the way it did in the State of Origin game on that same field a few months before. But it wasn't to be. It was one of those nights, unfortunately.

I've been asked a few times about what happened with Craig Wing and me in the rooms moments before the Grand Final. Television pictures showed us crash-tackling each other seconds before going out onto the field. Wingy and I worked together in defence, and we made this pact coming into the last ten games that, prior to each game, we'd hit each other harder than we'd hit any of the opposition in the match. There was a solemn pledge between us that no one would run over the top of us. They might beat us with skill, but not with strength. Then we'd go out and be right, if a little sore.

In the rooms before the Grand Final we lined each other up again, twice on the left side and twice on the right each — that's eight huge hits in all — and simply went at it. They reckon the impact was like two bull elephants sorting out their territory. I'll tell you now that there was nothing held back. We were hitting each other damned hard by the end. We found it worked unbelievably well — neither of us got hurt on the field as long as we did that pre-match ritual, as painful as it was. Whoever ran at me on the field could do no worse than Wingy had in the rooms. It made me superconfident in defence. Mind you, both of us had corked shoulders from it, but our confidence and faith in each other was rock hard. It might not work for everyone, but it worked for me. I can't remember anyone getting through us in those last ten weeks.

By half-time I was confident, of course, with that 13–6 lead. It might have been an even bigger margin without the disallowed try in which Anthony Minichiello was found to have impeded defenders by running behind his own player. When I was growing up you couldn't run behind anyone: that was a basic rule of footy. Then one day Brett Kimmorley did it, the powers that be said it was OK because no one was impeded, and the League changed the rule. In English League, if you run behind a player, and regardless of whether there's an obstruction, it's a penalty. Cut and dried. No controversy. Exactly as it should be. After the Kimmorley incident it became a quite stupid rule that evolved into a huge grey area in the game. Each time there was a similar incident it became open to interpretation. That's just creating a rod for your own back. I had no problems with disallowing Minichiello's try. None at all. Run behind, you get penalised. That's it for me. Do yourself a favour, guys — change it back the way it was.

At half-time Ricky made a point of warning us that they'd try to score straight after the break. And that's exactly what Matt Utai did, four minutes in. Then they got the lead with the El Masri try and everything we did to get back fell on its ear. Where it was so frustrating for me was that I didn't think the Bulldogs were on top of their game. They'd played a lot tougher than that. So the game was there to be won, and we really blew it. I'd never felt more like we were going to win a big game, not even in the Grand Final against the Warriors two years earlier. The Bulldogs were there to be beaten.

I didn't want to know about the stats afterwards, things like the fact that the Roosters realised only eleven of nineteen completions. I was living it right there on the field. I thought Michael Crocker was in until Andrew Ryan brought him down. Full marks to the Bulldogs, I suppose. They hung in. But I can't get over the feeling that we gave it to them.

It's not my intention to point the finger at anyone in our team; no one means to drop the ball. It's just that the execution under pressure was bad. That last twenty minutes of the game — effectively the last twenty minutes of the year and the last twenty minutes of my career — ought to be taken down and used as a model for how *not* to play under pressure. The ball would land into a player's breadbasket and simply pop out, or be lost in a tackle. Like I said, no one set out to make that happen. It just did because players were trying too hard, and the pressure continued to build as the clock ticked on.

I knew all along that we needed to score only four points. We needed only one good set of six tackles and the game was ours. There was no point being critical as the game wore down. We had to stay positive, at least outwardly. Anything else would not have helped. When I got the ball I tried to 'die' with it and then work a play. I felt in control of my own game. My defence was the best it had been all year.

When it was over, and the Bulldogs had won 16–13, I sat on the grass and watched them whoop it up in celebration. I had this all-over dead feeling. It sucked. What else can I say? No good shouting and screaming abuse at anyone. I've been disappointed in the past. I pretty much know all the after-match emotions. The worst thing was that it was so winnable. Credit to the Bulldogs: they played smart. Willie Mason had a great game; so did the captain, Andrew Ryan. He was fantastic, a tough country kid who turned in an awesome performance. And Sonny Bill Williams, coming fresh into the finals series, showed flair and maturity beyond his years. Also Matt Utai, scoring a couple.

After the presentations we returned to the rooms, and Ricky Stuart was blunt and honest. He said he'd like to concentrate on the good year we'd had, but he was too thoroughly disappointed and we'd blown it. Ten minutes later he came back and said all the nice things, but I'm glad he got the other stuff off his chest first. He was right: it had been a crucial game of footy and we hadn't handled it.

The only thing that took my mind off all the bad feelings was the thought that Demi had been somewhere in the crowd, and just thinking about her brought a smile to my face. I didn't know it then but Demi had carried on like a proper little she-devil the whole time, kicking and screaming. She'd never been like that before. Mostly she's a little angel. I wonder if she knew Daddy was in for an unhappy night and was making her thoughts on our team's performance known to the world. Poor Mum had to take Demi out behind the stands and watch the game on TV in the takeaway food area as she pushed Demi back and forth in the stroller. I was blissfully unaware of any of that.

I was seated on the cold floor of the dressing room, head between my knees, when Marie brought Demi in, and it was fantastic. My baby had a Roosters jumper on, with number 6 and Demi Fittler on the back. Her little eyes lit up when she saw me, and my spirits suddenly soared. She didn't care less whether we'd won or lost; it didn't matter a fig to her. And, suddenly, it didn't matter to me either. There'd be things in the future much more important than winning or losing a football game. And here was the most important of them all, looking as cute as a button and giggling in my lap, which was still covered in the dirt and grime of Telstra Stadium. For a couple of minutes I was the happiest bloke on earth, at the end of one of the unhappiest days of my football life.

Before the game I had to ask myself what was going to be enough. I placed my emphasis on playing well. After all my experience, I knew I could live with winning or losing. But, à la State of Origin 2001, I wouldn't be able to live with a poor performance. I feel I can hold my head high.

I reckon at that moment Demi came into the dressing room, I solved the ultimate question about the meaning of life: devoting yourself to your children. That's the answer. Funny how inspiration hits you at the most inopportune moments and the most inappropriate places. The PM, John Howard, came into the rooms and I introduced him to Demi. 'Now Demi,' I said, 'this is the head man, the Prime Minister.' Mr Howard said, 'G'day, Demi' and said 'Hello' to Marie and me, and I respect that enormously. He didn't need to acknowledge us. There was no one else around. He did it because he's a good man, not because it might impress someone. I wished him all the best for the election the following week. I've said before that I'm a supporter. The country has always been flying under his leadership.

Back at the club the feeling was pretty dead. But it was, in fact, a terrific day for the Roosters. Grand Final wins in Jersey Flegg and Premier League. A Grand Final appearance in first grade. It was testament to what a lot of people had worked hard to build up over the years. In a small way, it was part of my legacy as well. The club will be attractive to potential players in the future. I had a good night with my old school mates Shippo, Shorty, Boppa and Reddo. It would never have troubled them whether I won or lost. Our mateship was all that counted to them.

Mad Monday was a pretty good drink by my modest standards at that time, a party at the so-called 'house of grouse' occupied by a few of our single players at North Bondi, then to the Charing Cross Hotel in Waverley. It got a bit blurry after that. There was a small drink the next day at a Darlinghurst pub owned by the Australian gridiron player Colin Scotts, then some very nice things said again at the club presentation the next night.

During those couple of days following the Grand Final, I had one last decision to make. An English club, the London Broncos, weighed in with bids of more money than I had ever earned, even during Super League, for me to continue my career. Those offers were made to Wayne Beavis in the week leading up to the Grand Final. The problem was that I'd made a promise to Nick Politis that if I ever changed my mind and played on, it would only ever be with the Roosters. My time with the Roosters was over, but not my loyalty to the place. Quite simply, if I'd had any football left in me it would've been played with the Roosters. I was certainly tempted, though. Marie and I discussed it. It's hard to turn your back on so much money. I said to Beaver, 'Tell them thanks a million, but no thanks.' I discussed it with Tony Rey from London and he was very understanding. Maybe it's something I'll regret in the future.

So for a few days there was too much to do and too much to think about to concern myself with the fact that it was all over. The way I'd spent my life pretty much from the time I was four years old was done. It was all behind me. That notion didn't strike me till about the Thursday, though. Then — and I remember the moment clearly — I sat on the couch, and thought, *What are you going to do?* It was quite scary. Bloody scary. A shiver went up my spine, quite literally, as if someone had just walked on my grave. All those first-class games — 448 of them — and it was over. I'd ridden the 448 Express from Penrith to Sydney, and now it had ground to a halt. I was looking forward to retirement. I was. But I was nervous. I was apprehensive. How was I going to channel my energies into something else? How was I going to stop thinking about football?

starting over

Holidays: that's about all I could work up the energy to think about, in the near future, anyway. The thought of taking a complete break was all-consuming after the Grand Final. No end of season trips with the boys, just a seaside break in Queensland with Marie and Demi, and then a surfing trip to Fiji. If I could take a surfing trip each year with a couple of mates, and not have the worry about getting back in time to train for footy, I'd be the happiest bloke around. Sounds like a simple retirement plan, but I've never had a totally relaxing holiday. There was always the thought of pre-season training around the corner.

If the truth be known, I'm not much of a surfer. World champion Layne Beachley tried to teach me at Long Reef one day when I bumped into her. How embarrassing that was. I tried to convince her I could surf OK when that was a blatant exaggeration. She knew it, too, before we got off the beach. 'Brad,' she said, 'you're not very experienced at this, are you?' I replied, 'How do you know?' Layne looked at me and said, 'Because you've got your wetsuit on back to front and you're about to choke yourself to death.'

My first six months out of the game have mostly been spent renovating my house in Clovelly, in Sydney's east. I'm not much good at that either, but I'm learning from the experts. I'll have a role of some sort at the Roosters, and play a little golf. Maybe I'll coach down the track, although I'd find it terribly difficult to watch from the stands as a team I coached went through its paces. I know if I missed a match during my playing career, sitting on the bench was a nightmare of pain and suffering and frustration. It was just awful. They'd have to chain me up as a coach.

I'll admit to being more than a bit fearful as I look ahead to the next phase of my life. There's nothing like the massive rush of running out through the clearing smoke of fireworks and thundering applause to play a big match in front of 80 000 fans. It's a high no drug could ever give you. As captain you run out first, and whether it's State of Origin, a Test match or a big club game, the adrenaline surges like a tidal wave.

You're so revved up and hyped up, and there are all these people there for you. I can't imagine what long-term effect that will have on my psychological make-up. It can't be good for you. It's dangerous to feel that good, I'm sure. But what I've learned is to accept it for what it was and just be appreciative that I was in that position. There are times, standing there in shorts and jersey waiting for the kick-off, when your whole body feels like exploding. You're positively volcanic. Loved and hated by footy fans with equal and absolute passion. You're lauded in the media one day, kicked in the arse the next. My life has had those fantastic highs and then devastating lows through losses and injury. How do you come down from all of that and live what's a normal life to others, yet something I've not experienced since I was seventeen? The answer is . . . that I don't know the answer.

I think it's in my family and friends. I now get those highs from Demi, and from Marie, and from seeing more of my extended family and mates. When Demi crawled for the first time at eight months, the night I got back after my last home game against Parramatta, my spirits soared through the roof. I'll be banking on highs like that to get me down to normality. I had the other, and now it's time to adjust and move on. I'm told ex-players find they get bored or have too much time on their hands. Hopefully I'll have enough projects to keep me occupied. Sponsors like BMW and adidas are sticking with me. I've got investments, so money shouldn't be a problem.

Mates are important to me, and many of my closest friends have nothing to do with football, going right back to my very early teens. I can't wait to spend a little more time with them, to give back some of the support they've given to me unflinchingly over the years. One of them, Michael 'Shorty' Shortland, whom I've mentioned before as part of the group I met in the playground at St Mary's, came to share the Highgate apartment with me when I first moved from Penrith. Shorty has suffered my trials and tribulations on the phone, and still does, almost every day from most parts of the globe. He wanted his say in these pages and I promised I wouldn't cut anything out, good or bad. So, over to you, Shorty, and be kind:

I always found it extraordinary how Brad could live in this rarefied world of adulation on the footy stage, and then come back and talk about relatively stupid and trivial things with us. I guess that's what helped keep his feet on the ground. You always knew that a call from Brad was never far away.

I'm a futures trader on the stock exchange. Most of my work's done at night. And when Brad was away on tour, he knew that at least I was awake, and he could talk to me from Huddersfield or Paris in the dead of night over here. I'll never forget one call I got from the Kangaroo tour. I was in the middle of trading $10 million in bond futures. But Brad wanted to give me the rundown on this bar he'd just been to in England. I couldn't shake him. The deal went through, and it worked, but in the middle of it I had to pick up the phone from time to time and say, 'Yes mate, no mate', so he thought I was listening.

I can't begin to tell you how generous Brad's been with his circle of friends. Just one example from personal experience. I don't want to embarrass him, but people should know the kind soul that lies within Brad. I was short of enough to buy a house, and without even asking for it he wrote me a cheque for $80 000 — repaid later, of course, but it's just an indication of what he means to us, and I think what we ordinary blokes from his distant past still mean to him.

One thing I've been able to do is take a hands-on role with investments. With the house at Collaroy, I trusted builders and felt I was let down simply because I wasn't around to oversee what was being done. Maybe I was just twenty-three and naive. I saw the ugly side of the renovations craze sweeping Australia. Mistakes were made. I should have been checking up.

Major renovations were required at the Clovelly house, and I wasn't about to make the same error again. After I retired I went up to the TAFE college at Castle Hill in Sydney to get my owner-builder's licence. Can you imagine me sitting at a school desk all day in the heat of a summer afternoon? There I was, with my books and pens. It was hot ... *really* hot. All I can remember is losing focus pretty early. These days, as far as learning goes, I've got the attention span of a grasshopper. If I close my eyes now, all I can recall is the whirring of the ceiling fan overhead. *Voom, voom, voom.* Over and over. Like a horror movie. That and looking blankly out the window. I must have concentrated just enough, though, because I got the licence.

In retirement I've managed to do things I never had time to do when footy was the priority. I've gone parachuting, and I took Marie and my mum, along with a few mates. I'd been tandem skydiving before and knew it was a huge adrenaline burst. Oddly enough, Marie and Mum didn't need all that much convincing. They were apprehensive, but not scared. We all piled into this little plane, flew up to Albion Park south of Sydney, and then threw ourselves out — in tandem, of course, with an experienced skydiver — one after the other. Mum went first, pumped as all get-out. Then Marie. I went last. I reckon that's the worst, because you see people tumble out and go *whoosh* backwards at a hundred miles an hour.

We landed at North Wollongong beach, all safely, and we hugged each other and whooped it up. It was an amazing day. An experience I recommend to anyone.

And I had a chance to go surfing in Fiji with an ex-pro surfer named Rod Kerr, as well as mates Shannon Hegarty, Trent Langlands and Todd Byrne. We surfed a reef break called Cloudbreak in the middle of the ocean, the waves small enough for me at just over a metre. Rod guided us to a much meaner-looking shelf break, again in the open ocean, only this time it was 3 to 4 metres and not for a novice like me. I sat on my board at the edge of the break and watched him carve it up. If I'd tried, I wouldn't be here now, I'm sure. On that trip we ended up at a remote village where there was no running water — no services at all. Life was hand-to-mouth stuff. But I found it amazing because they knew all about rugby league, and my career, even though they lived here in this remote place with no electricity or plumbing, no newspaper, radio or television.

Mostly, though, it's been a family affair for me since I hung up my boots. I've come to learn that raising a family is a team sport. Or at least it should be. I never realised that until I retired. Until then, Marie did the hard yards. I can't imagine a better mother. Is there a harder, more time-consuming and daunting job in the world? I don't think so. Now I do my share, and find it unbelievably fulfilling. Like the time I had to nurse Demi through the night when she was sick. She eventually fell asleep in my arms after several hours, and the emotional rush, just looking at her resting comfortably wrapped up in my arms, was as big a boost as you could ever hope to get out of footy. I was buggered the next morning from lack of sleep, but floating on air.

As for watching kids grow and learn, that's another huge buzz for me. It's the simple things they learn and then master each day, like picking things up from the ground without falling over. One day I watched Demi throwing a tea towel, waddling over, picking it up, waddling back and doing it all over again a dozen times. I followed the whole exercise, engrossed, on my video camera. She's a determined kid, and was simply practising the art of picking stuff up on the run.

And learning to cope with stairs, too. There's a step leading onto our balcony that was preventing her getting out into the open air, where she wanted to be. I watched her for days, trying to swing her legs over it. First one, then the other. She tried and failed a hundred times, but kept at it. After a few days, and one tumble after another, she eventually got it down pat, and from that moment on she never missed. But that presented a problem in itself, since the balcony's fifteen floors up!

Speaking of which, you know they have to have accidents, but it's a harrowing experience when it happens. In Canberra, at Marie's sister Terri's house on Christmas Eve, Demi got all excited and ran headlong into a sharp join in the wall. I heard all these Greek women screaming and shouting, and found Demi with an egg-shaped lump on her head and a deep gash through the middle of it. The least flustered of all of us was the baby herself. If she was sobbing, it was only because these women were yelling and shouting and wailing in her face.

Now, I've seen some head injuries in my time on the footy field. I knew she just needed a small stitch and everything would be fine. It was almost midnight on Christmas Eve when we got to casualty at Canberra Hospital. They did a terrific job, patching up Demi and calming the women. I have a photo of her taken the next day, looking like a crime boss, in mid-stride, full of attitude, and with a bandaged head. It could be entitled, 'Don't mess with this miss!'.

As much as I dote on her, though, I can't imagine spending twenty-four hours a day, every day, caring for Demi. I'd melt from overwork. I have so much respect for Marie and all mums who do that. Especially single mums. My God, that must be tough. If I spend a full day looking after Demi, I'm done for. I crash and burn. After just one day! Demi's such a good kid because Marie is such a good mum — I'm certain of that.

One of the other things I'll be able to do in retirement is travel more. I'd like to spend time in New York, where I've never been. I love big cities. I could never retire and move to the quiet of a country homestead. I want to die living. I also want to spend time in Greece, and I think that's important from my viewpoint as well as Demi's. She's half-Greek, so I want her to spend some time there when she's older. I'd like her to learn the language and the culture. Marie and I want to get married in Greece, too — maybe next year.

Since I met Marie, I've come to consider myself half-Greek. Honestly, I have. Freddy Fittleropolous — it's got a ring to it, don't you think? More Zorba the Geek than Zorba the Greek, I suppose, but so what? I want to learn more about the Greek heritage. Half my social life is spent in the Greek strongholds of Sydney, like Marrickville, enjoying the company of Marie's family and friends. Cards and backgammon and Greek coffee and loud, back-slapping laughter. You can't beat it. Marie's closest friends, Angela and John, have us over on occasions, and the girls chat away animatedly while John and I play backgammon for three or four hours straight. I absolutely love it. Yes, I know it's a far cry from my wildcat youth, but there you are.

I want to learn to speak Greek. Some of the insults I know already, because Marie aims them at me sometimes and I've sought a translation from her relatives. What I love about Greeks is the close-knit nature of the families and the unbridled passion with which their lives are lived. I admire and respect that so much. And I want Demi to grow up to cherish her dual backgrounds. I've never been to Greece, but I figure I got a pretty good idea of it at a Greek Easter function at rural Riverstone in Sydney's west one day. I couldn't believe it: venison and chickens on the spit, fifty people on a long row of trestle tables, and food and wine and wonderful companionship. I've never laughed so much in my life, nor met so many wonderful people, nor been hugged and kissed quite so often by women and hairy old men.

I've embraced other things as well. Greek traditions that might make you think I've bumped my head once too often in tackles. I'm a firm believer in the 'evil eye', for instance. Demi was sick, and Marie said she would call her grandmother and ask her to cure Demi of the evil eye. I kid you not. I was so angry with her. But it worked. The evil eye is about as ancient a superstition as there is in the world; the Greek Orthodox Church won't even condone it. The Greeks call it *matiasma*. Those with blue eyes and green eyes are treated with suspicion. Infants are especially susceptible, apparently, and can suffer from sluggishness, nausea and a vague feeling of having something inside, like a lump in the throat. You need an old woman to provide the *xematiasma* or exorcism, and that's what Marie did. The cure has something to do with drops of olive oil in water and the sign of the cross on the forehead. I don't know. I just know that it worked, and I'm a believer. Then again, Demi might have recovered naturally. Who knows? Once when I got crook, Marie rubbed methylated spirits into my chest. That one *didn't* work. Give me the *xematiasma* any time.

It's not the first time I've dabbled in the occult and the stars. The week before the 2002 Grand Final, which we won, I read the stars for my sign, Aquarius, in the Sunday papers. It was as if the astrologer, Jonathan Cainer, was talking directly to me: 'You're going to win something big, something you've worked hard for all your life.' I tore out the page and referred to it every day until the Grand Final. And at the end of that year, in December, I consulted the daily stars again in the paper, and there was this:

> People love to watch others climbing the ladder of success. They cheer them on and do all they can to be supportive. Once they're near the top though, it's a different story. Suddenly, the world fills with folk anticipating your downfall.
>
> You have much to lose. Certain people would be only too pleased to help you lose it. Don't give them the

chance. Don't rise to the bait. Don't seek approval of others. And don't be afraid of change.

I swear the astrologer knew me and was writing for me. Nonsense, of course, but it was just so accurate, it was uncanny. I cut that out and framed it, and it's been sitting above my computer at home ever since.

Sometimes I think my life is like a scene from *My Big Fat Greek Wedding*. I've been to Greek weddings and danced with the best of them. No one gets to be a wallflower at Greek weddings. You're up and dancing whether you're three years old or ninety-three. Demi's christening, three days before the State of Origin decider in 2004, was just stunning. The rituals took place in a Greek church at Newtown. Her *nona*, or godmother, held her throughout the goings-on. The priest had a big long beard and, well, Demi's no fan of beards, so she screamed blue murder. Even more so when she was dunked under the water. Some will say these are just more examples of ancient superstitions, like the evil eye, that have no place in modern society, but I disagree. God's inside you, as far as I'm concerned, and traditional religions don't appeal to me, but I respect faith and ritual, and applaud it. Anything that brings family and friends together in such joyous celebration has to be worthwhile.

The christening party was held at Ripples, above North Sydney Pool, and right next door to Luna Park. Demi was calm by then, done up in the prettiest little dress I'd ever seen, and happy to be passed around from one friend and relative to another like a football at training. I'm not kidding: her smile lit up the harbour. I was the proudest dad on earth. I organised fireworks for the occasion, just as I did for our millennium New Year's Eve party. There was a barge in front of Luna Park, and come 9 p.m. the fireworks went off, and at the end of it there was Demi's name spelled out 5 metres high in sparklers.

If you'd looked out from any of those multimillion-dollar houses and apartments straddling the harbour to see what all the noise was about, you would've seen the name of my daughter writ large in bright lights out on the water with the Sydney Harbour Bridge, the Opera House and the heart of the Sydney CBD reflected in the Fittler name. Overhead, fireworks exploded and showered down in bursts of green and red and yellow.

If you'd looked below, you might have caught a lingering and tearful embrace between Marie, Demi and me.

From that moment on, I knew everything was going to be all right.

brad fittler

Born: 5 February 1972, Auburn, NSW

CAREER OVERVIEW

CLUB CAREER *1989–2004*

Penrith *1989–1995*	Games	Trs	Gls	F/G	Pts
Premiership *1989–95*	119	31	5	2	136
Pre-season *1990–95*	10	2	-	-	8
Sydney Roosters *1996–2004*					
Premiership *1996–2004*	217	91	9	8	390
World Club Challenge *2003*	1	1	-	-	4
Premiership Total	**336**	**122**	**14**	**10**	**526**
Other club matches	11	3	-	-	12

REPRESENTATIVE CAREER *1990–2004*

City-Country *1990–97*	Games	Trs	Gls	F/G	Pts
City Firsts *1990*	1	1	-	-	4
City Origin *1991–97*	7	1	-	-	4
TOTAL	8	2	-	-	8
New South Wales *1990–2004*					
State of Origin *1990–2004*	31	8	-	2	34
Australia *1990–2001*					
Tests *1991–2001*	34	14	1	1	59
World Cup *1992*	1	-	-	-	0
World Cup *2000*	5	4	-	-	16
Tour matches *1990–94*	22	13	1	-	54
TOTAL	62	31	2	1	129
GRAND TOTAL					
All senior matches	448	166	16	13	709

Fittler represented the Australian Schoolboys from McCarthy Catholic College in 1988 and 1989.

He toured with the Kangaroos in 1990, 1994 and 2001 (as captain) and played in the World Cups of 1992, 1995 (World Cup matches in 1995 were designated as Tests) and 2000.

He remains the youngest NSW State of Origin player (18 years and 114 days in 1990) and the youngest Kangaroo representative (18 years and 247 days when he played his first match on the 1990 Kangaroo tour).

He captained Australia in 20 Tests, winning 17 and losing three. He captained New South Wales in 14 matches, winning 8 and losing 6.

First grade debut: Penrith v Wests at Orana Park, Campbelltown, 1989 (Round 21)

Last club debut: Sydney City v Sydney Tigers at Sydney Football Stadium, 1996 (Round 1)

Junior clubs: Sadleir, Dayments, Mt Pritchard, Ashcroft, Cambridge Park

Fittler played more matches at club level in Australia and at representative level than any other player.

CLUB CAREER 1989–2004

Penrith 1989–1995	Games	Trs	Gls	F/G	Pts
1989	4	1	-	-	4
1990	21	8	5	-	42
1991	19	3	-	-	12
1992	20	6	-	1	25
1993	19	4	-	-	16
1994	21	6	-	-	24
1995	15	3	-	1	13
Total	119	31	5	2	136

Final Series: 1989, 1990, 1991
Grand Finals: 1990, 1991
Premierships: 1991
Captaincy: 1992 — 1, 1993 — 2, 1994 — 8, 1995 — 6 (17 matches)
Also played: Channel Ten Cup 1990, Lotto Challenge 1991, Tooheys Challenge 1992–93, 1995 (10 matches, 1 try, 4 points)

Sydney Roosters 1996–2004	Games	Trs	Gls	F/G	Pts
1996	21	5	-	-	20
1997	21	5	-	1	21
1998	25	17	-	-	68
1999	21	11	2	1	49
2000	27	9	-	-	36

Sydney Roosters 1996–2004 (cont.)	Games	Trs	Gls	F/G	Pts
2001	25	13	-	1	53
2002	25	9	-	1	37
2003	26	12	5	3	61
2004	26	10	2	1	45
Total	217	91	9	8	390

Final series: 1996, 1997, 1998, 1999, 2000, 2001, 2002, 2003, 2004
Grand Finals: 2000, 2002, 2003, 2004
Premierships: 2002
Captaincy: 1996 — 3, 1997 — 21, 1998 — 25, 1999 — 21, 2000 — 27, 2001 — 25, 2002 — 25, 2003 — 26, 2004 — 26 (199 matches)
Also played: World Club Challenge 2003 (v St Helens, won 38–0 — 1 try, captain)

Premiership matches	336	122	14	10	526
Official pre-season	10	2	-	-	8
World Club Challenge	1	1	-	-	4
CLUB TOTAL	347	125	14	10	538

REPRESENTATIVE CAREER 1990–2004

City–Country 1990–97	Games	Trs	Gls	F/G	Pts
City Firsts v Country Firsts 1990					
1990 at Sydney Football Stadium	1	1	-	-	4
City Origin v Country Origin 1991–97					
1991 at Sydney Football Stadium	1	-	-	-	0
1992 at Sydney Football Stadium	1	-	-	-	0
1993 at Parramatta Stadium	1	-	-	-	0
1994 at Marathon Stadium	1	-	-	-	0
1995* at Steelers Stadium	1	-	-	-	0
1996* at Steelers Stadium	1	-	-	-	0
1997* at Marathon Stadium	1	1	-	-	4
TOTAL	7	1	-	-	4

* Captain (3 matches)

New South Wales 1990–2004
State of Origin 1990–2004

30/5/90 at Olympic Park (won 12–6)	1	-	-	-	0
8/5/91 at Lang Park (lost 4–6)	1	-	-	-	0
12/6/91 at Lang Park (lost 12–14)	1	-	-	-	0
6/5/92 at SFS (won 14–6)	1	-	-	-	0
20/5/92 at Lang Park (lost 4–5)	1	-	-	-	0
3/6/92 at SFS (won 16–4)	1	-	-	-	0

New South Wales *1990–2004* (cont.)	Games	Trs	Gls	F/G	Pts
3/5/93 at Lang Park (won 14–10)	1	-	-	-	0
17/5/93 at SFS (won 16–12)	1	-	-	-	0
31/5/93 at Lang Park (lost 12–24)	1	-	-	-	0
23/5/94 at SFS (lost 12–16)	1	-	-	-	0
8/6/94 at MCG (won 14–0)	1	-	-	-	0
20/6/94 at Suncorp (won 27–12)	1	1	-	1	5
15/5/95* at SFS (lost 0–2)	1	-	-	-	0
31/5/95* at MCG (lost 12–20)	1	-	-	-	0
12/6/95* at Suncorp (lost 16–24)	1	-	-	-	0
20/5/96* at Suncorp (won 14–6)	1	-	-	-	0
3/6/96* at SFS (won 18–6)	1	-	-	-	0
17/6/96* at Suncorp (won 15–14)	1	-	-	1	0
22/5/98 at SFS (lost 23–24)	1	1	-	-	4
5/6/98 at Suncorp (won 26–10)	1	1	-	-	4
19/6/98 at SFS (lost 4–19)	1	-	-	-	0
26/5/99* at Suncorp (lost 8–9)	1	-	-	-	0
9/6/99* at Stadium Australia (won 12–8)	1	-	-	-	0
10/5/00* at Stadium Australia (won 20–16)	1	-	-	-	0
24/5/00* at Suncorp (won 28–10)	1	1	-	-	4
7/6/00* at Stadium Australia (won 56–16)	1	-	-	-	0
6/5/01* at Suncorp (lost 16–34)	1	1	-	-	4
10/6/01* at Stadium Australia (won 26–8)	1	2	-	-	8
1/7/01* at ANZ Stadium (lost 14–40)	1	-	-	-	0
16/6/04 at Suncorp Stadium (lost 18–22)	1	-	-	-	0
7/7/04 at Telstra Stadium (won 36–14)	1	1	-	-	4
TOTAL	31	8	-	2	34

* Captain (14 matches)

Australia *1990–2001*

Test Matches *1991–2001*	Games	Trs	Gls	F/G	Pts
6/10/91 v Papua New Guinea at Goroka (won 58–2)	1	2	-	-	8
13/10/91 v Papua New Guinea at Port Moresby (won 40–6)	1	-	-	-	0
12/6/92 v Great Britain at SFS (won 22–6)	1	-	-	-	0
3/7/92 v Great Britain at Lang Park (won 16–10)	1	-	-	-	0
15/7/92 v Papua New Guinea at Townsville (won 36–14)	1	1	-	-	4
20/6/93 v New Zealand at Auckland (drew 14–14)	1	-	-	-	0

Test Matches 1991–2001 (cont.)	Games	Trs	Gls	F/G	Pts
25/6/93 v New Zealand at Palmerston North (won 16–8)	1	-	-	-	0
30/6/93 v New Zealand at Lang Park (won 16–4)	1	1	-	-	4
6/7/94 v France at Parramatta Stadium (won 58–0)	1	1	-	-	4
22/10/94 v Great Britain at Wembley Stadium (lost 4–8)	1	-	-	-	0
5/11/94 v Great Britain at Old Trafford (won 38–8)	1	-	-	-	0
20/11/94 v Great Britain at Elland Road, Leeds (won 23–4)	1	-	-	-	0
4/12/94 v France at Beziers (won 74–0)	1	-	-	-	0
23/6/95* v New Zealand at Suncorp Stadium (won 26–8)	1	-	-	-	0
7/7/95* v New Zealand at SFS (won 20–10)	1	-	-	1	1
14/7/95* v New Zealand at Suncorp Stadium (won 46–10)	1	-	-	-	0
7/10/95* v England at Wembley Stadium (lost 16–20)	1	-	-	-	0
14/10/95* v Fiji at McAlpine Stadium, Huddersfield (won 66–0)	1	-	-	-	0
22/10/95* v New Zealand at Huddersfield (won 30–20)	1	1	-	-	4
28/10/95* v England at Wembley Stadium (won 16–8)	1	-	-	-	0
12/7/96* v Fiji at Marathon Stadium, Newcastle (won 84–14)	1	1	-	-	4
11/7/97* v Rest of the World at Suncorp Stadium (won 28–8)	1	-	-	-	0
24/4/98 v New Zealand at Auckland (lost 16–22)	1	-	-	-	0
23/4/99* v New Zealand at Stadium Australia (won 20–14)	1	1	-	-	4
15/10/99* v New Zealand at Auckland (lost 22–24)	1	1	-	-	4
22/10/99* v Great Britain at Suncorp Stadium (won 42–6)	1	1	-	-	4
5/11/99* v New Zealand at Auckland (won 22–20)	1	-	-	-	0
21/4/00* v New Zealand at Stadium Australia (won 52–0)	1	2	-	-	8

Test Matches 1991–2001 (cont.)	Games	Trs	Gls	F/G	Pts
7/10/00* v Papua New Guinea at Townsville (won 82–0)	1	1	-	-	4
13/7/01* v New Zealand at Wellington (won 28–10)	1	-	-	-	0
7/10/01* v Papua New Guinea at Port Moresby (won 54–12)	1	-	-	-	0
11/11/01* v Great Britain at Huddersfield (lost 12–20)	1	-	-	-	0
17/11/01* v Great Britain at Reebok, Bolton (won 40–12)	1	1	-	-	4
24/11/01* v Great Britain at JJB Stadium, Wigan (won 28–8)	1	-	1	-	2
TOTAL	34	14	1	1	59

* Captain (20 Tests)

World Cup Matches 1992, 2000 (Non-Test matches)

World Cup Final 1992	Games	Trs	Gls	F/G	Pts
24/10/92 v Great Britain at Wembley Stadium (won 10–6)	1	-	-	-	0

World Cup 2000

	Games	Trs	Gls	F/G	Pts
28/10/00* v England at Twickenham (won 22–2)	1	-	-	-	0
1/11/00* v Fiji at Gateshead (won 66–8)	1	-	-	-	0
11/11/00* v Samoa at Watford (won 66–10)	1	1	-	-	4
19/11/00* v Wales at Huddersfield (won 46–22)	1	2	-	-	8
25/11/00* v New Zealand at Old Trafford (won 40–12)	1	1	-	-	4
TOTAL	5	4	-	-	16

* Captain (5 matches)

Test Tour Matches 1990–94	Games	Trs	Gls	F/G	Pts
Kangaroo Tour 1990					
10/10/90 v Wakefield at Wakefield (won 36–18)	1	1	-	-	4
17/10/90 v Cumbria at Workington (won 42–10)	1	-	-	-	0
31/10/90 v Warrington at Warrington (won 26–6)	1	1	-	-	4

Test Tour Matches 1990–94 (cont.)	Games	Trs	Gls	F/G	Pts
6/11/90 v Halifax at Halifax (won 36–18)	1	-	-	-	0
14/11/90 v Hull at Hull (won 34–4)	1	-	-	-	0
27/11/90 v President's XIII at Paris (won 46–18)	1	2	-	-	8
29/11/90 v France B at Lyon (won 78–6)	1	2	-	-	8
5/12/90 v Languedoc at Carcassonne (won 38–9)	1	2	-	-	8
Papua New Guinea Tour 1991					
29/9/91 v Northern Zone at Lae (won 40–6)	1	-	-	-	0
2/10/91 v Islands Zone at Rabaul (won 42–25)	1	2	-	-	8
9/10/91 v Highlands Zone at Mt Hagen (won 28–3)	1	-	-	-	0
World Cup 1992					
9/10/92 v Huddersfield at Leeds Rd (won 66–2)	1	-	-	-	0
14/10/92 v Sheffield at Sheffield (won 52–22)	1	-	1	-	2
18/10/92 v Cumbria at Workington (won 44–0)	1	1	-	-	4
Kangaroo Tour 1994					
2/10/94 v Cumbria at Workington (won 52–8)	1	-	-	-	0
5/10/94 v Leeds at Headingley (won 48–6)	1	-	-	-	0
8/10/94 v Wigan at Wigan (won 30–20)	1	-	-	-	0
16/10/94 v Halifax at Halifax (won 26–12)	1	-	-	-	0
30/10/94 v Wales at Cardiff (won 46–4)	1	1	-	-	4
13/11/94 v Bradford at Bradford (won 40–0)	1	-	-	-	0
15/11/94 v GB Under–21s at Gateshead (won 54–10)	1	-	-	-	0
27/11/94 v Catalans Selection at Perpignan (won 60–16)	1	1	-	-	4
TOTAL	22	13	1	-	54
All matches for Australia	62	31	2	1	129

AWARDS

1992   Dally M Centre of the Year
       Rugby League Yearbook Team of the Year
1993   Dally M Centre of the Year
       Rugby League Yearbook Team of the Year
1994   Dally M Lock of the Year
       Rugby League Yearbook Team of the Year
1995   *Rugby League Yearbook* Top Five Players of the Year
       Rugby League Yearbook Team of the Year
1996   *Rugby League Yearbook* Team of the Year
1997   Nokia Provan-Summons Medal
       Rugby League Yearbook Top Five Players of the Year
       Rugby League Yearbook Team of the Year
       Rugby League Week Player-of-the-Year
1998   Dally M Five-eighth of the Year
1999   Dally M Five-eighth of the Year
       Dally M Captain of the Year
       Dally M — second runner-up
       Rugby League Yearbook Team of the Year
2000   Golden Boot Award
       Rugby League Yearbook Team of the Year
2001   *Rugby League Yearbook* Team of the Year
2002   Dally M Five-eighth of the Year
       Rugby League Yearbook Top Five Players of the Year
       Rugby League Yearbook Team of the Year

index

Richard Sleeman is a much-awarded sports writer and broadcaster, with a career in journalism spanning almost forty years.

In his early teens he attended rugby league matches as a newspaper copy boy and wrote about school sports for the *Sunday Telegraph*. He rose to be the Australian Associated Press London correspondent, and returned to Australia as columnist and feature writer on *The Australian* newspaper, and then *The Sun*. He has covered many of the major sports and news events in Australia and overseas over the past four decades, including five Olympic Games; the 1983 America's Cup win in Newport, Rhode Island; several Commonwealth Games; cricket, rugby and rugby league international series; world title fights; Wimbledon and US Open tennis; British Open golf, and the Port Arthur massacre.

Richard was named the National Press Club's sportswriter of the year. He has also presented radio programs on 2GB and 2KY. He has authored and contributed to a number of books, including a biography of controversial commentator Ron Casey, and *200 Years of Australian Sport*, celebrating the Australian bicentenary. Rugby league has always been one of his major interests, as a supporter of the Sydney Roosters from childhood, manager and adviser to many of the stars of the game, and observer of the great players from the late 1950s to the present day.

THE END